A practice of pleasure

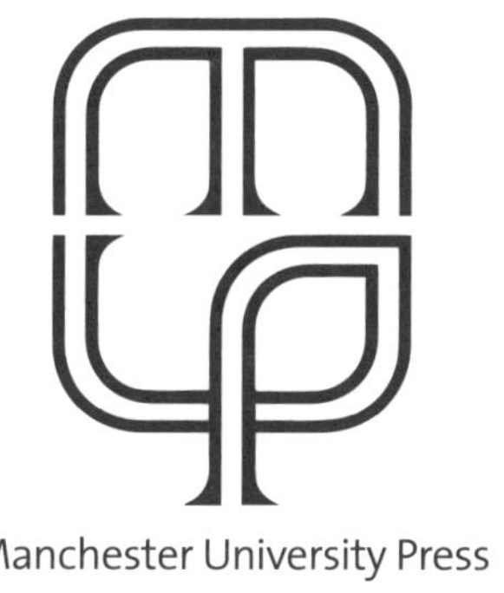

A practice of pleasure

Joanna Frueh's performances and writings, 2005–11

Joanna Frueh
edited and with an introduction
by Marsha Meskimmon

MANCHESTER UNIVERSITY PRESS

Published by Manchester University Press
Oxford Road, Manchester, M13 9PL
www.manchesteruniversitypress.co.uk

British Library Cataloguing-in-Publication Data
A catalogue record for this book is available from the British Library

ISBN 978 1 5261 8931 8 hardback
ISBN 978 1 5261 8932 5 paperback

First published 2025

EU authorised representative for GPSR:
Easy Access System Europe, Mustamäe tee 50,
10621 Tallinn, Estonia
gpsr.requests@easproject.com

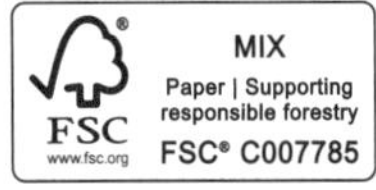

Typeset
by Cheshire Typesetting Ltd, Cuddington, Cheshire
Printed and bound in Great Britain by Bell & Bain Ltd, Glasgow

Contents

Part II The results of pleasure

Editorial introduction: a correspondence with critical intimacy

Marsha Meskimmon

A posthumous publication brings with it a palimpsestic tale of time and space.

In the absence of the author, it falls to the editor to map some of these imbricated and overlapping stories for readers who, inevitably, embark belatedly on the journey of the book. Joanna Frueh's *A practice of pleasure* was completed in 2011. A meticulous scholar and prolific writer, Frueh drafted a detailed and lucid introduction to her volume during the hot summer months of that same year from her home in Tucson, Arizona. From that point, the completed manuscript remained untouched until, shortly before her death in February of 2020, Frueh alerted her wife, Kathleen Williamson, and her close friend and collaborator, Jill O'Bryan, to the existence of the manuscript and her desire that it be published. It was through their attentive efforts to honour Frueh's wish that the digital files comprising the full draft manuscript of *A practice of pleasure* were located, and the documents prepared for submission to potential publishers. Thus it was that on a dull November day in 2023 Emma Brennan, the commissioning editor at Manchester University Press with whom Amelia Jones and I work closely as series co-editors, sent an email to us, opening with the words '*We've received something very interesting ...*'.

That is one of the stories of time and space that chart the course of this book, but it is certainly not the only tale to be told.

There is the story captured within the volume itself, of a richly transformative period of Frueh's life and work from 2005 to 2011. Frueh drew these lines with fine acuity throughout the text, sketching the significance of her move to Tucson in 2005 and her deep attachment to the Sonoran Desert, her decision to retire from her position as Professor of Art History at the University of Nevada, Reno, in 2006, the completion of a number of key publications, and the receipt of prestigious awards that, as she wrote, 'mark a career of accomplishment and longevity' (p. 3). To these geographical and professional markers she added friendships, love affairs, the study of yoga (including travel to India in 2008), and of course writing, performances, and a number of in-depth critical conversations she convened through monthly salons, commencing in 2010.

The volume unfolds in two parts, 'Practices of body and mind' and 'The results of pleasure', bringing together poetic and critical essays, reflections from salon conversations, and scripts from performances with descriptions of everyday practices of pleasure that make the quotidian profound. And at the centre always Frueh, the 'pleasure activist', using her explorations of *soul-and-mind-inseparable-from-body* to materialize living as fully sensual 'work in progress', and to invite her readers to share the possibility to do likewise. The authorial introduction to the volume that Frueh drafted in the summer of 2011 is the work of a consummate professional academic art historian, cogently explaining to readers how and to what ends the materials included in the final manuscript were produced, selected, and structured. In her introduction, Frueh drew a clear, concise, and compelling cartography that sustains the central thesis of the volume, articulated on its very first page: 'Pleasure matters'.

Narrated so eloquently by Frueh throughout the book, that tale of time and space requires no editorial addition, and so from here my stories take different turns.

Some of these concern the past, *presence*, and possible futures of the text. Disciplined art historians are probably most comfortable with narrating the past of a text, carefully situating it within the time and place of its production, and perhaps making a case for its historical significance. *A practice of pleasure* admits of such a tale. At the time of its completion, Frueh had enjoyed a long career as an art historian and feminist art critic, and had gained substantial recognition for her scholarly writing and her performance practice, both within the academy and beyond. The two volumes that she co-edited with Cassandra Langer and Arlene Raven, *Feminist*

Art Criticism: An Anthology (1988, reprinted 1991) and *New Feminist Criticism: Art, Identity, Action* (1994), remain markers of late twentieth-century Anglo-US feminist interventions into art's histories, while her evocative and challenging monographs, *Erotic Faculties* (1996) and *Monster/Beauty: Building the Body of Love* (2001), placed the fully embodied, corporeal-material desire and sensuality of the woman scholar, writer, teacher, and thinker at the heart of feminist explorations of art, life, body politics, and academic disciplinarity.[1] By the time Frueh was completing the task of compiling the performance texts and critical essays that would come to comprise *A practice of pleasure*, her major retrospective collaboration with Jill O'Bryan, *Clairvoyance (For Those in the Desert)*, an elegant and beautifully illustrated compendium charting a quarter of a century of Frueh's performance works, had been published.[2]

The present volume can be understood as a continuation of the trajectories of Frueh's earlier work and as a companion volume to *Clairvoyance*, but drawing the lines of this story with such stark linearity may too quickly consign its tale solely to the past.

A practice of pleasure was completed nearly a decade before Frueh's death from metastatic breast cancer and, perhaps even more significantly in terms of the writing, shortly before she received her initial diagnosis in 2012. Readers familiar with Frueh's work will be very aware of this timeline. While her work after 2012 did not abandon the central themes of her earlier writing and performances, the ways in which she applied her aesthetic engagement with beauty, pleasure, and eros – love, life force – became at once more pointedly focused on *healing*, and more broadly designed to articulate the exquisite experience of living and loving, *unapologetically*, in the full sensuous precarity of mortal human being.[3]

Arguably, the charged interval between the writing and the publication of *A practice of pleasure* serves to disrupt the seamless and unidirectional narrative of life and work that typifies scholarly and artistic biographies. Posthumous publications more usually signal the endnote of the life story; the final, unfinished book/article/work is edited and the scattered notes left on the scholar's desk are ordered, the better to bring the inevitable full stop to the life-in-art. But here, where the timeline had already been read as complete – the details of the 'life' and the 'work' digested, categorized, and filed for posterity in the archive – this volume creates a sudden and unexpected i(nte)rruption, a potential elaboration or critical disturbance moving across both the biographical and aesthetic registers. The existence and subsequent publication of this new/old material is excessive. It overspills the fixed parameters of the story-as-known and the tale *told*. It reopens the subject as a work *still* in progress, and I am moved to suggest that it could hardly be more apt that this completed, yet *untimely*, element of Frueh's *oeuvre* might cause bold and bodily trouble for readers seeking to tell a singular tale of the life and work by means of disciplined and disembodied critical distance.

And so a question emerges from drawing the contours of the work's past and future that recasts our imaginary map: does this critical i(nte)rruption tell a story of the *here and now* or of the *there and then*?

Of course there is no simple answer to this question, only an intellectual challenge and an imaginative opportunity. The text can be read anachronistically, searching for clues of what was yet to come in its brief references to healing, for example, or in its discussions of loss, grief, and mourning. And while reading in this way might secure the objectivity of the historian-editor behind a wall of disembodied critical distance, I would argue that using the text to prove what is already known relegates the work to little more than a missing piece of a jigsaw puzzle, belatedly set in place. Such a strategy forecloses the potential relevance of the text *here and now* by fixing it at a point along a flattened teleology – *there and then*. I want to suggest instead a critically intimate practice of reading this text creatively and corporeally as an entanglement of *here* with *there*, and *now* with *then*, capable of acknowledging the material coordinates of its writing in a specific time and place without reducing it to a knowable and distant past or an already storied future. Such intimate criticality engages with the much more dangerous and vital potential of the volume to perform disciplinary disobedience through explorations of haptic, sensuous textu(r)ality.

The volume is replete with invitations to read, and to write, in ways that enhance the corporeal and pleasurable power of scholarly and critical work as part of a vibrant life praxis. Perhaps most directly, the second section of Part I, 'Practices of body and mind', entitled 'Reading', gives an account of Frueh's transition away from the constricted practices of disciplined reading required by professional academic life, characterized in the text as acute forms of categorical accounting – bookshelves and bibliographies ordered more to demonstrate the completeness and correctness of the literature survey than to nourish the author or the work. By contrast, she describes liberating and life-enhancing practices of textual engagement under the heading 'How I read now':

> I read freely compared to before, and that freedom feels good. If a book doesn't interest me, I don't finish it. If a friend recommends a book, I thank her for the recommendation but I don't feel obligated to read it. Neither do I feel obliged, when I'm researching a subject for my writing, to read either the de rigueur or in-fashion publications on it. (p. 51)

Her call to read differently is not an excuse for failing to read widely and well, both of which Frueh demonstrates amply across the greater body of her critical writing and in this volume. Frueh's work drew variously on ancient Egyptian, Greek, Chinese, and South Asian literatures, Victorian artists and poets, poststructuralist critical theorists and feminist philosophers, cultural historians, and art historian/theorists to fashion what she called playfully 'lovestruck "multibridities"' (p. 24). But more than once in the present volume, Frueh challenged herself, and her readers, to recognize and refuse the negative and egocentric criticality fostered by the disciplinary regimes of the academy (including the power politics they support) and to reconnect with the generous bodily roots of subjectivity and aesthetics through writing – to become 'a scribe of beauty without being a conscript of academia' (p. 68).

In other words, the sheer joy of reading, writing, conversing, and performing, *soul-and-mind-inseparable-from-body*, that shimmers across the pages of this volume is not an academic exercise in intellectual mastery, nor is it evidence for an abstract feminist theoretical proposition *about* pleasure, eros, art, and life. In the texts that comprise *A practice of pleasure*, Frueh's love of reading, writing, and performing is reanimated, *after* professional academic work, and *outside* the authorization of the academy. The text is creative, aesthetic, and performative in the strong sense; it materializes the emergence of authorial agency as an embodied and sensuous work in progress realized by means of a practice of pleasure in, of, and with textuality. The work's focus on 'self-study' is thus not a conceit; neither is it a form of solipsistic presentism, nor an uncritical return to negatively conceived narcissistic intentionality. Rather, through a critical intimacy that unfolds over many different texts, *A practice of pleasure* seeks to study, understand, sanctify, and embody *presence*.[4]

Claiming a time and space of intellectual and imaginative presence *without* mastery, *after* and *outside* the academy, is a radical gesture for a woman scholar, artist, writer, and performer.[5] To do so through a corporeal-material aesthetics that yields to eros – sensuality, pleasure, love, spirituality – is not only radical, it is *disarming*. It is no mere coincidence that *A practice of pleasure* connects its 'pleasure activism' with peace, and draws sustenance from writings on nonviolence by Mohandas Gandhi and Martin Luther King, Jr. In its performative and poetic evocations of eros as *activism*, the volume speaks eloquently through *presence* with both the past and the potential to realize many different futures. Here, I would suggest, it finds kinship with the arguments and writing practices of some of the most politically and intellectually dynamic feminist, queer, and race-critical work of the past half-century. *A practice of pleasure* invites reading with and through earlier and later texts charting similar terrain, such as the poetic and activist praxis of Audre Lorde, bell hooks, and M. Jacqui Alexander, the creative theory texts of Gloria Anzaldúa, María Lugones, and Laura Pérez, and the transdisciplinary work of Nina Lykke and Trinh T. Minh-ha.[6] To read as a pleasure activist is to story history otherwise, to tell tales of material connections and imaginative possibilities as yet unknown.

While it may be possible to unfold myriad stories of time and space by thinking with *A practice of pleasure*, I am compelled to tell just one more.

This manuscript came to my attention through the ether in 2023, and it has been a privilege to be part of the collective effort to bring the work to publication. But this book was by no means my first introduction to Joanna Frueh, and I did not, and do not, come to the editorial task as a disembodied, all-seeing eye/I.

I first met Joanna at the turn of the twenty-first century, but I was familiar with her work before we met. Meeting Joanna is memorable, and our first meeting was filled with pleasure; to this day, the memory of Joanna fills me with pleasure, despite having been deeply saddened when contacted by her widow with the news of her death. I was brought up short many times in reading the manuscript for *A practice of pleasure*, as Joanna's voice is so present, so vivacious, so compelling that it is palpable in and of the text on the page. At various points in the work she played with self-naming, revelling in '*this* gala of many names' (p. 6). In thinking of how to name my relationship with Joanna, the better to make my investment in this project clear to readers, I too was faced with a gala of names – friend, colleague, conversant, fellow-traveller, interlocutor, inspiration – too many, not enough, not *good enough*.

My relationship with Joanna was not a thing, but a doing; we met in person only a few times, spoke by phone and video call a few more, and wrote messages to one another through the ether with fair frequency over the years. I was delighted to host her in performance at Loughborough University in 2001, was honoured that she reviewed my book *Women Making Art* in 2004,[7] drafted and shared with her a text slated for an anthology on her work that did not come to fruition, and happily wrote a different essay nearly a decade later that did.[8] I was touched when Joanna asked me to review plans for her *Unapologetic Beauty* project and charmed by her willingness to connect me with a small feminist bookshop in Arizona so I could give a copy of *The Glamour of Being Real* to my oldest and dearest friend.[9] Joanna and I talked, laughed, and shared confidences, professional and personal, often marvelling at our affinities despite differences of generation and geography – simply, we shared a long correspondence in and through the gift of critical intimacy.

And thus I come to draw the lines of this editorial map to a close from within its multilayered folds, as an inspired intellectual interlocutor of Frueh's work, and as a person touched in life by Joanna's *presence* and her astonishing ability to make others *present* in her company. One of our shared joys was gardening, and often our ethereal correspondence concerned what was in delicious or dramatic bloom in our respective gardens, nearly 5,000 miles and a world of weather apart. Early in *A practice of pleasure* Joanna wrote, 'In truth I am a gardener and a goddess' (p. 15). I take her lead and, as a fellow gardener tending to this text, I conspire – *breathe with* – the goddess, in the hope that these few words will continue to give forward Joanna's great generosity of spirit, from the soil to the stars.

Notes

1 Joanna Frueh, Arlene Raven, and Cassandra Langer, eds, *Feminist Art Criticism: An Anthology* (Ann Arbor, MI: UMI Research Press, 1988; second edition, New York: Harper Collins, 1991) and Joanna Frueh, Cassandra Langer, and Arlene Raven, eds, *New Feminist Criticism: Art, Identity, Action* (New York: Harper Collins, 1994); Joanna Frueh, *Erotic Faculties* (Berkeley and Los Angeles, CA and London: University of California Press, 1996); Joanna Frueh, *Monster/Beauty: Building the Body of Love* (Berkeley and Los Angeles, CA and London: University of California Press, 2001).

2 Joanna Frueh, *Clairvoyance (For Those in the Desert): Performance Pieces, 1979–2004*, with an introduction and photographs by Jill O'Bryan (Durham, NC and London: Duke University Press, 2008).

3 Joanna Frueh, *A Short Story about a Big Healing* (Tucson, AZ: ErneRené Press, 2013) and *Unapologetic Beauty*, photography by Frances Murray (Minneapolis, MN: University of Minnesota Press, 2019).

4 I am not the first to focus on *presence* in writing about Frueh's work; O'Bryan's eloquent Introduction to *Clairvoyance* brought this insight to the fore, and my use of the term echoes her with thanks.

5 Julietta Singh, *Unthinking Mastery: Dehumanism and Decolonial Entanglements* (Durham, NC and London: Duke University Press, 2018).

6 Frueh acknowledged the impact of Audre Lorde and Gloria Anzaldúa on her thinking in *Monster/Beauty* and referred elsewhere to the work of Adrienne Rich. For those interested in following these lines of thought further, see: Audre Lorde, *Sister Outsider: Essays and Speeches by Audre Lorde* (Berkeley, CA: Crossing Press, 2007 (first published 1984), esp. 'The Uses of the Erotic: The Erotic as Power', pp. 53–9, and *A Burst of Light and Other Essays* (Long Island, NY:

Ixia Press edition, 2017 (first published 1988)); bell hooks, *Love Song to the Nation* trilogy: *All About Love: New Visions*, *Salvation: Black People and Love*, *Communion: The Female Search for Love* (New York: William Morrow Paperbacks, 2016); M. Jacqui Alexander, *Pedagogies of Crossing: Meditations on Feminism, Sexual Politics, Memory and the Sacred* (Durham, NC and London: Duke University Press, 2005); Cherríe Moraga and Gloria Anzaldúa, eds, *This Bridge Called My Back: Writings by Radical Women of Color* (Watertown, MA: Persephone Press, 1981); María Lugones, *Peregrinajes/Pilgrimages: Theorizing Coalition Against Multiple Oppressions* (New York: Rowman & Littlefield Press, 2003); Laura E. Pérez, *Eros Ideologies* (Durham, NC and London: Duke University Press, 2019); Nina Lykke, ed., *Writing Academic Texts Differently: Intersectional Feminist Methodologies and the Playful Art of Writing* (London and New York: Routledge, 2014); Trinh T. Minh-ha, *Lovecidal: Walking with the Disappeared* (London and New York: Routledge, 2016).

7 Joanna Frueh, "Love IS the Answer," review, *Art Journal* 63:1 (Spring 2004), 87–90.

8 Marsha Meskimmon, "Art Matters: Feminist Corporeal-Materialist Aesthetics," in Hilary Robinson and Maria Elena Buszek, eds, *A Companion to Feminist Art* (Oxford: Blackwell, 2019), pp. 353–68.

9 Joanna Frueh, *The Glamour of Being Real* (Tucson, AZ: ErneRené Press, 2011).

Illustrations: editorial note

Marsha Meskimmon

Joanna Frueh did not leave a file of bespoke images with the manuscript for *A practice of pleasure*. Although a digital file on her laptop bore a name suggesting that she intended to create images, its contents were no more than a handful of test shots taken on a phone.

Thus, in the absence of a body of work curated by Frueh for *A practice of pleasure*, how or whether to illustrate the text became an editorial question – one that I was grateful to share with the two people through whose care the manuscript had come forward to the press in the first instance: Jill O'Bryan and Kathleen Williamson. We worked collaboratively to select images that would provide a visual counterpoint for the text; these brief notes make our selection process explicit for readers.

In seeking to follow the logic of Frueh's text, the first selection was straightforward: Frueh noted that two of her performances, the texts of which are included in this volume, had been recorded. It is with sincere thanks to Daniel Buckley and Paul Helzer that *Goddess of Roses* (2007) and *Sexual Advances* (2009) are accompanied by photos and video stills. In addition, Daniel Buckley's luminous photograph of Frueh waiting to perform *Goddess of Roses* appears on the cover of the volume.

Our second lead from the text was Frueh's enumeration of the three most significant artists she had collaborated with on photographic projects: Russell Dudley, Jill O'Bryan, and Frances Murray. Dudley's collaboration with Frueh had ended by the time *A practice of pleasure* was being written, but her close collaborative friendships with O'Bryan and Murray were of vital and enduring importance, both during and after this time. O'Bryan and Murray selected photographs from their personal archives for this volume, and through their gift have ensured that Frueh's vibrant visual presence accompanies the richness of her voice in the text.

The final group are images taken by Kathleen Williamson, Frueh's widow, and comprise the most intimate and interstitial of the selections, extending the archive to a time shortly after Frueh privately completed the manuscript, but before her death in 2020, when she disclosed its existence. Williamson and Frueh met during the time that *A practice of pleasure* was being written, and Williamson appears in the text with increasing frequency and ever greater intimacy as the volume progresses. At the end of Section 4, 'Conversation: salons', there is an extraordinary encounter, centred on a well-known portrait photograph of Frueh as Dante Gabriel Rossetti's *Venus Verticordia*. A large work, the portrait had dominated Frueh's living room in Tucson since her move, yet it was an image of her from the past, not of her present. As Frueh recounted the tale, it was Williamson's intervention that shaped her decision to let go of this past/image and embrace the present she practised, brought into being, and materialized in the interstitial work that is *A practice of pleasure*.

Williamson and Frueh coupled soon after the manuscript had been completed, and married a few years later. Williamson was both the photographer and intimate witness of Frueh's embodiment of what she called an 'art of uplift' and a 'practice of pleasure' during the challenging years between the completion and revelation of the manuscript. For Williamson, Frueh's shared love of joy and creativity is without end; hopefully, it will be likewise for the readers of this book.

List of figures

Introduction

Pleasure is the root of my work. Very consciously so since 2005. Experiences of pleasure and thinking about pleasure in ways that are sane and therefore healing. In my work the secular and the sacred, the erotic and the spiritual blossom from pleasure, and the corporeal is always in evidence, for without the body we cannot feel, sense, or perceive pleasure. We can neither experience, think, nor talk about it. Pleasure has always been the overarching impetus for much of my writing and performing.

Pleasure matters. Not as some kind of simplistic fun or amusement and not as an escapist counterpoint to the world's abundant horrors, but rather as a movement away from the unhappiness that people too often live with as their unconsciously accepted lot in life. That pleasure produces well-being is an idea and a feeling of utmost importance in my work. Pleasure can be an ever-present movement towards happiness. Pleasure produces love and love produces pleasure. This is a process of embrace and expansion, of opening the heart. Pleasure transmutes self-loathing and mourning, which so readily constrict human beings' hearts and their entire bodies, into the opening that is love.

I once knew a scholar who studied happiness. He did so because he wanted to be happy and was not. The only way to be happy is to *practice* being happy. Also, being happy is far more beneficial to ourselves and to others than is an intellectual pursuit of happiness, which can leave us obsessed about happiness and even miserable. Misery grows from the desire for happiness as an outcome of its study when that desired outcome does not manifest itself in our lives.

Studying happiness is ineffective. Experiencing it is essential, and experience happens in the body, which cannot be separated from the mind. When consciousness or unconsciousness, both mind, connect with something external to the body – from words in a book or a classroom to autumn leaves to the tunes a brother plays on the piano to the blood we see and the pain we feel after tumbling onto pavement from a bicycle to the fur we stroke on the back of a beloved cat – we feel that connection as a sensation in the body. Thus, body and mind are one. The sensation may be obvious, like the softness of an animal's fur on our fingers, the ache that remains from a fall, or sensation may be so subtle that we are unaware of it unless we have trained ourselves to feel subtle sensations throughout our bodies.

As with pleasure, most people think that happiness is an occasional and discontinuous experience. They're happy because they win a marathon or it's their birthday or they're eating a perfectly ripe peach. Race over, birthday gone, peach eaten, and they're back to the flatness, depression, vague dissatisfaction, or other non-happiness and non-pleasure that is usual for them. They feel pleasure because they're having an orgasm or sunning themselves at the beach, chatting with a close friend, or landing in a city that enchants them. Orgasm faded away, clouds covering the sun, conversation past, trouble with the taxi driver at the airport, and the pleasure has ended.

In the above examples I could exchange the happy ones with the pleasurable ones, because as I experience life and name its components, happiness and pleasure are equivalent terms that describe what can be the ground of living from which one thinks, acts, and speaks, the moment-to-moment feeling of one's daily life. Self-study and self-care as the observation of sensation, which is observation of the body as mind and the mind as body, takes one into that happy and pleasurable roundedness. For me, self-study and self-care shape a practice of pleasure.

In *A Practice of Pleasure* I discuss aspects of my personal and intellectual life that feed into my work as a performance artist, and I include recent performance texts of pieces that I've presented from 2006 through 2010. Having written and performed over sixty pieces since 1979, when I was 31, I'm observing, now at 63, practices of living and working that have been essential to me as a human being and an artist, and that remain so. (I generally perform each piece one to three times, and I co-authored and co-performed several early in my career.)

A Practice of Pleasure makes available to scholars and students of theater and contemporary art insights into the everyday life and the thinking of an artist well known for offering her own experiences as a means of embodying and speaking about pleasure: female pleasure, sexual pleasure, and the pleasures of prosaic and domestic beauties, such as enjoying the reality of her own body and the luxurious simplicities of the senses. Those pleasures continue to evolve, because, as I say in the first section of this book, I am a work in progress. *A Practice of Pleasure* will also appeal to readers who wish to learn about pleasure from an authority on the subject.

Now – as I write this introduction in June 2011 – is an intuitively right time for me to "collect" myself in the format of a book about my practice of pleasure. In the last five years much has come to fruition and much has changed in my life. I have been honored with a Lifetime Achievement Award from the Women's Caucus for Art (2008) and a section about my performance work in *TDR: The Drama Review* (2011). Duke University Press published my book *Clairvoyance (For Those in the Desert): Performance Pieces, 1979–2004* (2008), which contains essential performance texts and many photos from the beginning of my performance career into my maturity as an artist, and I retired from my position as Professor of Art History at the University of Nevada, Reno (2006). All of the above mark a career of accomplishment and longevity. Startling realizations have occurred over this period, from 2006 into 2011, and they arise from moving to Tucson, Arizona in 2005, with a semester left to teach (and a grueling commute, whose rigors I felt once it ended), traveling to India for the first time in 2008 to study mantra, renewing friendships with high school girlfriends (seven of us, who have now got together every summer since 2006), "breaking up" with a close girlfriend of twenty-six years (2009), intensifying my yoga practice after my move to Tucson, and undertaking Panchakarma, which is an Ayurvedic cleanse, in 2011, and continuing to eat Ayurvedically. I've also been awakened to myself through intimate relationships, one with an intellectual who barely felt his body (I was experimenting with a different kind of man from my preferred very bodily aware individual) (2005–07), another with whom I fell deeply in love but who didn't return my desire for a consistent, let alone committed, relationship (2008–10), and a third from whose self-knowledge came a momentous knowing, for me, of myself. He and I had a wonderful, very brief affair, and neither of us fell in love with the other (2010).

From 2006 through to now I have been changing in gently radical ways, letting old patterns dissolve, from ways of eating to ways of loving myself and others, to my process of writing, to my too-much-for-me-now ego investment in the career-making aspects of performing and publishing. And the performances themselves have changed. For instance, I debuted *Goddess of Roses* in 2007 and consider it to be the beginning of a new path that includes greater freedom of expression. Of the performance texts in *A Practice of Pleasure*, *Goddess of Roses* is the first one that I performed. (In 2006 I presented *A Flowering of Vision* in a contemporary art course that I taught at the University of Nevada, Reno.) Examples of a new freedom occurred in the writing of *Goddess of Roses*, a seamless weaving of the personal and the scholarly that happened without my thinking about it, and in the performance my spontaneous interaction with the audience was much more than usual and the comedienne in me emerged. Also, during the performance I experienced a clarity about myself in which the rational, the mystical, and the sexual felt perfectly compatible and fluent, and that feeling remains with me.

As I write this introduction, it is summer here in Tucson, an unusually hot June, which means temperatures are around 110 rather than 100 degrees. Tucson's sunny heat penetrates the body to the bones, and that sensory intensity, even with the comfort of air conditioning that I keep at 80 degrees, moves me into the bones of my life and art. So, now offers itself as a perfect time for self-reflection and organizing it for public view by gathering key material that I've written and performed during these past five years of a mature, intensely focused self-study and self-care that guide a passionately pleasurable creation of both artworks and myself. My life has become very spacious over these past five years, and my practices of pleasure have created that space, which keeps increasing. The spaciousness is changing my performances, and possible outcomes of this are my performing in my home, presenting a once-a-year extravaganza, and focusing for a while on self-portrait photos. The spaciousness is also in my body, for example pains leaving my left groin, hip, and sacrum, and people point out the spaciousness to me in subtle ways, such as a close friend who noted, "You need to remember that you've chosen to refine yourself." Self-refinement is a pleasure whose effects direct my performances, without any planning, and practices of self-refinement appear throughout this book. *A Practice of Pleasure* is a materialization of pausing and observing in a long career and a newly spacious life, on the way to fresh revelations and explorations of pleasure.

I create, write, direct, and perform my own pieces. They are intimate and embracing, and they engage the mind, the heart, and the spirit. Soul-and-mind-inseparable-from-body underpins my work, and that phrase recurs throughout my writing. Matter responds to how we treat it, to the ways in which we think about it, care for it (or not), and are conscious about it (or not). People tend to think of the body as profane and the soul as spiritual, yet the phrase soul-and-mind-inseparable-from-body indicates that the sacred and the sexual are unified. A person's genuine awareness of soul-and-mind-inseparable-from-body entails what I call dreaming the world into being, which is a process not only of personal transformation but also of social transformation. Dreaming in this way is activist. (See "Dreaming the world into being" in Section 4.)

I'm a writer and a scholar whose work expands into photo, video, and audio pieces. Writing is foundational for my performance work and for all of my work. In my writing I develop the ideas that drive and permeate my art. Many of my published writings are performance texts. Subjects and themes in my writing include but are not limited to love, beauty, pleasure, the body, creativity, eroticism, art, private and public power, the sacred, power, pink, vision, aging, and transformation.

Writing clarifies experience and writing is a way to create beauty. My writing is sensuous, poetic, and embodied, personal and philosophical. Sexual intimacies and intellect, prose and poetry, critique and romanticism, high emotion and scholarly persuasion recur, as do friends' and family's words from conversations. Personal reflection, autobiography, and lyricism are paramount. Graphic and sexual language are embedded in the lush terrain of words that convey an embracing – and bracing – authenticity and acuity of feeling and thinking.

Rich, graphic, and lyrical language spoken by my resonant voice characterizes my work, and I often sing, sometimes my own lyrics. I frequently revel in rich, delicious food, such as digging into a huge chocolate cake with a fork and then my fingers. The visual aspect of my performances is simultaneously spare and voluptuous. The staging is minimalist – a music stand, a pedestal that holds a glass of water and perhaps a cake, a vase of flowers on the floor. My costumes are elegant, simple, and conventionally sexy. These days I see each piece as a kind of contemplative prayer shared by the performer and audience.

We all have many identities, and I speak in different voices and personas, all of them me. Some of those identities are seer, goddess, little girl, lover, scholar, oracle, elegist, elder, art critic, daughter, mythmaker, wife, singer, hero, fairy, friend, and prophet. My narratives and arguments are multiple and fragmented, often unfolding in several literary genres as well as spoken in various of the voices listed in the previous sentence.

Writing and performances come about these days, since 2006, in unpredictable ways. They experiment with me – my patience, my habit-breaking happiness, my passion for the craft of writing, my love for men, my captivation by *sutras*, the excitement and peace I feel in friendships, my willingness to be who I am *now*, in *this* gala of many names.

In Part I, "Practices of body and mind," I discuss fun, favorite, and essential activities and disciplines in my everyday life that filter into my performances, either as obvious subject matter in the texts or as a foundational impetus for that subject matter or for what I choose to wear or ways I choose to move. I call these practices of self-care and self-study erotic, because eros as I define it includes life-enhancing thoughts and actions that enrich the life of the "erotic" and also of those around her. The erotic is a responsive human being, so I begin Part I by writing about responsiveness.

Section 2 is about reading. There I discuss my old ways of reading and the new ones that have developed over the past five years. The section also includes a very select list of readings over this period and comments on some of them. In Section 3, "Theory: on behalf of muses," I contemplate and analyze pleasure as it relates to my love for men, who have been muses for many of my pieces. Indeed, the man with whom I fell in love in 2008 – I mentioned him earlier in this introduction – is the muse for *Sexual Advances* and "The Dark Lord and his Wily Mistress," both included in this volume. Conversation is a supreme pleasure for me, and in "Conversation: salons" (Section 4), I provide the entry points for some of the best conversations I had in 2009 and 2010. In conversation I thrive, which is one reason why partying and small talk have never been my cup of tea. In conversation I learn about everything – politics, sexual dilemmas, the rewards and demands of others' relationships, any current event that fascinates me. I learn how to be a better friend, lover, and partner. I learn directions I wish to take in my art and life.

I held my first salon on December 19, 2010, and after that hosted one every month through December 2011. The first salon was a gathering of several women invited by me. Most lived in Tucson, and a couple of them were friends from out of town who happened to be visiting Tucson at that time. Our group decided that with more than seven people the kind of conversation that stimulates and satisfies us would become diffuse (although out-of-town guests could increase the number and that would be okay, as we guessed correctly that visitors would be infrequent). Usually four to five people, myself included, participated in each salon.

I use the word *salon* to describe the conversations that I hosted, because they partook of elements essential to the salons of eighteenth-century Paris, where women of intellect and education, called *salometers*, received guests and facilitated polite conversation – stimulating, fluid, focused, intelligent, and harmonious. Conversation is erotic, in contrast to small talk and chitchat. Conversation is an erotic art, by which I mean it is an art of connection.

My intention was to host a monthly get-together in which the same group of people would meet each time for casual yet concentrated talk, accompanied by light food and drinks provided by each participant on a rotating basis. The topic would be decided by me (though the topic of intimacy, which appears in this book as "Be perfect be perfect be perfect with me," was suggested by the group, and the topic of resurrection, presented here as "The ultimate tenderness of resurrection," was suggested by a member of the group who thought it would be great to talk about during the month of Easter), and I would present something that I had written and then facilitate the conversation, which would continue for around two hours. Any shorter would leave an insufficient amount of time to develop the topic through the kinds of unexpected exchanges and shifts that only conversation delivers, and any longer would likely disintegrate our attention. In my salons, I certainly directed the conversations, and at the same time I was a gentle facilitator who let talk take its own course and redirected the group only when the conversation went far afield. My presentations ranged from around five to twenty minutes in length.

We in the salon loved its freedom and pleasures (one of which, of course, was the food!) Sometimes our own vulnerability amazed us, our willingness to say things that felt risky and intimate. I especially appreciated my fellow conversationalists' abilities to nourish, contradict, express, and communicate with what appeared to be stunning ease. I know that such ease takes courage.

The salons in this volume are for the most part presented exactly as I read them to our group. They are a form of very intimate and informal performance in which I dressed up, greeted my guests, and helped them brew tea and arrange food and drink. We convened in my living room and I kept track of time on my phone. Often the conversation continued after the first guests left. I've added material to several of the salons, feeling a need to carry on the conversation about the topic. Other salons migrated into performance pieces in part or in toto. For example, the performance *I AM Desire* combines the salon from January 2010, in which the subject was plenty, with part of the original version of "The exceptional person." The performance *A Flowering of Vision* was the first salon. I thought that it was appropriate for beginning the salons, because conversation requires vision. *A Flowering of Vision* plays with literal and figurative definitions and ideas of vision, such as "I see" meaning "I know" and vision meaning the sense of sight as well as the force or power of imagination. Overall, vision in that piece is a profound kind of more than visual literacy whose pursuit demands courage and whose effects are far-reaching.

Practical matters of performing are the subject of Section 5 in Part II, "The results of pleasure," in which I explain why I present any one performance very few times, often only once, the difference between my performances and readings, and my use of audio, video, and photography. I also describe my experience of performing. Seven performance texts, written between 2005 and 2010, constitute Section 6 in "The results of pleasure."

The ability to move my performance audiences is based in the pleasure that they receive from my embodied writing and what I've been told is my charismatic presence. In both my performances and writing, I welcome people into a sensual and psychic openness made available through transformation. Pleasure transforms situations and experiences that seem to be personally or culturally difficult, such as the deaths of one's parents, loss of innocence, or the pressures that people feel from the fashion and beauty industries to look perfect. Pleasure consists of my playful and very human delving into the actual as well as intellectual terrain of pleasure, which includes beauty, sex, and eros, from a perspective that is uniquely joyous. When I'm performing I'm in an ecstasy of play, and when I write, the scholar's informed intelligence and attention to accuracy and the poet's lyricism are playing with language and ideas. The ecstatic performer is both an object of pleasure and a subject who delights in pleasure, playfully invigorated with the down-to-earth feelings and language of a person who enjoys her body, her mind, and her access to emotional, psychic, and cultural depths, and the ecstatic performer conveys to her audience that they are an object of *her* pleasure. I give them my lightness and grace: performing in beautiful fabrics (and, in my photos, the glamorous "dress" of nudity); eating cake, cookies, and ice cream; coloring the stage with flowers; laughing spontaneously as I'm eating or as I'm responding to the energy of the audience; saying something that just came into my head. In the play of performing I bring grace and lightness to my body, words, and actions. A strong intention is to communicate the pleasure of being alive. The pleasure of being alive heals disconnections that people feel between each other and within themselves.

Part I

Practices of body and mind

1

Responsiveness

Pleasure is the ground of responsiveness. I want to be closer closer closer, intimate with life because I am in love, not in a horridly romantic obsessive way, but in a light and fascinated way that propels me to want to know, see, and create the best and most beautiful that I can be. When I am in love, I am a work in progress, I am present, I am honest, I am a discerning body. When I am in love, I engage in lovestruck play and lovestruck unions, I am Aphrodite and I dress in the habits of love. When I am in love, I study myself through psychotherapy and yoga. When I am in love, I create a time defined by honey.

The performer as a work in progress

I return with every season, rose-fresh and fairy light, though I was born in winter: January 18, 1948; Chicago, Illinois. I am a Capricorn, born into a family of Aquarians: my mother Florence, my father Erne, and Renée, my sister, who arrived in the lush and lovely north eleven months before I did. Astrology tells us that Aquarians are creative and far-seeing – visionary. Capricorns: astrology tells us that we grow lighter as we grow older. January 18 is on the cusp of Aquarius. I thank the roses, stars, and fairies that I arrived in a house of Aquarius.

The lush and lovely north greeted me, the lush and lovely girl, with beauty. My family lived close to Lake Michigan, in the town of Highland Park, thirty miles out of the big city.

My parents were artists and intellectuals. Mom played piano, like an enraptured angel, and she knew English literature like she knew the literature of classical music. Dad had played clarinet in big bands, and when I was a little girl, he took classes at Moholy-Nagy's Institute of Design. Dad especially loved the Abstract Expressionists. His formally cool yet emotionally intimate collages are reminiscent of the works of the artist he admired most – Braque. Ren was a whiz at clarinet and saxophone. I sang, for I have a golden voice.

In my childhood winters, Dad, Ren, and I ice skated together. We warmed ourselves with the cocoa that he'd made. It filled the thermos that we left in the cabin at the edge of the ice. The smells of chocolate, smoke from the fire, and wood benches cuddled me, like the love of Dad and Ren. Like the love of Mom, whose lap I laid my head in well into my forties.

Over the Christmas and Chanukah holidays when I was a girl, I stayed up late in bed reading, and woke up early, reading in bed till breakfast. Mark Twain's *A Connecticut Yankee in King Arthur's Court* and *Great Tales of Terror and the Supernatural*, a 1,076-page volume of stories, provided my kind of entertainment. From playfulness to drama and sensuality, they stimulated my imagination.

In second grade I drew Picasso paintings from the art books in my parents' library. I wrote stories. I remember one in third grade about dogs traveling in outer space. I read Greek myths and let the histories of ancient Greece and Rome take me there, to places that felt remembered.

My first starring role in a play came in fourth grade. I myself was a space traveler, though my rocket landed here on earth in one foreign country after another. Up and away, down to earth.

The earth of the body, the ecstasy of eros. In fifth grade a boy touched one of my breasts – in the classroom! Our innocence embarrassed me, who for a number of years had been masturbating, gazing with love at every bit of my naked self, occasionally dressed in Mom's mink or Persian lamb and in her bright red lipstick. Masturbating in devotion to Aphrodite and to me, the lush and lovely girl.

As a girl, I read about sex. I read many novels, I read stories by de Maupassant, and I read Freud, because an edition of his works sat on a shelf in our library at home. Reading is my heart, like songs and sensuality.

In my teenage summers, I swam with my girlfriends at the beach below my family's house. We listened to the transistor radio, tanned ourselves to gentle browns, and talked about boys.

As I was growing up, Dad gardened. He knew himself through lilacs, roses, pansies, honeysuckles, tulips, petunias, impatiens, daffodils, tiger lilies, hostas, hawthorn trees, and a forest that he let be just that, groomed only now and then. Gardens are like the heart. When you love them, they bloom. I flowered into many things.

I call myself a writer, an actress, an artist, and a teacher. In truth I am a gardener and a goddess. In all my work I welcome beauty. It is a happy way to Know Thyself. A light, sure-footed Capricorn in the house of Aquarius.

The work in progress is life – that simple, that encompassing. I've always used my creative and intellectual work as a tool for the exploration of being alive, and now I see that the tools I use in daily living and the experiences, perceptions, and changes that emerge from them are as much my work as are writing and performing.

Although I just used the phrase "work in progress," it feels beside the point and inaccurate because it conventionally designates creative work that results in a product, a final result, ready for the marketplace: selling for money, working towards recognition and fame. However, in the process of self-creation, the creator *is* the art, soul-and-mind-inseparable-from-body. Neither that entity nor its actions is a performance. That creator is real, whether I'm presenting ideas at a conference or talking with a street person who's just asked me for money. In those and all situations I *am* my aesthetic and erotic self-creation, and creating that soul-and-mind-inseparable-from-body is happening every moment.[1]

Aesthetic and erotic self-creation comes about through self-care and self-study. Primary tools in my self-care and self-study include the body and mind practices that I discuss below. Some may seem more body-oriented and some more mind-oriented, but for me every practice I'm engaged in operates throughout soul-and-mind-inseparable-from-body. I am playfully disciplined about them all and they all affect me mightily.

Note

1 See Joanna Frueh, *Monster/Beauty: Building the Body of Love* (Berkeley and Los Angeles, CA and London: University of California Press, 2001), pp. 1–41, for my discussion of aesthetic/erotic self-creation.

Presentness

Soul-and-mind-inseparable-from-body underpins all of my work, and that phrase recurs throughout my writing. Matter responds to how we treat it, to the ways in which we think about it, care for it (or not), and are conscious about it (or not). People tend to think of the body as profane and the soul as spiritual, yet the phrase soul-and-mind-inseparable-from-body indicates that the sacred and the sexual are unified. A person's genuine awareness of soul-and-mind-inseparable-from-body entails what I call dreaming the world into being (see "Dreaming the world into being" in Section 4 of this volume). Dreaming the world into being is a process not only of personal transformation, but also of social transformation. Dreaming in this way is activist. And the dreamer, as I define her, can be a model of presentness, responsive to herself and to life outside of herself, and therefore aware of change and consequently capable of transforming herself. Presentness and change, impermanence, and transformation go hand in hand.

Erotic connection happens between people through presentness, which I'll here equate with authenticity. Authenticity connects the performer and her audience.

People tend to think of acting as inauthenticity: the performer is a character who pretends to be someone else. However, I perform myself. In my writings, which serve as scripts, I speak as myself and about myself and my friends, family, lovers, and experiences, and I speak with introspective honesty. I read my own language, because it indicates that I am not performing a character through memorized words or through *somebody else*'s words.

A friend confirmed that my acting expresses authenticity. He connected my acting with a statement made by the actor and director André Gregory. In an email from 2004 my friend wrote:

> The actor/director/teacher ... Andre Gregory of *My Dinner with Andre* fame ... said ... that 100 years ago most people were characters, enjoyed being themselves. The job of the actor then was to be able to portray vastly different characters; today most people are pretending to be someone other than who they are, so the job of the actor is to be nobody-but-herself on stage or film.

Makeup and hair also communicate my authenticity. Rather than wearing stage makeup, I slightly intensify my everyday look. For example, in performance I'll color my lids with two shades of gold, whereas I usually wear no eye shadow. I generally wear my hair long and loose when I perform, exactly as I do every day. In several performances I've pulled my hair back, the way I wear it when I'm in a yoga class. (I'm always amazed by hair stylists, whether my own or one who knows me casually and learns that I'll be performing soon, who want to do my hair for a performance. But I shouldn't be surprised, because they don't know that I like my hair how it is, no more dramatic or sexy or special than normal, when I perform.)

My friend the scholar and artist Jill O'Bryan, who has published pieces about my work,[1] calls me "The Queen of Presence." In an unpublished writing, she addresses the effects of my presentness:

> Frueh performs so that there is no distance between the viewer and the performer. You are undulating together like the air and the water. Her incredible gift for writing intimate prose takes you here – you can smell her, feel her – in short, it is a sensuous experience. It is also terrifying, embarrassing, fascinating, and exhilarating.

I'm sure that Jill would agree with me that my intimate behavior, such as the gestures of my body, the warmth and melodiousness of my voice, my looking confidently and these days, often with a smile, at the audience overall and at individuals within it, my intimate behavior, which is presentness, is as powerfully sensuous, terrifying, embarrassing, fascinating, and exhilarating as is my intimate prose.

Note

1 Jill O'Bryan, untitled essay, unpublished, 2006.

The honesty of a "provocateur" and an "iconoclast"

In March 2010 I gave the keynote presentation for an art history graduate student symposium held at the University of Arizona. I was checking sound, lights, and computer equipment a couple of days beforehand with the assistance of two students, one of whom casually mentioned that a professor of hers had spoken of me as a "provocateur." The student who introduced me at the keynote event said in his introduction that he'd contacted two art world figures for some words about me. One of them is an acquaintance who I met in the 1970s, an artist. In her words of praise she referred to me as an "iconoclast."

I felt odd being named a provocateur and an iconoclast. I'm sure it's not the first time someone has called me those names, but now I heard them applied. I'm also sure that some artists would love being seen as both a provocateur and an iconoclast, or as either one, because those words may connote powerful and revolutionary creativity and effect.

I'm reminded of a colleague many years ago, my senior in the art department in which we both taught, who called me a "rebel." He said that the students loved me because I was a rebel. The term was not meant to be especially complimentary. So I sat there with him in his office listening, taking in his taking to task my "rebellious" thinking and scholarship as evident (to him) in my teaching, and doing my best to clarify *for* myself what I was *to* myself. Silently I heard this: I'm a revolutionary, not a rebel. That was my internal self-defense at the time.

I think that provocateurs intend to provoke and iconoclasts intend to make war on convention.

Never have I intended to attack. Revolutionaries can hold in common with iconoclasts their attack on beloved (or dogmatic) institutions, concepts, and beliefs.

Never have I intended to be a revolutionary. Revolution, as I wrote long ago, can be going around and around, never really creating or building a social order, an art, or ways of thinking that are truly new.

Never have I intended to provoke, to cause irritation, offense, or resentment.

Never have I intended to be provocative – to be a seducer or a sexually inflammatory presence.

Simply, I think differently from a lot of people. That thinking is familiar to me. I'm not going out of my way to deal with taboos or extremes or uncomfortable ideas or outrageous feelings and outlandish behaviors. I'm thinking the way that I normally think and acting the way that I normally act. I'm being as authentically and honestly myself as I can be. I do understand that such authenticity and honesty can push the buttons of people who think and live more conventionally.

The other person contacted by the student who introduced me is an art historian who was a good friend of mine many years ago. She talked of my "unflinching honesty" in both my art and my life. "Unflinching honesty" struck a very different chord in me than did "provocateur" and "iconoclast." It rang true – because I want to live up to it. She also said that I have "a talent for friendship." What a beautiful thing to say about someone. I want to be a friend to my book and performance audiences. I want to be honest with the people in my life, those I know well and those I know little. The art historian's name is Janet. Janet's perceptions inspire me, to be myself.

Perceptions from a discerning body

A sign in a shop window reads “Pray less. Think more.” Seeing it on Tucson’s Fourth Avenue, a commercial street in a socially and politically liberal neighborhood, had me imagining that the dual directive is an anti-fundamentalist or anti-evangelist corrective, perhaps to a sign or bumper sticker that reads “Pray more. Think less.” If my supposition is true, then praying less and thinking more offers itself as a solution to people’s self-serving, egotistic, and mindless, or simple-minded, requests of a deity.

“Pray less. Think more” implicitly defines thinking as rational – sensible, reasoned, and analytical – and implicitly assumes that reason produces good outcomes. However, thinking defined differently, as in “You think too much,” is obsessive and unproductive. Or “You think too much” can operate as an anti-intellectual’s trashing of an intellectual, if we define an intellectual as a mentally active person.

Being a scholar and having had a career in academia, my impression is that intellectuals tend to believe that thinking, the rational kind, presents facts accurately and leads to considered opinions and calm deliberation. Consequently, thinking is the best and most realistic way to solve problems – presumably even the “problem” of pleasure! Reasoning is surely better than beating people up or yelling at them. Yet reasoning, because it’s a human activity, has the human quality of being reactive, even when used by someone who can critique her own positions and arguments, because everyone is subject to their own persuasions, whether we call them biases, ideologies, or just likes and dislikes. Persuasions can be hidden to oneself or so embarrassingly glaring and incriminating to ourselves that we are ashamed to own up to them. Reactivity indicates imbalance. Thus the supposed balanced nature of reasoned argument falters.

To state the obvious, thinking avoids or dispenses with the body, but the obvious needs stating in this case. In our society, which encourages thinking things through before acting, whether personally or governmentally, the body is untrustworthy. Despite the growing respect for holistic tools, such as integrative medicine, our society considers the body to be unreasonable – cramping, aching, or getting gravely ill without any cause or explanation that people can pinpoint or, often, even vaguely affirm. By dismissing the body, thinking dismisses direct experience, without which a person can never come to equanimous terms with reality. The indirectness of thinking adds and subtracts from reality. Selectivity both establishes and limits a fine argument.

People tend to be remarkably undiscerning when it comes to the body with which they go about their lives, often in blithe oblivion, despite the assertion "I know my body" from people who strike us as inexperienced in little more than gross sensations, such as acute recurrent pain or genital orgasm. (Orgasm *can* be felt in various parts of the body and throughout the entire body, and intercourse or masturbation aren't necessary for that to occur.)

In appreciation of the rational, we may praise it for bringing us to awareness. Ah, the surprises and satisfactions of awareness built on explaining, theorizing, and justification. Thinking can bring me to an awareness of social problems, of literary brilliance and the beauty of dead leaves and bougainvillea petals that blow to the front door of my house, of justifications as well as excellent reasons for leaving a relationship or entering one. But thinking cannot get rid of feelings, which, alive in the body, even when submerged within it and out of range of a person's thought because he has not tuned himself to greater sensitivity, substantially direct a person's life, no matter that he is profoundly forgetful of them, let alone unable to name them. (Naming can be beside the point, an exercise in the kind of interpretations that may promote self-recriminations or undue pats on the back.)

I do find thinking to be fun. Right now, as I'm writing. Yet the body's very subtly ever-changing nature, which a person can feel when being still and silent, gives the thinker – and I don't mean that in *any* highfalutin way – a chance for the mind to stop commenting, to stop confiscating the reality, which the body feels, of impermanence.

Dogmas, doctrines, theories, beliefs – people hold firm to them, as if those products of thinking are real, real as in unchanging and not to be changed. Talk about hard thinking, thinking in a really hardened way. Holding thoughts, whether dogmas, doctrines, theories, or beliefs, in an iron grip. People are also capable of holding thoughts softly, the way that a grown-up holds a child, whose tears, moods, and actions the adult sees changing quickly. Thinking is a useful tool, used for both serious and playful purposes, which the body enhances.

Lovestruck play and lovestruck unions

I am a lovestruck person, a lovestruck woman, a lovestruck friend, a lovestruck artist, writer, and scholar who once practiced art history as one of her chief professions. The art historian James Elkins wonders throughout his book *Pictures and Tears: A History of People Who have Cried in Front of Paintings* about the meaning of art historians not being lovestruck: with probing heart and intellect he studies the phenomenon of scholars who are art historians who do not fall in love with art. Art historians analyze, and according to Elkins analysis kills emotional response to art. That saddens him, and on the last page he asks, "What does it mean to say you love paintings, and yet never be in love with a painting?"[1] "Lovers" who are not lovestruck keep their distance from the objects of their love, whereas those of us who are in love cannot keep ourselves from involvement, drawing the "object" close to us through our own subjectivity, which is our consciousness. Indeed, we cultivate it. Scholars can develop a fully feeling and fully functional criticism in which the heart entrains the well-honed intellect and the intellect embraces an opening heart. Hybrid cultivations, such as that of the heart and mind, occur throughout my work and they are playful as they create unions among practices and theories that individuals, professions, and social conventions tend to keep separate. "Hybridities" seems an insufficient term. I create lovestruck "multibridities."

Only recently have I realized that the tools that have attracted me during my adult life, such as yoga and psychoanalysis, are tools whose powers and properties have become embedded in my work. I use the word "tools" rather than "techniques" because techniques implies a step-by-step method, one kind of thought or action following another or necessitating such thought or action through a formula, whereas tools blend together to multibridize of their own accord. They are the mothers of their own inventions, which is why play and labor of love readily characterize those tools. For me, play and labors of love are tools of pleasure. Note that one person's tools are not necessarily those that serve another – gardening, cooking, hiking, or playing guitar may serve *you* – and that any tool can become a hindrance to pleasure if used compulsively and obsessively.

Note

1 James Elkins, *Pictures and Tears: A History of People who have Cried in Front of Paintings* (New York and London: Routledge, 2001), p. 217.

Being Aphrodite

I'm not a devotee of Aphrodite, with pictures or statues of her around my house. Although I chose "aphrodite" as my website and email name, dedicated my book *Monster/Beauty* to her, and collaborated with Russell Dudley, one of my two ex-husbands, on photos of myself after Greek sculptures of her (which appear in *Monster/Beauty* and elsewhere), she is a symbol for me, not anything to which I pray. She is a figure of pleasure, and as such Aphrodite inspires me, so I take her name, as a bride might take the name of her beloved.

During a conversation in 2010 with my good friend Kat, who often calls me Aphrodite, she pointed out that the Greek goddess in her original configuration is pretty neurotic and therefore not befitting my intentions for either my art or my life. I saw that her capriciousness, vanity, and ill temper, her neurotic tendencies, clog the intention of my project, which is to advocate for pleasure, especially in the forms of love, beauty, creativity, and eros. Also, Aphrodite never grows older, and I do! Lightheartedly, Kat addressed me as "Yogic Aphrodite," and I thank her for her humor and insight. Kat and I go to the same yoga studio and became friends through meeting there. Yogic Aphrodite is a more complex, useful, and satisfying model than is the sometimes spleenful ancient goddess.

Beauty, economy, and necessity

Beauty, economy, and necessity are essential pleasures for me. These days they spontaneously apply themselves in writing and performing as they do in eating, cooking, moving my body, connecting with people, choosing and arranging the material elements that create my home, buying and wearing clothes, picking a book, an aesthetician, acupuncturist, yoga studio, or travel destination, be it the Missouri Ozarks or Tamil Nadu.

Beauty is a cultivation of self and surroundings through feeling the subtleties of each.

Economy means attentive management rather than sparing use or scarcity.

Necessity ensures, to the best of my ability, that *shoulds* and *have-tos* dissolve before they lead to wasted energy, time, and words, and such selectivity and discrimination unfix ways that I've written and performed, so that my own flexibility surprises me, letting ideas and texts reshape themselves, freeing me from forms and processes of writing and performing that have become routine and redundant to me.

Necessary privacy is part of that new freedom. R. Crumb, the brilliant comics artist, doesn't talk about projects that he's currently working on, because doing so dissipates a project's energy. I'm paraphrasing from an interview with him that I heard on National Public Radio. The interview focused on new (at that time) work by Crumb, and the all but inevitable question came. How often do people – whether they are interviewers from the most respected media or individuals from the public attending a reading or an art exhibition – ask artists, writers, or musicians who are in the midst of debuting or speaking about their most recent work, "What's next? What are you working on now?"

Such questions needn't offend the artist, but they point to a cultural assumption or projection of inadequacy: no matter how prolific an artist is or how significant her work, she has not done enough. Not contributed sufficiently to her field or to the world at large, not produced an amount of work that meets an undefined but patently asserted standard of plenty. Because scarcity, lack, and absence drive a good deal of behavior, such plenty is out of reach, so I shouldn't be surprised that scarcity, lack, and absence seem to unconsciously motivate even very intelligent interviewers and aficionados of the arts.

Crumb's response woke me up to a personal reality as well as to the cultural one that I state above. Hearing him, I thought that I've been too loose sometimes about describing works in progress or ideas that are newly forming. Like me, artists I know feel dissatisfied and a bit undone describing or explaining any of their work *enough*. The only enough is the work itself.

I'm liking a necessary privacy in the building of aesthetic power. Since 2008 I've been letting my ideas and their public reality take shape very fluidly, more than ever before. So when I've spoken with someone, even a close friend, about writing that's fresh in my head or about a new way to stage and deliver a performance, an interference takes place. It can burden the spaciousness of creativity, and I'm liking *a lot* of space. The more space, the more anything can enter it. When I pay attention to that anything, power builds. I equate power with balance and center (more likely verbs than nouns). I enjoy talking with close friends, who happen to be mostly artists and scholars, about my work or theirs as a whole, or about ideas that interest us and explorations that we're making into any part of life – and those are ways of talking about current work, but without specifying that as the subject of the conversation.

I'm also liking a necessary privacy in not using names of my lovers in my work, lovers who entered my life from 2006 on. Sometimes I don't name friends either. I've found that the intimacy of my work can exist through other means.

I foolishly hoped that beauty, economy, and necessity would be in evidence on Facebook when I opened two different accounts, both of which I've since deleted. One I kept for around a year and a half and the next one for less than two months. I'd been wondering for a while what to do with the first one, which I opened because I thought Facebook would be fun professionally more than personally. I said to friends soon after I opened the account that Facebook was "fascinating and dorky."

I thought that as a person who is public in terms of her art and writing I could post ideas, perceptions, and experiences and then conversation would ensure. Not so. The reason? Dullness. Due to limited space in which to articulate anything. I like conciseness (as well as beautiful elaborations) but not the confinement that Facebook imposes. Also, the superficially mundane things that people report bored me. I'm all for prosaic detail, noticing, loving, enjoying, and feeling its beauty and depth. The prosaic is pretty much the content of our lives – including our relationships with our computers and phones – but on Facebook the prosaic lacks the extensiveness that makes both the earthly world and life in it interesting. Understand that I *am* a very flesh-to-flesh person. The physical reality of someone's body – voice, clothing, skin, and what they all convey – stimulates me. The substance of physicality, which includes the seemingly insubstantial reality of a person's or an event's energy, the force field that we can feel in the material world.

Another reason for lack of exchange was the number of friends. Because my intention had been to use Facebook professionally – posting information about new performances and publications, along with having "conversational" contact – my friends list grew to a cumbersome and unfriendly size. Too much stuff and not enough substance.

On my first go-round, Facebook, whose purpose is to bring people closer to one another, felt removed and removing. So I needed to remove *it*. I sensed my energy being drained, not by being on Facebook but by staying away from it while imagining that I wanted to be making use of it. Responding to real life rather than an imagined one refreshes me.

On the second go-round, I intended to have very few friends. I just wanted to be in contact with them in a very quick and easy way – everyone in the same house, as it were. But as I was filling out the profile I was balking. A favorite book and movie? My education? The insistent expectation of a picture. Well, I love several movies. And books? I love many. My education? Anyone who'd be my friend at that time knew or, I'm sure, didn't care, and it seemed very beside the point. As for a picture, I wanted something very recent that I liked, and I had none. I'm not into taking snapshots of myself or having them taken – whereas I LOVE the process and products of working with other artist collaborators on photos of me. I'm very photogenic, and I'm also very particular about pictures of me. I left a number of the profile questions unanswered and I didn't post a photo. Know, too, that since I was a child, I've intensely disliked filling out forms – applications and questionnaires that reduce possible responses through a multiple choice format or the demand to say who you really are by responding to what the form presents as important. Blech! It all felt like duress: DO IT MY WAY. No! You're wanting me to be a person who doesn't exist, a bare, bare outline of someone who I no longer know when I see her on the profile page.

Furthermore, near the end of my first Facebook experience, I discovered that I could look at pretty much everything of someone who had never friended me, who didn't know me, and who had a tiny batch of friends. That creeped me out. The lack of privacy, even with Facebook's new privacy settings. I used a lot of them and deleted a backlog of information on my wall and elsewhere, and then I thought, "Why are you here anyway?" Delete the whole account! When I went back I was thorough in the privacy arena, but I shortly felt uncomfortable anyway. I'd rather be seen on the street, in all my glamour in my very ordinary neighborhood, than flatly and duly obedient on Facebook.

Dress/habits

We think of everyone as having habits, and we think of monks and nuns wearing them. We think of performers, whether in Shakespeare's plays or in the circus, wearing costumes. Costumes indicate a role, or something other than what one really is, and a habit (presumably) indicates something that a person truly is, the monk and nun having chosen to serve the spirit every instant of their lives.

The habits of religious orders are distinctive. The clothing of monks and nuns declares them to be different from other workers, communities, and mini-cultures, who wear Everyman and Everywoman attire, like suits, or jeans and a T-shirt, or any of the wide array of casual or semi-dressy outfits that we see in the workplace and on the street. Of course, the iconic clothing of religious orders is long, flowing, and supremely simple, and that clothing is worn every day.

I was talking with a fellow performance artist who used to be a monk and he suggested, "What if you wore every day what you wear in performance?" We were talking about performance gear as habit, in other words as a serious spiritual choice, neither as a fashion decision nor even as an aesthetic one, and his idea, elaborated, was this: what if a performance artist wore her costume as a habit while going about her daily business, indoors and out?

"You're always in costume!" asserted a male friend of mine several years ago when we were standing on a New York subway platform. What brought on that comment I don't remember, but it surprised me, because from my perspective I just get dressed.

Certainly I like clothes and choose them carefully when shopping or picking them from my closet, but I'd never thought of my everyday apparel as costume. My performance habit, such as higher heels than usual or naked feet, bare arms and legs, or translucent fabric without underwear, is more revealing and less easy to live in on the street than is my regular clothing. In performance habit, I imagine that I'd be uncomfortable living my ordinary life in Tucson, visiting New York or the Missouri Ozarks, where my sister lives, and walking long distances or in rain or wintry weather, because the habit would appear extreme, ostentatious, or way too partyish in everyday public life. Yet, I hear my performance friend's idea ... not as a challenge but as an invitation.

Or maybe I'll just have a party where everyone is invited to come as a character. I asked my friends Frances and Harold, "Wouldn't it be great to have a character party?" Characters being distinctively, and for the party, pleasurably unusual people. Of course, that definition includes all of *us*. Later, as Frances and I were walking to a neighborhood cafe for our weekly treat together, she suggested, "What about everyone wearing a costume?" A costume associated with a famous character? She wanted to go as Georgia O'Keeffe, about whom she was reading, and she imagined Harold in Alfred Stieglitz attire. Nothing for me leapt into my imagination, and then Frances offered, "Bettie Page!," seeing along the lines of numerous people who've said "You look like Bettie Page." That began in the late 1990s, when images of Page began to show up in mainstream culture. My response was slow and a little reluctant, "Don't know what I'd wear ...," and as we described a few possibilities, another character appeared and I said, "The Buddha. Not that I think I'm a buddha. I admire him." I could enwrap myself in something simultaneously monkish and sensual, robbing that conjures up the Buddha in saffron and Bettie in an animal print. I would, of course, wear bright red lipstick.

When I was a child, rouge, not blush, denoted the cosmetic that colors the cheeks. I think that rouge, along with red lipstick, powder, mascara, a brow pencil, and a fairly large bottle of Chanel No. 5, was one of the products that my mother used to further empower her natural beauty.

Mom wore the rouge so rarely – did she ever wear it? – that I question my memory of the little round (square?) tin even existing on Mom's side of the medicine cabinet in her and Dad's serenely clean and lovely bathroom. Yet I do remember applying rouge when I was a girl. (If it wasn't Mom's, it was Gram's.) Powder, lipstick, and brow pencil were Mom's standbys. A piano student of Mom's had given her the perfume, and I don't recall any instance of smelling it on either her clothing or skin. (Sometimes in writers' accounts of their mothers and their beauty, a signature scent figures prominently.)

I take after Mom – I'm a minimalist with products. I've tried wearing foundation a few times, but like Mom, I prefer powder. In my younger years I wore perfume regularly. I do love the scent of rose, and these days I'm feeling caressed and cozy in Jurlique's Rose Body Oil, which smooths my skin and nourishes its luster. I've used Jurlique's Rose Silk Finishing Powder, a loose powder, for a number of years, and its floral body, which is both light and lavish, indulges my sensuality while disappearing quickly or blending easily with the scent of my body. I agree with Jurlique's description of the powder and its effects: "A silky translucent facial powder that refines the complexion and helps reduce unwanted shine. Leaves the skin fresh and radiant. Ideal for maintaining balance."

Wearing products that feel good as well as look good is essential. Part of their feeling good is a woman's enjoyment of a product's application. Do you like to use a brush, a puff, your fingers? Do you like liquids, creams, powders? Do you like muted color on your mouth while darkening your eyebrows?

I realize that someone might perceive my red lipstick as harsh and my all-but-bare skin as unpolished – both unattractive in their eyes. I realize, too, that my minimalism – for myself, in terms of number of cosmetics, and in regard to other women, my veering away from makeup looks that disguise a woman's features rather than revealing them – may seem doctrinaire or ultra-purist. Red lipstick does cover the color of my mouth, but the color emphasizes my lips' voluptuous shape. So, my minimalism is at once understated and intense, like the romantic rouge in my mind from long ago, whose hue in its tin was very strong and whose application called for subtlety. Nuanced power is one adequate description of glamour.

Passing by my dining room table not long ago, I noticed two images, one of Ava Gardner in her Hollywood prime and the other of a human shape in a coif of chain mail.

Spectacular beauties and warriors – how I wish to rise to the occasion of their glamour!

My hair was growing in the direction of Gardner's coif – parted on the side, with luscious waves, a little frizzy, below the shoulders. "Coif" derives from the Middle English and Old French *coife*, which comes from the Late Latin *cofea*, a cap or hood, though I've also seen helmet. Gardner's coiffure is her helmet of glamour: it protects and projects her allure, she who is at the helm of beauty, in a contrapposto lean on a table in her long gloves and full-length gown, shoulder-baring and mermaid snug, sweet and sexy.

A coif is also a mail head covering, continuing down over the shoulders, like a glamour girl's lush hair. The bust-length warrior figure, viewed from the back and completely covered in links whose lit-up magic had my eyes running over them as if they were the skin of a lover, takes up most of the dust jacket of a bilingual edition of *Beowulf* translated by the Irish poet Seamus Heaney. Mail makes many appearances in *Beowulf*, and it is bold, direct, and still utterly mysterious, like the mesh and the mystique with which it overlays both the materiality and the iconic courage, which is a kind of etiquette, conveyed in the cover photo by Seth Rubin. O, the charisma of metal rings that weigh on the body yet shine like nobody's business!

Gardner's coif, a masterpiece of the film noir era, is come-hither, while the warrior's coif warns "Stay away." Both images communicate this: I am my own person, beauty-soaked.

Psychoanalysis and psychotherapy

In psychoanalysis and psychotherapy I have explored with brilliant teachers the depth of myself. Both have been men. My psychoanalytic experience was from my late twenties into my early thirties and took place in Chicago. I've mentioned my psychoanalyst, Dr. Robert Fajardo, in some of my published writing. My realization that pleasure is a way of living began in the office of Dr. Robert Fajardo. Psychotherapy began in 2001 in Reno, Nevada, and continues, when I feel that I need it, into the present. Larry Barnum, my therapist, and I talk with one another on the phone since I moved to Tucson in 2006. Larry is very romantic and very practical, and makes what for me are memorable statements, like "Everyone is leaking all the time," and "The way you do relationships is the way you do relationships … until you change it." So, if I pay attention to my responses to people, to their leaks, I can be assured that I'll be acting in my best interests and be kind to them as well. Also, I can change if I want to.

Yoga (with some words about bodybuilding)

The word "yoga" derives from a Sanskrit word often translated as *joining* or *union*. Looking retrospectively at my yogic practices, I am deliciously surprised by the sense that yoga, *the* essential tool for me, makes in my life and art, which is the erotic centrality of unions.

I began a home practice of yoga over forty years ago, after my boyfriend George, who was a little older than me, taught me some yoga postures when I was 21. As a bodily practice, yoga felt wonderful from the git-go, and the flexibility and strength that it produces continue to amaze and delight me. How interesting in retrospect that my yoga "training" began with an amorous relationship. George and I lived together for a couple of years.

George "initiated" me in hatha yoga, the physical exercise – postures (*asana* in Sanskrit) – that has become the most popular form of yoga in the United States, and he also introduced me to readings, which, because I tend to become a playfully disciplined student of tools that feel good to me, began for me a lifetime of reading about yoga and of reading sacred texts that originated in ancient yoga or evolved from it. Prior to meeting George I'd read the *Bhagavad Gita*, which is a key text for yogis (not only Hindus). As a sophomore in college I wrote a paper that treated similarities between the *Bhagavad Gita* and William Blake's *Songs of Innocence and of Experience*. Because I don't especially like the *Gita*, I've read a number of translations over the years, contrary as that may seem, because its translators and scholars, as well as some yoga instructors whose classes I've taken, praise the *Gita*. My latest attempt to like the book happened in 2010 with Stephen Mitchell's translation, published in 2000. No go. The visual spectacle feels as over the top as always.

Asana is one of the traditional eight limbs of yoga, and in my late fifties I began to attend hatha yoga classes regularly. Yoga is a system of soul-and-mind-inseparable-from-body health and balance, and it includes and branches into many avenues of self-care and self-study. Most engaging for me are the *yama*s and the *niyamas*, which are ethical principles, nada yoga, which is the yoga of sound and includes mantra (I studied mantra in India in 2008), Bharata Natyam, which is a form of Indian classical dance, and meditation. Bharata Natyam requires great stamina, coordination, and agility, and young girls learn it, so the one class I happened upon in New York (where no regular classes are taught) may be my only one. I practice a form of *vipassana* meditation in which bodily sensation is the opening to insight and equanimity.

My love of yoga is informed by reading, from ancient tantric and Taoist texts to yoga *sutras*, the history of yoga, and the thinkings of modern and contemporary yogis. Some of these readings appear in the Selected Bibliography in Section 2.

So, practices of yogic self-care and self-study are paramount for me. According to the *Yoga Sutra of Pantañjali*, "Yogic action has three components – discipline, self-study, and orientation toward the ideal of pure awareness."[1] The *Yoga Sutra*, almost 2,000 years old, is practical philosophy. Pantañjali sets forth 196 concise and illuminating observations about consciousness and awareness, and offers techniques for freeing oneself from the pain that comes from human beings' habitual (mis)applications of mind, which are clumsy in relation to yogic skills.

Yoga requires neither ritual nor ceremony. It is not a religion. All of that suits me. As does the silence of meditation. During the ten-day silent retreats that I attended in 2009 and 2010, all one needed to do was to meditate. You could keep a non-ticking watch or clock that you brought, but phones and other handheld devices, along with reading and writing materials, had to be turned in – they were kept safe – until the end of the course. Vegetarian food was cooked for meditators and served, buffet style, with much to choose from at breakfast and lunch. Dinner was tea and fruit. You were indeed unto yourself, with your appetites, projections, pains, and pleasures.

I can be such a monk – and I do identify with monks not nuns. I loved the gong that signaled meals and wake-up hour, which was 4 a.m., and called us to meditation in the center's hall. Lights out at 9:30! If in medieval Europe or further centuries and civilizations from my birth, if in nearer decades prior to my birth or in cities no longer visible and audible to human senses, energies coalesced that have brought this Joanna into being, more than once those energies materialized as a monk, one who lived in near-silent orders or conditions. At the retreat I loved the silence. A community of silence.

Silence has been one of my natural habitats since childhood, so it came easily. As did the silencing of communication through facial expressions or bodily gestures during the retreat. Silence guides a person into herself and sustains her solitude among a community of other silent meditators, silence that leads her to her clearest voice.

Analyzing, contemplating, and theorizing remove a person from yogic awareness. They interfere with it by contracting the sensuousness and spontaneity of living in the world and in the body. Analysis, contemplation, and theorizing come easily to me, and I do enjoy them, and at the same time, the elegant simplicity and directness of yoga create a peace and beauty in my life that more intellectual practices do not provide.

I built muscle in gyms from around the age of 30 till I was 60, discontinuing bodybuilding in 2008 because the movements, which I sometimes performed in a meditational way, were feeling rigid and formulaic. I loved the effects of bodybuilding, my muscular strength and shape, and had thought, even after a few years of yoga classes (in which I exerted myself more strenuously than in my home practice) that I became strong and shapely through bodybuilding. I discovered that hatha yoga gives me just as much if not more strength, and shape for sure, plus stamina and, of course, flexibility and grace.

Note

1 Chip Hartranft, *The Yoga Sutra of Pantañjali: A New Translation with Commentary* (Boston, MA and London: Shambhala, 2003), p. 21.

Everyday life

A Hug. I realized how unusual a real hug is, one in which bodies share the flesh in an intimately corporeal and emotional way. Even with friends and family that is not common. Bodies barely connect, and if they do, the touch is light, so the bodies are avoiding one another in both fleshly and feeling ways.

Not long ago a man and I hugged, briefly and fully clothed. We had met in a group situation a few hours earlier, and if we see one another again it would be delicious, but I'm not expecting it. We live in different cities and communicating seems unimportant. Before we hugged neither of us said anything like "Is it okay if I hug you?," "I'd like a hug," or "Give me a hug," which signal an awkward or extortionist origin. We hugged the way you do when you're making love with someone, in a full-on and deep embrace. Deep from and into soul-and-mind-inseparable-from-body. In other words, lovingly.

Those hugs cannot be given unilaterally, because mutuality defines them.

Stupor, Torpor, Girlfriend, Mom. A close girlfriend visited me for several days, and after I drove her to the airport I could only describe my state, to myself and other friends, as stupor. Although stupor generally means apathy, or insensibility, such as suffered due to narcotics or shock, I like turning to *stupefy* in order to articulate the grounds of my *sensibility*. *Stupor* and *stupefy* both derive from the Latin *stupere*, to be amazed or stunned. I like, too, their relation to stupendous. I loved my friend's and my stupendously splendid visit!

Stupefaction can bespeak astonishment or mental dullness. Struck silly – so you're dazzled or dumb, and even if you're dumb, perhaps it's because you're dumbstruck: nothing to say because something beyond expectation has happened and words have flown, for the time being or forever.

During and after my girlfriend's visit, I felt the way I do when I've fallen in love with a man.

The word stupor reminds me of torpor. The day that my friend left, Tucson was hot and humid, so torpor – due to the weather as well as to the intensely cleansing emotions that we both felt as a product of our pleasures, which included conversations, chosen hours of silence, yoga at home and in classes, writing, her cooking, long coffees at a neighborhood cafe, and having no schedule – was suitable to the occasion of living by myself again.

My friend and I talk on the phone and text and email, but we had not stayed in each other's homes before, and in fact had only visited in person with one another twice, in New York. The morning after her arrival I mentioned that we were figuring out how to live with one another. My sister and her partner, male and female friends, and a lover had stayed with me, but I'd not said to them that we were figuring out how to live with one another. My dear friend, she reminded me that already we had the essentials of closeness and comfort and now we'd be adding the topical, which I'll call the daily, like doing laundry and hearing the trains and church bells in the distance.

Besides sharing time, food, personal history, and emotions, we shared products. Weleda Wild Rose Deodorant, SkinCeuticals C E Ferulic and its Ultimate UV Defense SPF 30 cream, Aveda Dry Remedy moisturizing conditioner, Sonya Dakar Omega-e Repair Complex, products that we both used already and she'd left at home, or new ones to each of us, like the SPF cream for her and the omega complex and deodorant for me. I hadn't used deodorant in years. None seemed to have any effect and I sweat lightly, so why bother? Well, my friend's deodorant so impressed me that I bought it for myself during her stay. Weleda Wild Rose Deodorant works, and because it smells so good – organic rose leaf extract and other tantalizing scents – and it's a spray, my armpits receive the benefit of an unobtrusive cologne.

I could say that after taking my friend to the airport I was recovering, from stupor and torpor, but why? I was in better health because of my friend's visit, and why re-cover the territory that we both consciously helped each other detoxify? Territory largely inhabited for her by matters concerning family and her upcoming wedding, territory largely inhabited for me by a departing romantic attachment – indeed, the third term in Going going gone.

As I came out of my stupor, Mom came to mind, and my thoughts digressed from my girlfriend's visit into the sound of words, and from there to the fun directions in which homonyms can take us. When irritated by someone, Mom might call him a stupe. No one I know uses that epithet, and I love Mom's singularity in doing so. Then … *stupe* reminds me of *stoop*, and I think of Mom's girlhood in Chicago: she, her family, and their neighbors sitting on their apartment building stoops in the summer. Which led me back to my friend and me, who wanted to sit, drinking tea or coffee with toast and jam or a cookie or two, in the white, Victorian-looking wrought iron chairs on the porch outside my bedroom door. Torpor, however, overcame us.

Proliferating ecstasy. "… the Department of Paranoia." I swear that's what I heard on National Public Radio. I was in the bathroom, the radio was in the dining room, so … maybe I heard something different. Of course I did, but I love when the ears hear a twist on the words in the media or in a public gathering or private conversation. The twist gives the hearer insight into herself, and I bet that some combination of sounds had touched my wonder and sighs about billboards that I was seeing in Tucson that advertised (prevention of) disaster. I drove by one of the billboards regularly. It asked, "ARE YOU READY FOR A DISASTER?" The question presumed that disaster was on its way and that readiness was the key to one's well-being. The website on the billboard was www.ready.gov

"Be prepared" is the Boy Scout motto. That's it. All by itself, it conveys no urgency, anxiety, or paranoia. I can imagine being prepared in a Buddha-like way, whose foreground and background are balance, very different from readiness coupled with catastrophe.

Do you think that within the bowels of a government building the signage on a door reads "Department of Paranoia"? Maybe it's Department of Paranoiac Emergencies" – DOPE. No. The Department of Paranoia would have no signage at all. Its officials wouldn't want to draw attention to the mission – the dissemination of mistrust, suspicion, and hypervigilance. The more subterranean the officials keep the mission, the better it works. More likely, the Department of Paranoia is ensconced in the hearts of people you encounter every day, at work, on the internet news sources that you frequent, even in your family.

Like all feelings, paranoia extends beyond the person from which it emanates. Feelings fill space, so others' feelings waft our way and invade us, anger us, calm us, caress us. Others' feelings enter as do words in the ears, smells in the nostrils, tastes on the tongue, lotions on the skin, and the touch of others' hands there too, hands filled with anything from rage to tenderness.

Beauty exists in human beings, beauties exist in the world. Danger exists in human beings, dangers exist in the world. Perceptions, which derive from feelings, create the world.

Imagine the Buddha-like dope, meaning "information," that would come from here: the Department of Proliferating Ecstasy.

Mystic/realist. No one lives more in reality than the mystic. Forget asceticism, altered states of consciousness, transfiguration, or idealistic foolishness. The mystic enjoys the everyday world because its marvels fulfill her.

Marvels – the voice of a cashier, the color of brewed tea; a man sleeping in an outdoor alcove of a church, the sheen of a polished wooden chair; the scowl of a woman who looks at you when you board the bus; ice cream and butter at the temperature of their perfect softness. No dark night of the soul, à la St. John of the Cross. No flash-in-the-pan epiphanies.

Experiencing everyday anything as a marvel, the mystic doesn't linger in an experience in order to prolong its pleasures or discomforts or to agitate, vilify, or congratulate herself. When feeling moves along at its own pace, everyday anything is new, instantly and continuously, and the body and senses freshen themselves. When disappointment, dread, anger, sorrow, anxiety, delusion, projection, envy, stupefaction, cowardice, yearning, or frustration arise, they pass quickly, as does any perception or feeling, because she does not oppose them.

The mystic practices ordinariness – the mind untrammeled, unraveled from discursive embellishments. She lives in a palpable, sensuous world which includes her body. You may call the mystic's ordinariness extraordinary if not impossible. For her, gliding and loving are synonyms, as are smoothness and peace.

A time defined by honey

My practices of body and mind create a time defined by honey. A sweet life.

I return home from visiting friends and family who I love and who love me. I am sated from conversation and food. Travel has sapped my energy.

For close to twenty years I've traveled a lot, for work and pleasure, in the United States and internationally. I travel easily and come home full. Now, for a while, home is the only place to be.

At home it is hotter than seven suns. I entertain my cool head.

A tow truck driver verbally displays to me, who sits in the passenger seat of his vehicle, a passion for guns. He mentions his high IQ. Then karma. I say, at the end of our short trip to a tire shop, "It was fun talking with you."

In a waiting room two workers in residences for the old and the infirm talk of low income, comparative shopping for an axle fluid change, and administrators who they like and dislike.

A fat woman with the energy and skin tone of health teases herself about her love of food.

Unwanted immigrants and other citizens wait for rain as the clouds build every afternoon.

I soften like the girl I was, I am, in my mother's arms.

I am quiet like the sky as the rains get ready to test the strength of rooftops.

Sacred tantric texts reveal what every yogi knows: mind rules the world, mind bends it, mind in its ordinary state is clear and empty of concoctions, intellectual or fantastical (which *can* partake of each other). Yogis may read tantric texts. They may be scholars of Buddhism, Taoism, or embodiment. They may theorize and philosophize. They may write books about the history of yoga. None of that matters. Practice does.

People try to hold their world in place, to keep it from changing so that it can stay what it is, which nothing can. The rain does not hold back – a drop over there on the patio, a torrent for miles with bolts of lightning.

I eat Greek yogurt, densely rich like sour cream, a little less tangy, with local honey from a 12-ounce jar. The label reads "Sonoran Desert Honey." Beneath the words an illustration of saguaros and prickly pears and a tree, ironwood perhaps, conveys the expanse of the land in which I live. I like knowing, from the information to the side of the picture, that Sonoran Desert Honey "is a pure natural blend of mesquite, catclaw, ironwood, saguaro and other springtime honeys." The reddish gold liquid is the infinitely sexy complement to the thick dairy. The honey is startlingly sweet even after my eating it days in a row, a most desirable partner for the mildly tart yogurt. (Before buying the Sonoran Desert brand, I hadn't eaten honey in years.)

An attractive man helps me choose a gunpowder green tea, the smokier of two choices.

I water the plants until the rain comes.

In New York I met a man who's a delight. I don't think that I've called any man but him a delight. Our romantic interlude at his home was completely satisfying. I feel no desire or need to spend more time with him. I tell my friends about it all. "I feel like I've just heard a novel," one says, and they and I accept the mysterious goings-on of a happy heart.

I'm listening to a clock and birds.

I'm drinking that smoky tea.

I'm living in a time defined by honey.

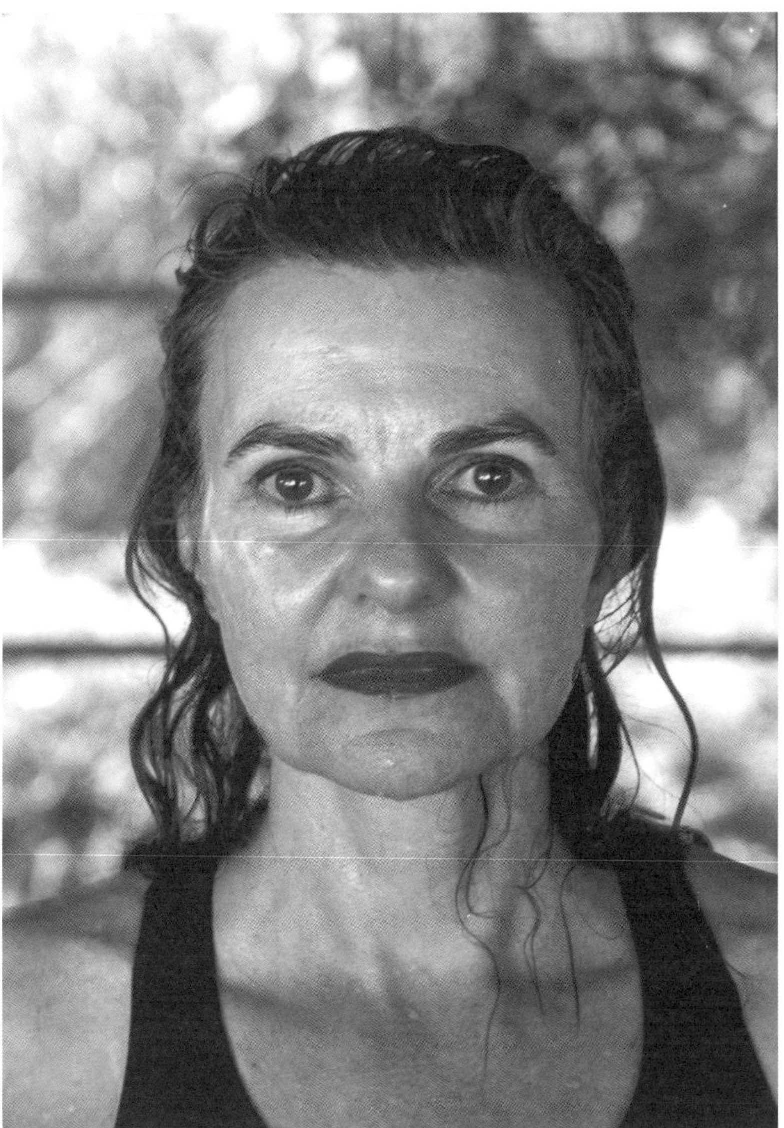

Figure 1 *My friend Joanna*, 2005 © Jill O'Bryan, reproduced by kind permission

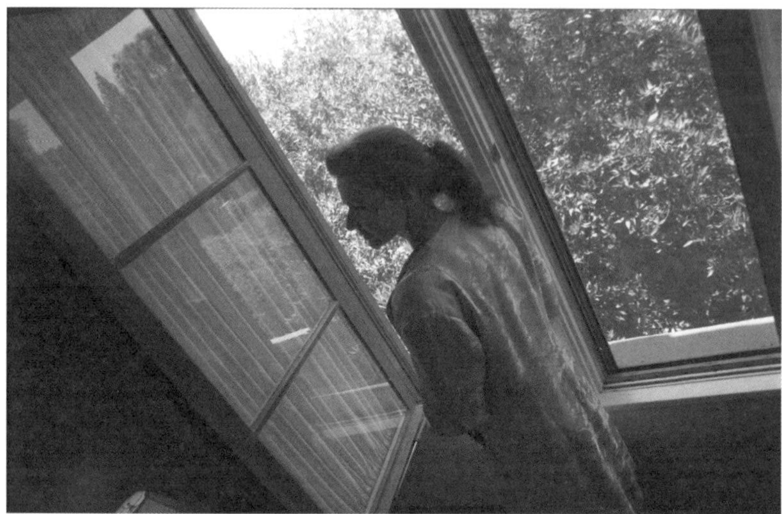

Figure 2 *Seeing Joanna*, 2005 © Jill O'Bryan, reproduced by kind permission

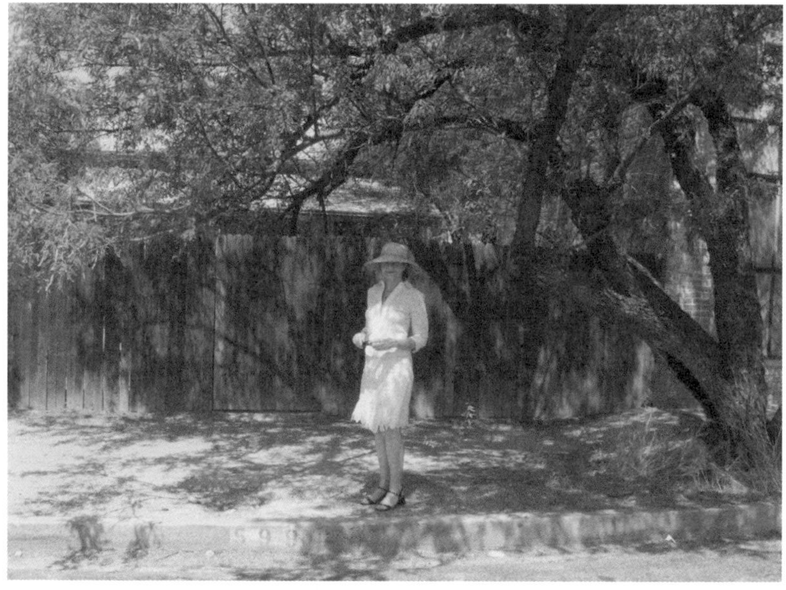

Figure 3 *Joanna arrives in Tucson*, 2005 © Jill O'Bryan, reproduced by kind permission

2

Reading

I've been a studious person since my childhood, an avid reader who loved libraries and bookstores and read the newspaper, the *Chicago Tribune*, every day, and the magazines to which my parents subscribed. *Saturday Review* was my favorite of those subscriptions. Reading has, of course, been basic in my scholarship, whose requirements of reasoning, analytical thinking, and interpretation draw me to a love of learning through books and the mind. Pleasure also comes through the accuracy and precision necessary to fine scholarship and the excitement of seeing both the forest and the trees. I continue to reside in reading as one of my greatest pleasures. Hanging out in the homes of books – libraries and bookstores – and hanging out with books in my home. Talking with people about ideas and what they're reading, knowing that my sister loves current events and American history, one friend loves Heidegger, another Anaïs Nin, and another sticks a lot with contemporary Irish fiction. Sharing book recommendations and books themselves.

How I used to read

I used to read pretty much anything I began all the way through. That was a habit from childhood, and when I was a professor and being the "good" scholar, I read all of each book and article that I'd chosen on the subject I was researching, and those sources would appear in books, essays, and performance texts of my own. The scholar must record her reading, tend to an inventory of her intellect. In that vein I began a list of my reading in around 2004 and kept it up till sometime in 2010 when I started to remove items that weren't all that important to me, meaning that they hadn't moved me, profoundly fed my work, and stayed with me. If a book didn't generate all three of those effects, it left the list. From 2004 into 2010 I also read around in a number of books, skipping here and there or starting at the beginning and reading half or less. Those books generally were written in a style that I found unengaging. They include both scholarly and popular books, and I didn't list them anywhere.

Along with the paring down of a bibliography, I also pared down my library. Some might say severely, I'd say radically, in that the books on my shelves had to adhere to the three requirements of books on the changing bibliography. I sold and gave away *many* books in spring 2009, and the shelves no longer look like those of a normal scholar. In both cases of choosing what mattered deeply to me, Yes and No served me well. If something was a maybe, I had to realize that I didn't want it, either in my home or on my list. However, I did keep nine books, distinct Maybes, lined up on a shelf next to my desk, and they stayed there for nearly a year and a half. Every author was a woman, and whether or not each one called herself a feminist, the content of her book identified her as such for me. I intended to write something about these nine before giving them away, but they spoke to me so little over their coexistence near where I write, that I didn't even open any of them over their months within feet of me during the many hours that I spent at my desk. Finally, I so wanted them gone, so wanted the Maybe turned materially to a No, that I wrote a line or two on each.

Nine books

One of them I used to love, even though its rage at men is way beyond that of most very angry feminists. I'd considered the writing, which cuts to the core of emotion, not only pain, to be brilliant. Valerie Solanas, *SCUM Manifesto*.

One of them irritated me strongly because the author's intent is to give shame a good reputation. No, thank you. Elspeth Probyn, *Blush: Faces of Shame*.

One of them is full of acute, wry thinking that puts me off because the author so negatively critiques intimate love relations. Laura Kipnis, *Against Love: A Polemic*.

One of them claims that conflict in the female psyche is feminism's biggest problem. Laura Kipnis, *The Female thing: Dirt, Sex, Envy, Vulnerability*.

One of them delivers advice, pallid in racy clothing, to couples in conditions of forlorn eros. Esther Perel, *Mating in Captivity: Reconciling the Erotic and the Domestic*.

One reads as a woman's and Woman's plaint about men and women being different, and embeds the stuff that it laments further into the critiqued system of love, sex, and gender. Luce Irigaray, *Elemental Passions*.

One bored me on skimming it, and I read only one whole page, around two-thirds of the way through. Violet Blue, *The Smart Girl's Guide to Porn*.

One has a sentence/idea that appeals to me: "It is my definite impression that some people are good at sexuality, take to it easily and confidently, and seem to have a talent for it." Leonore Tiefer, *Sex is not a Natural Act and Other Essays*.

One is disembodied writing about the body. Elizabeth Grosz, *Volatile Bodies: Toward a Corporeal Feminism*.

Even with the paring down of the bibliography, which was ongoing, I intended to denote the remaining readings as important (a double asterisk) or unmemorable (a single asterisk), but I didn't get around to doing that because I began an entirely new list in 2010, recording only the most memorable of the latest items I'd read. So, rather than the scholar's detailed account of her research, I documented only what I loved the most and learned the most from. A bibliography of everything I'd read didn't serve me. Why do I need to know everything I've read? The true archive of knowledge is within me, so what purpose does a complete listing serve? Now I've combined both lists into the one that appears in this chapter, the very select bibliography of my most loved books.

How I read now

I read freely compared to before, and that freedom feels good. If a book doesn't interest me, I don't finish it. If a friend recommends a book, I thank her for the recommendation but I don't feel obligated to read it. Neither do I feel obliged, when I'm researching a subject for my writing, to read either the de rigueur or in-fashion publications on it. I'm inclined to read classics on a subject, but I no longer need to prove that I know the literature on it. I keep adding to the very select bibliography.

A very select bibliography from 2004 to 2011, with some comments

I continue to read a lot – mostly books and the news – and on various subjects. Top ones include fashion, health, the female pelvis, Indian classical dance, beauty, *sutras*, ancient Greek art and life, traditional Chinese medicine, Ayurveda, and yoga. Every now and then I read a biography, a novel, a play, or a book on current events and issues, like James Stewart's *Tangled Webs: How False Statements are Undermining America*, about Martha Stewart, Scooter Libby, Barry Bonds, and Bernie Madoff; Nicholas Carr's *The Shallows: What the Internet is Doing to our Brains*, about inroads that the digital world is making into people's minds and into culture at large; and Yasmina Reza's *Dawn Dusk or Night: A Year with Nicolas Sarkozy*, about his presidential campaign. I often read more than one book on any subject and more than one book by an author, and some of that reading doesn't appear on this list at all, such as on ancient Greek warfare, Alexander the Great, diet, and the decline of American higher education.

Armstrong, Carol. *Buddha*. New York: Penguin, 2001.

Armstrong, Carol. *The Great Transformation: The Beginning of our Religious Traditions*. New York and Toronto: Alfred A. Knopf, 2006.

Barthes, Roland. *Mourning Diary: October 26, 1977–September 15, 1979*, trans. Richard Howard. New York: Hill and Wang, 2010.

Batchelor, Stephen. *Confession of a Buddhist Atheist*. New York: Spiegel and Grau, 2011.

Bentley, Toni. *Sisters of Salome*. Lincoln, NE and London: University of Nebraska Press, 2005 [first published New Haven, CT: Yale University Press, 2002].

Beowulf: A New Verse Translation, trans. Seamus Heaney. New York: Farrar, Straus and Giroux, 2000.This is one of the most beautiful works I've ever read. I remember a version of it when I was a child – what a "Grimm" fairy tale! – and hadn't looked at *Beowulf* again till 2010, wanting to read another premodern hero classic of Western literature after falling in love with *The Iliad* (also on this list). I found the Heaney translation serendipitously, at my neighborhood used bookstore. When I mentioned to my sister that I'd just read the Heaney translation of *Beowulf*, she told me that she had it too!!

Bernstein, Carl. *A Woman in Charge: The Life of Hillary Rodham Clinton*. New York: Vintage, 2007.

Bolton, Andrew, with contributions by Susannah Frankel and Tim Blanks. *Alexander McQueen: Savage Beauty*. New York: Metropolitan Museum of Art, 2011.

Brown, Norman O. *Love's Body*. New York: Vintage, 1966. A perennial favorite that I reread.

Carney, Elizabeth. *Olympias: Mother of Alexander the Great*. New York and London: Routledge, 2006. Having read a number of books about Alexander the Great and watched Oliver Stone's *Alexander* numerous times, I felt impelled to read about Alexander's mother. I wanted to know how a woman of power lived, and survived, in a cutthroat world of men. My conclusion: what a difficult life! On guard, strategic, and hard to imagine – the emotional tenor and the parameters of feeling – from the perspective of a twenty-first-century middle-class American woman.

Chia, Mantak. *Chi Nei Tsang: Chi Massage for the Vital Organs*. Rochester, VT: Destiny Books, 2007.

Chia, Mantak. *Healing Light of the Tao: Foundational Practices to Awaken Chi Energy*. Rochester, VT: Destiny Books, 2008.

Chozanshi, Issai. *The Demon's Sermon on the Martial Arts and Other Tales*, trans. William Scott Wilson. Tokyo, New York, and London: Kodansha International, 2006.

Cranz, Galen. *The Chair: Rethinking Culture, Body, and Design*. New York and London: W. W. Norton, 1998.

Daniélou, Alain. *The Hindu Temple: Deification of Eroticism*, trans. Ken Hurry. Rochester, VT: Inner Traditions, 2001.

de Clario, Domenico. *A Calvinian Architecture*. Melbourne: Monash University, 2001. Dreams and dreaming caught my attention early on while reading the book and I began to underline their occurrence – until less than halfway through, I stopped, because they appeared so regularly that I understood dream-space to be a paradoxical bedrock of de Clario's world. Or, more precisely, the foundation of a Domenican (from the writer's given name) architecture. De Clario has said that within the fine arts, architecture is his first love. Over and over, de Clario's emotions surge in ecstasy as he lets himself be taken by life – yielding to its unfolding forms. Like when he knows for the first time, in Urbino at the age of 20, that "*I'm Italian!*" and that "I cannot contain any of this" sensual glory that gives him "this primal understanding," which is a keystone – *the* keystone? – of Domenican architecture. In de Clario's awakening to Italian-ness, the senses collide and resonate: taste – wine; smell – "frying artichokes," "cypress trees fresh hay," and goats; sound – voices laughing, "a few muttered curses," and the goats' bells; vision – the architecture of Urbino, the "little lights in a hundred kitchens being switched on," and the rising moon "full golden"; touch – buttocks seated on a chair, skin absorbing the atmosphere of a spring evening. Soul-and-mind-inseparable-from-body completely invested in each changing moment. Here, as in my reading of many of de Clario's moments of fluid consciousness, I experience his feelings as thousands of blossoms blooming simultaneously, the centrality of sensation.

de Clario, Domenico. *A Tertiary World*. Melbourne: Monash University, 2008.

Deng, Ming-Dao. *Chronicles of Tao: The Secret Life of a Taoist Master*. San Francisco, CA: HarperCollins, 1993.

Deng, Ming-Dao. *Scholar Warrior: An Introduction to the Tao in Everyday Life*. San Francisco, CA: HarperCollins, 1990.

Devi, Ragini. *Dance Dialects of India*. Delhi, Bombay, Bangalore, Kanpur, and London: Vikas Publications, 1972.

Foucault, Michel. *Fearless Speech*, ed. Joseph Pearson. Los Angeles, CA: Semiotext(e), 2001.

Gathorne-Hardy, Jonathan. *Sex the Measure of All Things: A Life of Alfred C. Kinsey*. Bloomington and Indianapolis, IN: Indiana University Press, 1998.

Goenka, S. N. *The Discourse Summaries: Talks from a Ten-Day Course in Vipassana Meditation*. Onalaska, WA: Vipassana Research Publications, 2000.

Gordon, Mary. *Spending: A Novel*. New York: Scribner Paperback Fiction, 1999.

Graham, Martha. *Blood Memory: An Autobiography*. New York, London, Toronto, Sydney, and Auckland: Doubleday, 1991.

Grilley, Paul. *Yin Yoga: Outline of a Quiet Practice*. Ashland, OR: White Cloud Press, 2002.

Gupta, Roxanne Kamayani. *A Yoga of Indian Classical Dance: The Yogini's Mirror*. Rochester, VT: Inner Traditions, 2000.

Haberman, David L. *Acting as a Way of Salvation: A Study of Raganuga Bhakti Sadhana*. New York and Oxford: Oxford University Press, 1988.

Halpern, David. *Saint Foucault: Towards a Gay Hagiography*. New York and Oxford: Oxford University Press, 1995.

Hawkins, David R. *Power vs. Force: The Hidden Determinants of Human Behavior*. Carlsbad, CA: Hay House, 2002.

Hawksley, Lucinda. *Lizzie Siddal: Face of the Pre-Raphaelites*. New York: Walker and Company, 2004.

The Iliad of Homer, trans. Ennis Rees. New York and Oxford: Oxford University Press, 1991. The first lines of this translation gave me chills, and they so excited me that I had to read them to a few friends. Over and over this book gave me pause for tears and contemplation. (Other translations did not have that effect.) *The Iliad* dazzled me, and I took my time absorbing its beauties, one of which is its intensity of grief, so I read slowly, putting off finishing the book. People who know me might be surprised by my speaking of beauty and grief in the same breath, because my gravitating towards pleasure, equatable with happiness, is part of my friends' knowledge of me. Ennis Rees, the translator, notes the purity and intimacy of *The Iliad*, and I think that those qualities of Homer's expression of grief are the aspects that brought me to tears as I read about death after death. I don't remember the last time I cried while reading of characters or their actions and emotions. In *The Iliad* people and deities experience "unspeakable grief," "grief overwhelming," and "unbearable sorrows." Their grief transfers into this reader. Zeus, the Father god, cries "a shower of bloody tears"; great heroes, champions, and rulers cry. I was in good company as I grieved along with them, over the grimness of war, the absurdities of its continuation, and the loss of companions and kin. Greaves are a kind of leg armor that primarily protects the shins, worn by the ancient Greeks, and Homer more than occasionally describes the Greeks in *The Iliad* as "well-greaved." Indeed, well-greaved and well-grieved are they.

Joshi, L. M. *Lalita-Sahasranama: A Comprehensive Study of One Thousand Names of Lalita Maha-Tripurasundari; with Original Text in Sanskrit, Roman Transliteration and Critical Explanation of Each Name*. New Delhi: D. K. Printworld (P) Ltd., 1998. This inspired my performance *Sexual Advances*.

Kashner, Sam and Nancy Schoenberger. *Furious Love: Elizabeth Taylor, Richard Burton, and the Marriage of the Century*. New York: Harper, 2010.

Keeney, Bradford. *Shaking Medicine: The Healing Power of Ecstatic Movement*. Rochester, VT: Destiny Books, 2007.

Kennard, Edward A. *Field Mouse Goes to War: Tusan Homichi Tuwvota*, Hopi text by Albert Yava, ed. Williard W. Beatty. Palmer Lake, CO: Filter Press, 1999 [first published by Branch of Education, Bureau of Indian Affairs, 1944].

Kent, Tami Lynn. *Wild Feminine: Finding Power, Spirit & Joy in the Female Body*. New York: Atria, 2011.

Khan, Hazrat Inayat. *The Mysticism of Sound and Music*, revised edn. Boston, MA and London: Shambhala, 1996.

Kinder, Terryl N. *Architecture of Silence: Cistercian Abbeys in France*. New York: Harry N. Abrams, 2000.

Knapp, Caroline. *Appetites: Why Women Want*. New York: Counterpoint, 2003.

Kothari, Sunil, ed. *Bharata Natyam*. Mumbai: Marg Publications, 1997.

Lao-Tzu. *Tao Teh Ching*, trans. John C. H. Wu. Boston, MA and London: Shambhala, 2003.

Lawrence, Robyn Griggs. *The Wabi-Sabi House: The Japanese Art of Imperfect Beauty*. New York: Clarkson Potter, 2004.

Maharshi, Ramana. *The Spiritual Teaching of Ramana Maharshi*. Berkeley, CA and London: Shambhala, 1972.

Marin, Gilles. *Healing from Within with Chi Nei Tsang: Applied Chi Kung in Internal Organs Treatment*. Berkeley, CA: North Atlantic Books, 1999.

Marsh, Jan. *The Legend of Elizabeth Siddal*. London: Quartet Books, 1989.

Martin, Agnes. *Writings*, 6th edn. Ostfildern-Ruit: Hatje Cantz, 2005.

Martin, Judith. *Common Courtesy: In Which Miss Manners Solves the Problem That Baffled Mr. Jefferson*. New York: Atheneum, 1985.

McLuhan, Marshall and Quentin Fiore. *The Medium is the Massage: An Inventory of Effects*. Corte Madera, CA: Gingko Press, 2001 [first published 1967].

Odier, Daniel. *Yoga Spandakarika: The Sacred Texts at the Origins of Tantra*, trans. Clare Frock. Rochester, VT: Inner Traditions, 2005.

O'Shea, Janet. *At Home in the World: Bharata Natyam on the Global Stage*. Middletown, CT: Wesleyan University Press, 2007.

Patai, Daphne. *Heterophobia: Sexual Harassment and the Future of Feminism*. Lanham, MD, Boulder, CO, New York, and Oxford: Rowman & Littlefield, 1998.

Paul, Russill. *The Yoga of Sound: Healing and Enlightenment through the Sacred Practice of Mantra*. Novato, CA: New World Library, 2004.

Pollan, Michael. *In Defense of Food: An Eater's Manifesto*. New York: Penguin, 2008.

Prakash, Prem. *The Yoga of Spiritual Devotion: A Modern Translation of the Narada Bhakti Sutras*. Rochester, VT: Inner Traditions International, 1998.

Rao, Gopinath and S. V. Ramana. *The Classical Dance Poses of India*. Madras: Natana Niketan Publications, 1955.

Rosenberg, Marshall B. *Nonviolent Communication: A Language of Life*, 2nd edn. Encinitas, CA: Puddle Dancer Press, 2003.

Rosenzweig, Rachel. *Worshipping Aphrodite: Art and Cult in Classical Athens*. Ann Arbor, MI: University of Michigan Press, 2004.

Sarabhai, Mrinalini. *Longing for the Beloved: Songs to Siva-Nataraja in Bharata Natyam*. Ahmedabad: Darpana, 1976.

Sarabhai, Mrinalini. *Understanding Bharata Natyam*, 3rd edn. Ahmedabad: Darpana Academy of Performing Arts, 1981.

Sartwell, Crispin. *Six Names of Beauty*. New York and London, Routledge, 2004.

Schaef, Anne Wilson. *Escape from Intimacy: The Pseudo-Relationship Addictions*. San Francisco, CA: Harper & Row, 1989.

Schaef, Anne Wilson. *When Society Becomes an Addict*. San Francisco, CA: Harper & Row, 1987.

Schulman, Sarah. *Ties that Bind: Familial Homophobia and its Consequences*. New York and London: New Press, 2009.

Schumann, H. W. *The Historical Buddha: The Times, Life and Teachings of the Founder of Buddhism*, trans. M. O. Walshe. Delhi: Motilal Banarsidass, 1989.

Smith, Patti. *Just Kids*. New York: Ecco, 2010.

Sri Ragini. *Hindu Dances (Nritanjali)*. Delhi: Sumit Publications, 1982.

Steele, Valerie and Jennifer Park. *Gothic: Dark Glamour*. New York: Yale University Press and Fashion Institute of Technology New York, 2008.

Stieber, Mary. *The Poetics of Appearance in the Attic Korai*. Austin, TX: University of Texas Press, 2004.

Taleb, Nassim Nicholas. *The Black Swan: The Impact of the Highly Improbable*. New York: Random House, 2007.

Tao Te Ching: A New English Version, trans. Stephen Mitchell. New York: HarperPerennial, 1992.

Thurman, Robert A. F. *Anger: The Seven Deadly Sins*. Oxford and New York: Oxford University Press, 2005.

Trungpa, Chögyam. *True Perception: The Path of Dharma Art*. Boston, MA and London: Shambhala, 2008.

Alcoholics Anonymous. *Twelve Steps and Twelve Traditions*. New York: A.A. Grapevine, Inc. and Alcoholics Anonymous Publishing, 1953.

Werner, Kenny. *Effortless Mastery: Liberating the Master Musician Within*. New Albany, IN: Jamey Aebersold Jazz, 1996.

Williams, Margery. *The Velveteen Rabbit*. New York: Doubleday, 1922.

Yogananda, Paramahansa. *Autobiography of a Yogi*. Los Angeles, CA: Self-Realization Fellowship, 1959.

The Yoga of Spiritual Devotion: A Modern Translation of the Narada Bhakti Sutras, trans. Prem Prakash. Rochester, VT: Inner Traditions International, 1998.

The Yoga-Sutra of Pantanjali, trans. Chip Hartranft. Boston, MA and London: Shambhala, 2003.

3

Theory: on behalf of muses

Why I love the boys

I love the boys because they give me pleasure.

I call men boys, you husbands, students, lovers, thinkers, fathers, friends, and artists, men who I love in the flesh and from a distance that is centuries, cities, blocks, or the vagaries and factual black holes of written history, because I like being playful. I call you boys, flirtatiously and a bit factiously, because it's lighthearted, like calling my women friends, who range in age from their twenties into their seventies, girls. Play and pleasure are effortless companions.

In 2009 I completed a performance text called "Why I love the boys." It has remained unperformed, and I'm glad, because when I looked at it in 2010, the text felt scattered, insufficiently focused. However, from that piece I saved the first line and the paragraph that followed it, which open this piece, and they do feel fitting, because men have been my muses, and pleasure *is* the overarching reason why I love the boys.

I like being a woman who articulates love for men, and while I would never deny men's invasions of women's peace of body and mind, brutalities which can be blatant or insidious, nor disappointments with men in my own life, I gravitate more naturally to loving and celebrating than to excoriating either men or life, and men need women's love more than they need our criticism. Not fluffy, mindless, babying, I'll-die-for-you romanticism, but rather mature and flourishing love, which is love that means kindness and compassion for oneself as well as others, that entails self-care and self-study so that individuals can grow, in relationship and unto themselves. Elucidating pleasures with men helps me to elucidate pleasure, period.

The "problem" of pleasure – solved!

People tend to misunderstand pleasure in both daily and spiritual life. The misunderstanding happens through limited definitions and practices that paradoxically minimize the place of pleasure by maximizing some of its conventional intensities, thereby demoting pleasure from its all-encompassing magnitude into a narrow if not tiny, though often obsessive, goal or craving, a stance in which pleasures can be enjoyed, but they can be a big problem! The authors of Hindu, yogic, Taoist, and Buddhist texts, for example, present pleasure as a major cause of suffering. Pleasures are fleeting, and because they feel so good, one grasps after them, wanting the same pleasure as previously experienced or another of an even greater intensity. The obsession with a particular pleasure results in the obsession taking up a lot more space and time than the pleasure ever did, and in the pleasure-craver's "living" for the past and future rather than in the present. The authors of texts such as those I have mentioned advocate living in the present, which, they say, is the only time and reality in which human beings actually exist. Change and impermanence, they declare, define the essence of reality, and pleasures are simply facets of that flux.

After studying many sacred and spiritual texts in which I, the reader, was being admonished to desist from pleasure, which had become foundational in my life as a constant of happiness, I realized that the problem with pleasure was a problem of belief and practice. Pleasure needs help – it needs people to proclaim and articulate its necessity and subtleties. Misunderstanding arises from people's believing that pleasure is special – events and actions that stand out from the usual, ordinary, and daily. Rather than being at the center of living in general and therefore of one after another activity and experience every day, pleasure, people believe, is short-lived and a peak. It is party food rather than the staff of life.

We feel pleasure in our bodies: a taste; a sound, which may be a bird's twitter, coo, or melody, or a word grouping, in our own language and in ones that we don't know; or an impact or innuendo received in any of our five senses. Pleasure is often subtle, because our bodies are subtle chemistries. Obvious and gross pleasures are well known, and their familiarity may override sensations that seem to be merely pleasant, lesser because too prosaic to be sufficiently special. Intoxication through alcoholic beverages is obvious after a certain pitch is reached, but that intoxication may be drunkenness, which is often *un*pleasurable. Intoxication, whether through drink, love, or beauty, can be *subtly* exhilarating, variable, mutable, and changing, like a Sonoran Desert sky when a few clouds are humming their way through its reverberant blue, but intoxication often results in hangovers, whether physical or emotional, and the emotional ones can last a long time as obsessions.

For most people, the verbal articulation of pleasure's subtleties is an undiscovered vocabulary, and the sensation of pleasure's subtleties escapes notice. For many people, pleasure means high pleasure, and if "low" were to modify pleasure, that modifier would in effect deactivate pleasure, reduce it to ho-hum pleasantness, such as a "nice" meal or person or drive into rural America or outback Australia. Odd as it may seem, high pleasure is the reductive condition, because expecting or needing – craving or clinging to – high pleasure makes pleasure repetitive and redundant, a status quo of supposed specialness. Don't think that I'm reducing pleasure to niceness. All pleasure is pleasure to me, and pleasure is beyond measure. Like love, pleasure is or it isn't. You don't sort of love someone, and you don't sort of experience pleasure.

Pleasures range from the prosaic poignancy of observing a dead butterfly on my front porch to the high intensity of vaginal orgasm to the welcome that I find in sacred space, which rests in pleasure rather than in designated parlors of worship. The salons that I held were sacred space, as are walks by the Santa Cruz River with my friend Kat. Pleasure, as I experience it and offer it in my performances, is the substance of living, so it is ecstasy and ease, making love and making dinner, without making believe, as is the conventional thinking and modus operandi, that we must regularly experience and know the bad, which is *un*pleasure, in order to experience and know the good, which is pleasure, and that a life of pleasure would be bland. In ecstasy and ease, while making love and making dinner, a person can feel shifting balances of unforced appreciative engagement, simultaneous peace and stimulation, and those shifting balances are pleasure, one pleasure after another, so that pleasure itself becomes a foundation of existence. Attuned to those shifting balances, which means, attuned to her body, a person has no inclination to distinguish one or another pleasure as being better or more, for she perceives and experiences pleasures as simply and exquisitely differentiated from one another.

Pleasure is always a discovery that is a process, though people name their pleasures as things outside of themselves: it's the coconut cream pie, the Botticelli painting, the kiss, the century bike race, the sojourn in Paris, the Nietzsche book, the leaf drifting from a tree, the butterfly that flew right their way, the generosity of friends or strangers. Naming pleasure as outside of ourselves is a convention, yet it also demonstrates the fact that people do not feel the sensations within the body that indicate the delight in the heart, the arousal of the soul, and the expansion of the mind, or that they have no words to talk about those pleasures. Maybe pleasure for them is as shallow as their breathing.

Pleasure includes well-being and self-discovery. Pleasure is a fluid way of living rather than a static state that is the perfect completion of a process. Fluidity calls on a person to have faith. People often confuse faith and belief. Belief is a category of idea, often held so strongly, though perhaps unconsciously, that it structures an individual's thinking and leads to rigidly ideological ways of being – about pleasure, for example: pleasure is simplistic fun, superficial, something to do on Saturday night, or an orgasm as the necessary outcome of sexual arousal. Belief can be industriously static, ever working to keep soul-and-mind-inseparable-from-body (a term I began to use in the late 1980s) in place, unpleasurably. Soul-and-mind-inseparable-from-body: each of the three needs the others in order to function well, which is to function pleasurably, and faith is an act of imagination.[1] To have faith is to enjoy infinite acts of imagination. My work is the enjoyment of some of those acts, many realized.

I hope that my awareness and considerations of pleasure's subtleties stimulates both an audience's faith in the value of their own pleasures as well as their expanded experiences of pleasure and their desire and ability to talk about those experiences.

Impressing me with pleasure

I seem to have been born into the impress of pleasure, aware of it from infancy, in my first memory. There, my mother's sensuous touch impressed me, her communication of love as I lay naked in sunlight. Pleasure impressed me when I was a little girl: the warmth of our home in Chicago winters, Dad's hot cocoa, dressing up in Mom's mink and her gorgeous red lipstick, masturbating in undisturbed luxuriousness, Thanksgiving and Christmas celebrations, reading classics such as *Little Women* (which was one of the first books that wasn't a children's book that I read), matzoh ball soup, and Dad's rose and rock gardens and the shady bed filled with bleeding hearts. I could name many more pleasures, and they continued as I grew up, into adulthood and now maturity. I have not led a perfect life, whatever that means in national myths and in individuals' beliefs and yearnings. I suffered with depression in my teens and into my later twenties, a state of consciousness healed by psychoanalysis with Dr. Robert Fajardo, in whose office, lying on the couch, I first realized that pleasure is the point of living. I articulated that, either in Dr. Fajardo's presence or later one day after a session with him, and "Pleasure is the point of living" has remained foundational for me, no matter the difficulties I've experienced, from divorce to the deaths of my parents, which were three of the most painful difficulties that I've suffered. While I attribute my healing from depression to psychoanalysis, understand that since my early twenties I've gravitated towards tools such as psychoanalysis, and practices that I discuss earlier in this volume that contribute to my growing healthier, and that I've known innately, and certainly by my twenties, in an articulable way that the essence of healing comes from within oneself and her state of soul-and-mind-inseparable-from-body, which is a state of consciousness.

Some artists (in any of the fine arts) intentionally present in their work "what reality *feels* like."[2] So says Jonah Lehrer in his book *Proust was a Neuroscientist*. I am one of those artists who, as Lehrer notes, deal with consciousness – their own – and through that, truths of human consciousness. For me, investigating and enjoying pleasure opens just such truths, and my performing what the reality of pleasure feels like offers reflective, analytical, and philosophical considerations of pleasure. Several or all of those aspects frequently exist together in my work.

The tool of pleasure in the territory of deep camouflage

Being an artist, scholar, and writer, I am used to fine arts and academic studies that present and reflect on individuals', societies', and civilizations' problems and miseries, without solution. Around 2004 I began wanting an art of uplift, to see and read it, to write about it. I was looking for the erotic in art – eros being the deepest and richest connections in life, which may occur while making love or just as readily while stepping outside to collect your mail. Connections that many people would call mundane rather than special. Connections that are happening every instant if a person perceives them. Eros includes sex acts and sexuality, but erotic experience is much larger than that. One definition of eros is life force, and when a human being lives erotically, experience itself is pleasure, and pleasure organizes her life. Organize derives from the Latin *organum*: instrument, tool. Eros is an instrument of pleasure, a necessary tool for foundational happiness, and when pleasure gives order, which is a kind of sanity, to the human being by vitalizing the organs and the entire human organism, pleasure itself is the order of existence.

My wanting an art of uplift meant not only that I wanted it from other artists and writers, but also that I had to give it to myself, and through me, to my audience. In the high theory of academia and the avant-garde of art in which I've made my living and lived many pleasures, an art of uplift is generally considered to be sentimental, unchallenging, idealizing, and insufficiently edgy. People have written about my work as unclassifiable, even wildly so, yet, despite my unconventional status within art and academia, I've sometimes felt displaced and a little unnerved going against their grain of supposed innovation and originality and of anti-spirituality as I began to listen more and more to myself and less and less to the customs, dogmas, and conformities of those professional worlds with which I'm familiar. Since around 2006 I have been increasingly comfortable with my own artistic and personal capacity for pleasure, and I associate pleasure with sanity and healing. In 2009 I read *True Perception: The Path of Dharma Art*, written by the legendary Buddhist teacher Chögyam Trungpa. He severely criticizes contemporary art that offers its audience sickness as subject matter, content, or gestalt, and he understands that such work receives rewards from the art world. His gift to the reader? The assertion that an artist must give the world basic sanity.

Art can open space or close it, can be roomy or claustrophobic. Art can give people bright dreams or grotesque nightmares by which to live. In each of those possibilities, art can show us where we stand in our own shoes, and in my art of uplift, which is my mature work, I wish to show that we can stand in pleasure.

How important that is, for human beings live in the territory of deep camouflage. Some may think that pleasure itself camouflages the holes in people's lives. Pleasure as camouflage equals hollow pleasures, but the phrase "hollow pleasures" is itself hollow, because pleasure is fullness itself and no one can fake it. If they try to, *they* are the hollowness, not pleasure. Deep camouflage: it is the mask of fashion – "flawless" skin, shape-shifting surgeries, perhaps the short bangs that shaded my forehead over many years of my adult life. Deep camouflage is the misleading words of amorous cads and of politicians and of anyone too cool in the heart to tell the truth. Deep camouflage is the blur of scandal-mongering "news." Deep camouflage is the disguises that we wear for fear of inadequate protection against pleasure, whose power invites the relinquishing of our bullshit. Deep camouflage is the opiate that maintains people's defenses against pleasure.

Pleasure activist

I knew a man who wanted very much to be happy, which meant to me that he wanted to feel pleasure, but he was miserable. He was a scholar and a professor, and the following statement of his astounded me: "I'm a head without a body." Or maybe he said he was a body without a head or that he walked around with his body and his mind separated. I talked about this with several friends – my surprise and my difficulty in imagining how that state of being would feel, as it is alien to me. Months after his sad assertion, while talking with my friend Jill and because of her insights and humor, I realized, with a revelatory profundity and clarity, that most people (in contemporary Western culture) feel more or less the way that the disconnected man did, and in the whirl of that realization I perceived a major difference between myself and a lot of people in how we feel, sense, absorb, and move towards or away from any experience or person. Prior to Jill's and my conversation, another friend told me that the meaning of soul-and-mind-inseparable-from-body was beginning to dawn on her. I was shocked, because we'd been close since the 1980s and she'd read a lot of my writing, so I'd presumed that she understood, at least intellectually, soul-and-mind-inseparable-from-body. Her statement about beginning to get what to me was primally Joanna all of her life unlocked my acknowledgment of a big and basic difference between her and me. The unhappy man, the old friend, and the conversation with Jill – I thank her for her inimitably loving humor – affirmed that I certainly experience life in an unusual way.

I do have a compatriot – from the nineteenth century: Walt Whitman, who wrote from a consciousness that experienced body, soul, and mind as one and who Lehrer calls an empiricist and a lyricist – I identify! – seen in his time as "erotic and audacious."[3] I have found that people often perceive me and my work as erotic and audacious. How times don't change in regard to the reality of soul-and-mind-inseparable-from-body! Maybe those perceptions arise because I'm a woman, and sexuality expressed first-person by a woman in direct, honest, passionate, and romantic language remains taboo, despite the availability of numerous and overt samplings of sex, from news to entertainment sources. The taboo enlarges when a woman is long beyond childbearing years, because if she still likes men and sex with them after all her years of dealing with them, her imagined or real authority as a sexual being – an erotic being – is conjured to be intimidating and beyond the pale. The taboo enlarges even more when that woman embodies and expresses pleasure shaped in both the "energy, confidence, and sensuality of a newly desirous twenty-year-old" and the experienced confidence of maturity.[4] Hey, let's think about this phenomenon as a wonder rather than a taboo. (I specifically address that wonder in the performance *Maiden Elder* in this volume.)

Feminism is often no more welcoming of female eroticism and pleasure than is society at large. In many writings from differing feminist perspectives and in various genres since the late 1960s, and from academics' theories to novelists' characters, feminists have written about women as victims of sex and love. While the long record of physical and emotional cruelties and violence that women have endured when loving and making love with men continues to grow, as do the unrecorded abuses, and I understand reasons for feminists' rallying to the side of the oppressed and damaged, raising awareness of women's pains and problems, and acting politically and socially to alleviate if not eliminate them, pleasure with men is paramount in some women's lives or equally present with conflict, strife, and even trauma in regard to a woman's entire history with men. Yet a full-on embrace of pleasure by feminists as an unobstructed state of consciousness to which women can attest and which they can celebrate appears to be untrustworthy. The idea conveyed by the title of a classic feminist book from 1984, *Pleasure and Danger*, appears to be as "popular" today as it was then. (The book, edited by Carole Vance, came out of a famous conference, "Towards a Politics of Sexuality," held in 1982 at Barnard College.) One of today's insidious dangers regarding the soul-and-mind-inseparable-from-body pleasure of sex is the conflation of sex with naughtiness – a truly trivializing word in this case – and scandal. I read and hear the conflation in news and entertainment media and in conversations with acquaintances and friends. When sex is naughty and scandalous, pleasure as a state of consciousness is likely not its foundation or focus.

I laugh in awe: people think that because they feel one way or another, everyone else does! I'll call that the fallacy of familiarity. Our unthinking and unconscious familiarity with our own way of being allows us to think that others live the same way, or ought to, or are very peculiar and even wrong if they don't. My recent insight into knowing that I've always felt myself as soul-and-mind-inseparable-from-body and that the feeling is pleasurable helps me to see way beyond the misunderstandings, shortsightedness, and even ire through which some scholars and critics have seen this scholar's and critic's work, though, as a scholar, for my work has met with their distrust of ecstasy, eros, and intimacy and their unwitting enforcement of cultural taboos against spirited, direct, explicit, and sophisticated discussion of bodily and sexual sensations, especially for women. Criticism had no power to dissuade me from pleasure, so I am a scribe of beauty without being a conscript of academia, I am a magician without resorting to illusions, I am a goddess in this very skin. I am at once magisterial and common, as in common courtesy and common woman: Everywoman. I can tell you about dreams and visions, joy and blessing. Because I am and do such things, I manifest pleasure and I am its activist. Pleasure activist: that's what the performance artist and former porn star Annie Sprinkle called me as we were standing next to one another after I received one of the 2008 Lifetime Achievement Awards from the Women's Caucus for Art. She said that she was happy to see such an award go to a pleasure activist, and I acknowledged both her name for me and its designation of her too, with "There aren't a lot of us!"

Stealing the lady while leaving the beasts

I have not always been sanguine about men, and these days, even though I'm standing in pleasure, I sometimes feel frustrated and disappointed or just plain mystified by them.

Every day mystified right here in my Tucson neighborhood. Short men in long sleeves and chinos with holsters holding guns, ordering food in an Asian restaurant. Do they all have jobs in security? A homeless man in black who looks very fit. The demeanor of a seriously tough ice or rock climber. I see him regularly and wonder if he thinks of himself as a ninja. Ha! *My* fantasy. I call *him* "Mr. Ninja." Men spitting on the sidewalk – and my Mom's father spitting on the sidewalk comes to mind. It angered me for a while – in my teens? – and I thought that maybe I'd start spitting on the sidewalk too. Perhaps I did once or twice. An experiment in gender. Then, while he was still alive, I laughed inside at this weird behavior of men.

More difficult to process are the peculiarities of men with whom I become intimate. In the first half of 2010, I found two men intriguing, both of them sensual, smart, creative, and in lovely physical shape, all necessary characteristics for generating and maintaining my interest in a man. Neither of them lived anywhere near Tucson.

Travel ended up being minimal, ultimately not enough, so emails, phone calls, and texting sufficed for a while. Pleasures of the mind and body, and in one case, the spirit (very maximally) kept me involved, but no enduring relationship developed with either lover. I knew quickly with one man that despite his warmth, kindness, wit, and amazing sexuality, we didn't have a primal connection, one that creates emotional depths that call for exploration. "Primal bond that I've never felt before" was the other man's description of our connection, and I agreed with it, as if our responsiveness to one another were that of twins.

I let eros in spades, with its potential for expanding pleasure, direct a lot of my behavior – Aargh! Potential above reality, not a good idea – so I continued to initiate communication, many times, and let his more than occasionally unpredictable responses throw me into what I called "twits," little angers that I could tease myself about when talking with close friends, one of whom I asked in an email, "What's there to enjoy?" about men. "What is there to enjoy?" she responded. "Have you seen Joanna Frueh perform *Sexual Advances*? Please!"

Sexual Advances, in this volume, is a paean to pleasures with men, and the twit-inducing man was the muse. My friend knew the whole story about him and me, and her email had me laughing as she gave me insight of the kind that only an attentively loving friend can give, insight into the obvious, which is that I enjoy men a lot in my work through praising the pleasures that they provide. Not an iota of twit appears in *Sexual Advances*. And, before concluding this tale of vexation, but, more interestingly, of mysteries, I must tell you that my therapist, a heterosexual man fairly close to my age, as are the two lovers in this tale (earlier in life I tended towards intimate connections with younger men), wondered if something about the demographic of older men who had been in serious relationships once upon a time and not partnered for over ten years, which described both my lovers, brought about the behavior, considered odd by both my therapist and me: those lovers never stated clearly that they didn't wish to explore our connection any further. Such statements would have been the mature thing to do. Oh, well,

I bear them no anger. Nor did I ever feel beastly in my relations with them.

Beastliness belonged to a Joanna who, while friends called her sensual and even a hedonist, had not at all surrendered to foundational pleasure. In the mid-1970s, soon after Hollis Sigler began the fanciful and poignant drawings that originated her signature work, she was showing me what I think was the first batch of them as we sat at a table in her and her partner's loft. We were in our twenties (Holly died in 2001). The drawings came from profound honesty, and Holly didn't have to tell me that. Her honesty moved me, and I remember crying. The entire body of work that she showed me, which featured The Lady as a human figure, in symbols, or in words, may have drawn my tears, or maybe it was the piece showing three animals – one at a broken window – an emerald green chaise lounge, and a couple of shoes in a room whose pale yellow and blue contributed a lot to its bleakness. Holly had printed at the top of the image "men stole the lady and left me the beasts." I probably said "I love this" through my tears, and maybe I asked if I could buy the drawing. Holly simply said "It's yours," and I took it home that night.

Holly's soulful beauty amazed me. I wanted to stare at her, and most likely I did, the lady in her pink sweater with her dark, wavy hair, her elegantly bony facial structure, the large and sexy mole on her face, her thin form and eloquent fingers. Holly was such a lady, and I identified with that. Two ladies, she lesbian, me heterosexual (mostly), both feeling like beasts, left by men to fend for ourselves in a bereft nostalgia for our femininity, though we were both very feminine – indeed, consummate ladies – and, speaking only for me, left to fend for myself in my wild angers towards men. Holly's great understanding of the beastly, and more resonantly, of love, recovered and vitalized the glamorous, self-revelatory, and achingly brave and delicate Lady throughout the rest of Holly's career, and I, in my work, evolved from a turbulently emotional, uneasily satisfied female force into a goddess of pleasure and innocence. That transformation is apparent in my book *Clairvoyance (For Those in the Desert): Performance Pieces, 1979–2004*, and my evolution in pleasure continues.

Allowing the lightning

The goddess of pleasure and innocence loves the lightning as much as does the Greek god Zeus. It is a perfect metaphor for pleasures that flash in charges and discharges of power in her relations with men, the lightning quick degrees of sensations in continual transition. Allowing the lightning, rather than resisting its brightness and the nuances of existence that it reveals, is a mode of loving pleasure.

When I am attracted to a man, I feel undulantly responsive. A fluid joy in the body. Immediately my lumbosacral joint, which is the center of coordination in the body, begins a micromovement. It generates waves through my fluids, circulating around and into organs and my sphenoid and occipital bones, refreshing all that vibrates through those bones and everything that those organs flush out. Movements, small or large, from the lumbosacral joint, are erotic. Erotic movements are inseparable from erotic feelings, and in the center of both erotic movements and feelings (which is the only place from which a human being can truly feel them), I feel connections within my body, within soul-and-mind-inseparable-from-body, and so with beings, events, and objects that exist outside of my body as a container.

In lumbosacral micromovement, I am actively receptive for lovemaking, I am smiling through and through, in soul-and-mind-inseparable-from-body. Questions and internal conversations may occur, but they obscure and even squelch pleasure. The analytical and speculative mind, when overriding the body, compensates for a person's fear of sensation – the vortex and wave, the flash and flicker inside the body that moves her to tears, to her feet, to ecstasy – right out of any habitual thrall to thinking more than feeling. Right out of the structures of thinking and being that create a discoordination, a fragmentation of soul from mind from body.

In dance, in sex, in daily movements from washing dishes to stepping into a car, pelvis and sacrum move as one. The experience of their fluid physicality, swaying while I'm singing, instinctively snaking in synch with a lover's powerfully gentle hips (all the way out of the crown of our heads and all the way through the bottoms of our feet), going about my everyday activities in graceful comfort, enhances my love of life. When I am attracted to a man, first time, any time, I sense our fluidities entraining one another. That unity of being is ready for actual fluids, male and female, to meet and then dissolve in a heart-to-heart discovery of pleasure.

Helpings of pleasure

Pleasure as the center of living takes some doing for most people, perhaps a major healing. I am not at all certain that my work performs such healings, but I am sure that it provides or initiates for its audience the kinds of insights about oneself that catalyze pleasure as a state of potential or actual consciousness.

In its exposition of pleasures and of ways to experience, think, and talk about them, my work expands the meaning and parameters of pleasure from the conventionally imagined and lived categories into which people confine it. So doing, my work heals through the ample presence of pleasure itself. It also heals through the reality of another person's – this author and performer's – experiences, one who presents problems of her own, very real ones with which people can easily identify, that pleasure has resolved.

Both implicit and explicit in my work are challenges of the self, and pleasure meets those challenges and effects beneficial change.

My audience may learn and heal through a person who learns and heals through pleasure, and especially, over a range of pleasures, from the sexual to the spiritual to the everyday, and through my opening up a spectrum of feelings that includes humor, hurt, confidence, joy, and tenderness, with no guilt or shame. Certain words recur in my work and center it in pleasure. They charge it with pleasure. All belong to that spectrum of feeling, and they (and variants of them) indicate major paths on which I lead an audience. Generosity, beauty, love, simplicity, intimacy, spontaneity. Gorgeous, dazzling, delicious, playful, erotic, romantic, elegant, delicate, everyday, sweet. Clarity, enthusiasm, excitement, glamour, intensity, delight, gratitude. Spaciousness, receptivity. Embrace, engage, transform.

Enter. The very real humanity of pleasure.

Notes

1 Matthew Fox, *Original Blessing: A Primer in Creation Spirituality Presented in Four Paths, Twenty-Six Themes, and Two Questions* (New York: Tarcher/Putnam, 2000), p. 319, writes, "Faith is in imagination."
2 Jonah Lehrer, *Proust was a Neuroscientist* (New York: Mariner Books, 2008), p. viii.
3 Ibid., pp. 2–3.
4 Nona Willis Aronowitz described me this way in Nona Willis Aronowitz and Emma Bee Bernstein, *Girldrive: Criss-Crossing America, Redefining Feminism* (Berkeley, CA: Seal Press, 2009), p. 209. I'm pretty sure she'd say the same things right now.

Two pearls and many kisses

Melancholy is pleasurable to some people. It is palpable in their art, and I've even fallen in love with a few of those artists, for instance, the Two Rs, Russell and Rossetti.

Barely able to see at all, too mysterious to control

The glamour of materials and images produces paradoxically spectacular and intimate effects under Russell Dudley's touch. Russell is an artist in photography, sculpture, and installation. He sometimes uses video. In the late 1980s and early 1990s he presented performances. Russell was my second husband. We performed our collaboration *Amazing Grace* in 1989 and worked together on photos in which I am the subject, a number of which appear in my books and on their covers.[1] The painful times that occurred in our past relationship recede for me in relation to the memory of the welcome and very particular perceptions and insights about one another's families that only partners who are psychologically sensitive and also mutually sensitive can let arise and then share in silent acknowledgment and in speech.

A hand-polished steel teardrop trailer, fabricated by Russ, reflects the viewer who walks close to it. Overhead, a 5 by 5 by 9 foot "cloud" of clear pushpins seems to float. Russell melted the plastic heads, placed them together, and eased their points into other melted heads, leaving some points sticking out. A 10 by 16 foot screen of eight steel panels displays a video of several monumentally sized golf balls, into which he has hammered nails, which are exploding in slow motion. A real Suzuki SV650 motorcycle looks surprisingly like a toy in a 45 by 76 inch color photo. An 11 by 25 inch black-and-white image of Russ in the Great Basin Desert, poised mid-step on a dirt road between his dog and a shack, exudes the heart-speeding expansiveness of the western United States and the comforting solitude of home-sweet-home. Russ and I met in Tucson, which is located in the Sonoran Desert, our first home-sweet-home together and a place that remains beloved to both of us, having captivated him and me individually before we ever met each other.

All of the aspects of Russell's art, except performance, were exhibited in a concisely articulate mid-career survey of his work, at the AM Project in Los Angeles in March 2007. Besides the pieces described above, it included two more large photographs that, hung to the left of the motorcycle image, formed a triptych; several groupings of black-and-white photos; and small sculptures in various metals. The exhibition included works from 1993 to 2007.

The haunting sheen, glitter, glow, and luster of his material world, both actual and photographed, draw us into a disquieting estrangement from the heaviness of steel and bronze, the wicked spikiness of nails, the cactus-like prickles of pins. I stare, bewitched, at a gorgeously detailed still life, in the triptych, of two pearls and their mirror images on a metal tray. A couple of fuzzy pin-ups, each 8 by 10 inches and appropriated from a cheap porn magazine, printed as negatives, and conventionally sexy in their playful poses, fill the exhibition space with a shady sensuality.

Russell presents discombobulating incongruities of objects, scale, and imagery, and through masterly workmanship and observation, he integrates each particular, showing us that we can see so very clearly. Using the same means, he ensures too that those incongruities reassert themselves to disrupt stable perception, thus urging our renegotiation of reality because we may feel barely able to see at all. The world is too mysterious to control – infinite – and that is its glamour, which Russ knows so well.

Sung by Rossetti

When I first read Jerome J. McGann's *Dante Gabriel Rossetti and the Game that Must be Lost*, long after I wrote my dissertation on Rossetti, for McGann's book was published in 2000 and I read it in 2005, I bracketed many passages, underlined many sentences and parts of sentences, and wrote numerous comments in the margins. I feel McGann's soul-and-mind-inseparable-from-body response to Rossetti's art and writing, a response whose scholarly brilliance, artistic gorgeousness, and animal intensity are wildly and elegantly human. I am so taken by them all, so in tune that I write "Me" and "Like me" beside the text, asterisk many points – an asterisk is the mark I use to indicate my passionate interest – and, already, on page 17, in the top margin state my excitement: "Over and over ~ all of this is me/my work." I am being sung when the Rossetti Woman sinks into me, and I am being sung by McGann's thoroughgoing and lyrically conceived interpretation and analysis of Rossetti's art and writing. No feminist scholar has done for Rossetti what McGann does. They do not appear to love him.[2] McGann so evidently loves Rossetti.

I see and find myself in the words and images of men, as with McGann's lyrically intellectual mastery of Rossetti. Below are only several of many such happy sightings and discoveries.

> For Rossetti, ... artists come neither to represent real worlds nor to fashion imaginary ones. Art's *poiesis* brings revelation, not creation: not to make things, but to make things happen.[3]

> ... an idea (and an ideal) ... that received its classic expression in the synthetic idea of the union of soul, body, lover, artist, and God.[4]

> Rossetti's works comprise arguments for the truth-functions of art and poetry. They may not *look like* arguments because they come in forbidden poetical forms.[5]

> Texts and pictures come to challenge and confront, thereby developing a rhetoric of unmediated presence.[6]

> The most successful "interpretations" of Rossetti's works, of the paintings in particular, ... come as imaginative forms in their own right.[7]

One of the most playful results of Russ's and my photographic collaborations is *Venus Verticordia 2004* (2004), which honors Rossetti's painting *Venus Verticordia* (1864–68) and exchanges its gentle gloom for joy.

Because *Venus Verticordia* is one of Rossetti's double works of art – a sonnet and a painting elaborate one another – I also wrote a sonnet, based on his, for Russ's and my photo. I titled my sonnet "On Love's Sweet Track," which is where any success of his and my "interpretation" takes me.[8]

McGann is a professor in the English Department at the University of Virginia. He is a renowned Rossetti scholar and the engine that drove into existence the Rossetti Archive, a website that holds a compendium of Rossetti material. McGann was one of the most influential professors for me at the University of Chicago. Not only did I learn a lot about nineteenth-century English literature and poetry from him. He was one of those literature instructors who had the enchanting ability to recall and then ardently recite poetry, but to do so as a performance of love – for the poet, for the words, emotions, and ideas. He had the ability to convey the sacred depth of language, English syllables as *mantra*. I learned that a researcher's and thinker's obvious passion for his subject has a place in scholarship – for me, a necessary place – and I learned from him, as I had from one of my undergraduate professors, the art historian Carol Duncan,[9] that a scholar could dress and style herself in aesthetic and erotic beauty. My memory of Jerry is that the regular guy clothes he usually wore, like jeans and a white, long-sleeved shirt buttoned all the way up, were a smart contemporary complement to his Romantically tousled dark hair. Like Carol, he was flame and sparkle. His eyes flashed. He wore his excitement about being alive.

McGann writes poetry, so he experiences and understands Rossetti (and other poets) from that close range of creativity.

Ladies and love goddesses, you are my yogini *sisters*

I deeply identify with Rossetti's devotion to sensuality and spirituality, to his erotic and ecstatic understanding of the world, to his lover's intellect, which adores what it knows, and with the Rossetti Woman of full red lips, large moist and luminous eyes, mystically inward gaze, long, luxurious hair, and clear complexion – a woman who apparently cannot live without flowers, most frequently roses, because they surround her, because she is a flower and they are her companions, because she, like them, is an epitome of pleasure. Granted, she is also an epitome of danger, and I used to unconsciously and strongly identify with that characteristic. Today, I write only from the pleasures that she and Rossetti give me. Before 1859, Rossetti's female figures were thin, and they often feel pinched to me, as if they are recoiling from the world into despair and agoraphobia. His female heads with flowers, post-1858, which some of his contemporaries loved and others scorned for their fleshliness, are indeed robust.

Venus Verticordia and Blessed Damozel, Veronica Veronese and Beata Beatrix, La Ghirlandata and Regina Cordium, Fiammetta and Fair Rosamund, Mona Pomona, Mnemosyne, Astarte Syriaca, Mona Vanna, Sybilla Palmifera, Lady Lilith,[10] and other ladies and love goddesses in the trees and in the bowers, by the sea and most often by yourselves, sitting in still beauty, looking to yourselves for answers to the questions of Life, Death, and Love that Rossetti implicitly poses throughout his poems,[11] you are my *yogini* sisters, hands in *mudra*-like positions that seal into soul-and-mind-inseparable-from-body the courage to be beautiful while simultaneously offering it to me. You are deep in an *asana*, awakening your aptitude for pleasure. You are in contemplative prayer, which is silent and experiential: feelings, images, sensations, and reflections pass through you as you come back to one word of your choice.

> Beauty.
> Beauty. I come back to you.
> Beautiful *yogini* sisters, you are prayer itself, God incarnate as beauty.

How curious that Rossetti painted his dead wife Elizabeth Siddall in his famous *Beata Beatrix* (1864–70)[12] with her hands in a position very much like *dyhana mudra* – seated with elbows close to the body, hands, palms up, resting in her lap, right hand in left. Their grace, confidence, gentleness, and perfectly conscious placement frequently draw attention to the Rossetti Woman's hands. In order to perform classical Indian dance, a student learns many hand gestures, *mudras*, which function as spiritual, aesthetic, and narrative components of her art. Sometimes I pose or move in an action from that dance tradition, complete with hand gestures, and I feel that the hands of Rossetti's women could float right into those *mudras*. Though I think that those bodies could never do the dance, which is a very strenuous kind of yoga. The Rossetti Woman is so ethereal.

Rossetti, who never traveled to India and who I see as his own guru, envisioned a *yogini*, she who practices release from *dukha* (suffering, constriction). (Developing intuition and wisdom from within and having faith in oneself, develop the inner guru. According to the Vedas, which are Hindu scriptures dating to the first two millennia BCE, the inner *guru* is a person's most important source of knowledge.) Rossetti, a man who left England only three times and lived most of his life in London, wrote, "Thy soul I know not from thy body, nor / Thee from myself, neither our love from God."[13] Eros, the great connector, and in the gliding one-syllable words, in the alliterations and many soft consonants, I hear a mantra that a *yogini* would love.

A virgin and a sensuous gentleman in lumbosacral movement

In Elizabeth Hickey's novel *The Wayward Muse*, which delves into the relationship between Rossetti and Jane Morris, Jane experiences him immediately as a sensuous gentleman, and skin-to-skin the erotic charge is mighty. His sumptuous clothing is a synecdoche for his soul-and-mind-inseparable-from-body. The first time that they make love, she is still Jane Burden, a virgin from the lower class, not yet married to Rossetti's friend William Morris, a foundational figure in the British Arts and Crafts movement.

Lovemaking with Rossetti is much desired by Burden and it happens quickly. Hickey writes the novel from the perspective of Burden/Morris. Rossetti's grace and confidence, his dark eyes, his "face as smooth and chiseled as honey-coloured marble"[14] all attract her. He is "so beautiful she had trouble catching her breath,"[15] and between a kiss and intercourse, her following perception occurs: "His body was cool and smelled of bergamot and anise."[16] Rossetti is electrically gorgeous and sensual. Although Hickey says nothing about the movement of Rossetti's body during that episode of intercourse, I imagine that his lumbosacral movement, electrically erotic in its fluidity, is a powerful element of Burden's not knowing her lover's soul from her own body.

Sweet dirges prolonged by fallen angels

For several years I've been looking for art of uplift. Art that blesses me. That's the only art with which I want to spend a lot of time. Not a Francis Bacon or a Max Beckmann, who in their art feel to me like inmates of their psyches. Not a Richard Prince or a Vanessa Beecroft, who tinker with the platitudes of contemporary culture. Not a William Holman Hunt, one of Rossetti's fellow Pre-Raphaelites, whose often histrionic iconography and head-swimming detail seem to compress my senses, readying them for explosion.

I think that many viewers of Russell's and Rossetti's art would apprehend the melancholy there, probably more quickly than I did. They would see the Rossetti Woman as zoned out, sad, and self-absorbed, and sense within the hushed though urgent anxiety of many of Russell's photographs and installations some lurking, sharp, or looming danger that occupies the lonely landscapes and objects. Russell has written that his art provides "the kind of sense you make when you have stayed too long alone."[17] The Rossetti Woman, too, seems to be in the midst of making that kind of sense. And wafting from both men's art we might hear a sweet dirge prolonged in the voices of fallen angels.

Because of the melancholy in the two men's art, one might perceive beauty there as an object of yearning, which associates beauty with loss and lack. Crispin Sartwell defines and discusses the English word "beauty" in just that way in his book *Six Names of Beauty*, and melancholics who resonate to the theory that melancholy generates creativity might resonate too in a companionate, paradoxically brooding bliss with the two artists.

Eric G. Wilson, a professor of English, might reflect on Rossetti and Russell in that way if they were subjects in his book *Against Happiness: In Praise of Melancholy*. He compiles what he terms an "august list of melancholy innovators," from writers to musicians to entrepreneurs and actors, scientists, military leaders, philosophers – and artists – which does no justice, he declares, to the "honor roll" of brilliantly creative, melancholic men and women with whom he identifies.[18] That melancholy unto depression and other severe psychological disorders are a source of artistic inspiration is a familiar idea, one of whose most famous expositions is *Born under Saturn: The Character and Conduct of Artists*. Written by Rudolf and Margot Wittkower and originally published in 1963, *Born under Saturn* became a classic study of the visual artist's unhappiness and eccentricities. Saturn rules the sign of Capricorn, and in astrology one of the characteristics of Capricorns is said to be melancholy. In the words of a famous blues song, "born under a bad sign."[19]

I am a Capricorn, and beauty as the pleasure of *yapha* (Hebrew; bloom and glow), *hozho* (Navajo; harmony and health), and *sundara* (Sanskrit; holy and whole) resonate for me. Loss and lack permeate Rossetti's major literary work, the 101-sonnet sequence *The House of Life*, yet the poems that I reread because they give me the most pleasure are the ones in which the bloom of love, the harmony between lovers, nature, and God, and the holiness of human bodies are paramount. Like "The Lovers' Walk":

> Sweet twining hedgeflowers wind-stirred in no wise
> On this June day; and hand that clings in hand:–
> Still glades; and meeting faces scarcely fann'd:–
> An osier-odoured stream that draws the skies
> Deep to its heart; and mirrored eyes in eyes:–
> Fresh hourly wonder o'er the Summer land
> Of light and cloud; and two souls softly spann'd
> With one o'erarching heaven of smiles and sighs:–
> Even such their path, whose bodies lean unto
> Each other's visible sweetness amorously,–
> Whose passionate hearts lean by Love's high decree
> Together on his heart for ever true,
> As the cloud-foaming firmamental blue
> Rests on the blue line of a foamless sea.[20]

I perceive the rapture and romance and the reverberant imagery of "The Lover's Walk" when I look at the Rossetti Woman.

I am aware in each man's art of its "visible silence, still as the hour-glass."[21] Those words of Rossetti's pinpoint a quality inherent even in some melancholic art, a profound quietness that slows me into a stop. Russell said a number of times over the course of our relationship that such a pace is exactly that of his art: "slow to stop." That pace is the flow and the focus of meditation.

A complete pearl; I kiss myself

Thank you, Russell, for a pearl whose glow glides right to heaven. Thank you, Rossetti, for red lips that teach me I can kiss myself.

Notes

1 The text and a photograph of *Amazing Grace* appear in Joanna Frueh, *Clairvoyance (For Those in the Desert): Performance Pieces, 1979–2004*, with an introduction and photographs by Jill O'Bryan (Durham, NC and London: Duke University Press, 2008).
2 A case in point is Griselda Pollock, "Woman as Sign: Psychoanalytic Readings," in her *Vision and Difference: Femininity, Feminism and Histories of Art* (London and New York: Routledge, 1988). As Pollock writes on p. 121, the essay is an "interrogation of this unremarkable oeuvre labeled 'Rossetti'."
3 Jerome J. McGann, *Dante Gabriel Rossetti and the Game that Must be Lost* (New Haven, CT and London: Yale University Press, 2000), p. 4.
4 Ibid., p. 116.
5 Ibid., pp. 16–17.
6 Ibid., p. 17.
7 Ibid., p. 21.
8 "On Love's Sweet Track" appears on the back cover of *Joanna Frueh: A Retrospective*, ed. Tanya Augsburg (Reno, NV: Nevada Museum of Art, 2005).
9 I write about Carol in *Erotic Faculties* (Berkeley and Los Angeles, CA and London: University of California Press, 1996), pp. 44, 49, and in *Monster/Beauty: Building the Body of Love* (Berkeley and Los Angeles, CA and London: University of California Press, 2006), pp. 161, 165, 166, 168, 175–6, 192, 197.
10 Each name that I list is the title of a painting by Rossetti.
11 Throughout *The House of Life*, Rossetti's major work of poetry, Love frequently appears.
12 Six replicas of *Beata Beatrix* also exist. The first painting, from 1864–70, is in the collection of Tate Britain.
13 Dante Gabriel Rossetti, "Heart's Hope," in Jerome H. Buckley, *The Pre-Raphaelites* (New York: Modern Library, 1968), p. 99.
14 Elizabeth Hickey, *The Wayward Muse* (New York, London, Toronto, and Sydney: Atria Books, 2007).
15 Ibid.
16 Ibid., p. 55.
17 This statement appears on the cover of *Finding Russell Dudley* (Los Angeles, CA: AMProject Publishing, 2007), and also in the catalog's biography of Dudley.

18 Eric G. Wilson, *Against Happiness: In Praise of Melancholy* (New York: Sarah Crichton Books, 2008), p. 101.
19 Booker T. Jones and William Bell wrote "Born under a Bad Sign," which was first recorded by Albert King in 1967.
20 Rossetti, "The Lovers' Walk," in Buckley, *The Pre-Raphaelites*, p. 103.
21 Rossetti, "Silent Noon," in Buckley, *The Pre-Raphaelites*, p. 106.

Bless you, boys, I wish you well

The unorthodox Christian theologian, activist, and teacher Matthew Fox states that "'blessing' is the theological word for 'goodness.'"[1] That's all it is.

Giving and receiving blessings is available to everyone. Wishing someone or something goodness is not religious or mysterious.

Humanly numinous

In early March, 2008, a discussion about feminist spirituality began on the Women's Studies LISTSERV, whose subscribers are feminist scholars. I read many of the posts all the way through and took interest in the sources and ideas that my colleagues offered. Some hailed spirituality as personally healing, and some, perceiving such healing as insularly individual and dumbly, smugly self-satisfied, so neither building nor participating in community, asserted the necessity of analyzing religious structures and discourses in order to expose ways in which they have demeaned, ignored, or oppressed women. Well into the debate its initiator Diana Blaine, an instructor in the Writing and Gender Studies program at the University of Southern California, asked some questions to which I responded. These are her questions:[2]

> How can feminism change the self … [?] What do we get out of it as "practitioners," if you will, besides rocks to throw at monuments to sexism? If the personal is political, … how is my personal reorganized by my political? If feminism doesn't provide a pathway to healing the self as well as addressing structural inequity, well, what's to attract a new generation?

Here is my response:

> Spiritual practitioners can be activists: activist mysticism, activist prophecy. Spirituality can be practiced by oneself and in community – chanting, praying; speaking in private and in public, writing and publishing from a position that promotes love, justice, and joy. And, very importantly, not simply talking the talk but walking the walk, in other words, being a spiritual activist in every moment of one's life.

> This requires a soul-and-mind-inseparable-from-body consciousness: it extends beyond intellectual concepts, beyond any kind of body work, any regular attendance at a temple, church, or mosque. Soul-and-mind-inseparable-from-body is a term that I use throughout my writing, which is spiritual, intellectual, erotic, and very much of and from the body.
>
> My understanding of religion is that it often devolves into doctrine, even dogma, and that people in a religious community can end up letting words pass over them lightly, like a lovely breeze that quickly passes by, or go in one ear and out the other.
>
> Gandhi and King were activist prophets. Practicing what they preached. The theologian Matthew Fox notes that feminism is a prophetic movement and names Adrienne Rich, for example, as a prophet. (See his book *Original Blessing*.) Wayne Teasdale, a lay monk, writes about the importance for society of being a mystic in the world, which, for him, means being at once a social and a spiritual activist. (See his book *A Monk in the World*.) The historian Karen Armstrong writes about the divinity of human beings. (See her book *Buddha*.) To be human is to be numinous. Sadly, religion, as an often stony social edifice, separates the numinous from the human. Healing the self sounds sentimental to intellectuals. As a spiritual activist, I say, it's the only way to go. The world transforms because individuals do, and I don't think that that's any more strange an idea and feeling than believing that blood-shedding revolutions change the world. Healing the self is more radical, as it operates in the roots of daily life – in the family, on the job, in leisure hours. Healing as transformation takes faith, and faith is an act of imagination. What if half the people on Earth were healing themselves, soul-and-mind-inseparable-from-body? Imagine the effects. A foundation in that kind of radical reality is one reason why feminist thinking and practice can be so energizing and transformative, in one's home life, in the classroom, and in public spheres, whether they are the books that we publish, the greetings that we give people on a walk in our neighborhoods, or the language understood by others in our bodies' gestures and alignments wherever we are on this planet.

On the same day that I responded to her questions, Blaine replied privately, "bingo bingo bingo." Later that day, and in contrast, Ophelia Benson, a co-editor of Butterflies and Wheels, a website that aims to show that logical argument is the best way to demonstrate, explain, communicate, and spread truth, expressed dissatisfaction:

> So what exactly is spirituality? It seems to be more or less everything
> ...
> It all sounds very resonant and deep, but it seems to have no actual meaning at all.
> I can't help thinking that feminism needs rigor a lot more than it needs hand-waving about spirituality. It's so easy to dismiss women if they get identified with woolly empty pretty feel-good verbiage.[3]

Strictly defined, spirituality leaves out corporeality and thinking. Strictly defined, mind leaves out spirit and corporeality. Strictly defined, corporeality leaves out thinking and spirit. Benson seems to have been looking for something less simplistic than those definitions, but also concise and equally clear. My own disappointment with such definitions is that they allow for the compartmentalization and dissociation of soul, mind, and body and thus the intellectual distortion that human beings can, do, or should function within those separate realms. That situation does not fit my experience, which is why soul-and-mind-inseparable-from-body became part of my vocabulary.

I do tend toward mysticism, though not the airy-fairy, out-of-body, no-sex, fasting, literally and figuratively self-flagellating kind. No one lives more in reality than the mystic. Forget asceticism, altered states of consciousness, transfiguration, or idealistic foolishness. The mystic enjoys the everyday world because its marvels fulfill her.

Marvels – the voice of a cashier, the color of brewed tea; the scowl of a woman who looks at you when you board the bus, ice cream and butter at the temperature of their perfect softness. No dark night of the soul, à la St. John of the Cross. No flash-in-the-pan epiphanies. Experiencing everyday anything as a marvel, the mystic doesn't linger in an experience in order to prolong its pleasures or discomforts or to agitate, vilify, or congratulate herself. I'm no paragon, so I – or you! – can catch this mystical sensualist more than occasionally lingering or prolonging, but those times are mild – not so when I was younger! – and I can usually laugh at myself during them.

The mystic/realist practices ordinariness – the mind untrammeled, unraveled from+ discursive embellishments. She lives in a palpable, sensuous world that necessarily includes her body. You may call the mystic's ordinariness extraordinary if not impossible, but for a person in the fluidity of pleasure, feeling moves along at its own pace, everyday anything is new, instantly and continuously, and the body and senses freshen themselves. When disappointment, dread, anger, sorrow, anxiety, delusion, projection, envy, lethargy, cowardice, yearning, or frustration arise, they pass quickly, as does any perception or feeling, because she does not oppose them.

Some feminist scholars, with their academic training in objectivity, struggle with their mistrust of lived experience, even women's, as either truth or its foundation. Lived experience is subjective. But if one is a feminist, shouldn't one trust women's experience? On the other hand, doesn't the variability of women's experiences and women's ability to articulate those experiences disallow lived experience as evidence for scholarly consideration? Family history, economic class, education, projection, health, and many other factors can be understood to interfere with truth and also to create many truths (and foundations) in contradiction with one another.

Bless you, Diane and Ophelia.

A logic of infinity

The *Bhagavad Gita*, which is the most widely read scripture in Hindu literature, expresses over and over, and from various angles, the reality that spirituality includes everything. Translated as "Song of the Lord" and originally attributed to a sage named Vyasa, the *Gita* is a 700-verse poem written between 500 and 200 BCE that recounts a dialogue between Arjuna, a warrior prince who figures importantly in Indian myth and legend, and Krishna, his friend, who is an incarnation of the god Vishnu. The scene takes place before a battle that Arjuna does not want to fight, as he will be causing the suffering and deaths of beloved family members, and he asks Krishna in one way and another, "What shall I do?" Because the *Gita* is a spiritual poem, the battle is, of course, within Arjuna and the questions are about how human beings are to live in peace, joy, and goodness.

Arjuna perceives that Krishna is "behind me and in front of me,"[4] in other words, inescapable. No surprise, since Krishna also speaks as Brahman, the Supreme Reality, whose "face is everywhere."[5]

You can't get more "everything and at the same time ... beyond everything" than Supreme Reality! Arjuna sees within Krishna "all the gods and every kind of living creature," in other words, "the entire cosmos turning within."[6] Krishna's "presence fills the heavens and the earth and reaches in every direction."[7] Krishna names what he is, giving only a partial yet exponential list, so that the reader understands that Krishna/Vishnu/Brahman is certainly *every* name, for based on his list, he is every season, flower, mountain, seer, tree, priest, mind, force, animal, element, and effort; he is logic, radiance, and gambling; he is all beginnings, middles, and ends – EVERYTHING. "Just remember that I am,"[8] Krishna reminds Arjuna, which, on one reading, elicited a laugh from me. "Just remember that I am": what an understatement.

Useful as it is for questioning and examining, scholarly skepticism balks and falters with the paradoxes and the poetic language of spiritual experience and concepts. As the *Gita* lyrically explicates in elaborate imagery, which I've read and heard described as majestic and beautiful (though I remain emotionally unaffected), all and one – actually, All and One (Ophelia, you aren't liking this) – are the same: here is a logic of infinity. Soul, self, flowers, sages, Divine Reality speaking to human beings, who are awed and thankful for the speech: here is "woolly empty pretty feel-good verbiage" or a "resonant and deep" Hey, okay! into which I can relax. That okay is the wonder of a mystic/realist.

Bless you, mystics and Arjuna.

Sight through the third eye

Dear Fellow Travelers,

It is two weeks after our return from India, and I woke up at a quarter of five today with this image in my mind: a flame-like shape, blue tinged to lavender at the bottom, then orange, then yellow – all deeply saturated and compellingly brilliant. The flame filled my mind's eye comfortably and at the same time floated around a foot in front of my forehead, at the level of the third eye. Third eye: inner eye, clairvoyant eye, to whose images one would do well to pay close attention. I'm sure that more than one of you could give me meanings for the colors using information about *chakras*, traditional color symbolism, and the relation between colors and emotions. I know a little about all of those things, and your knowledge would help me to expand mine, or certainly to affirm it, and, what is more important, to see myself more clearly, to trust where clairvoyance guides me and to walk with ease to those destinations and destinies.

I miss your generosity, your help. You're all far away, and here, in my bed, is what came to me. A week ago an acquaintance happened to mention that blue and orange are healing colors. "Orange?" I asked, because I'd known about blue for ages. In my dream the orange was truly that, just like the skin of the fruit. Another simile that came right to mind was *yogini* orange. On one of those typically steamy days, when the sun was heating up stones and cement almost too much for my bare feet to enjoy, we participated in a healing ritual at the *yogini* temple, in which the priestesses were wearing the orange in my dream. Ha! It was also close to the orange of the T-shirt, of tissue-thin cotton, that I wore when hearing about the color's healing property and that you may remember me wearing on our travels. Where I sat during the ritual was extremely hot – within a foot or so of the fiery pit into which the main priestess threw herbs from over fifty metal bowls – each a separate throw – during her dizzying recitation, for close to two hours, of Vedic texts from memory. Heat upon heat, and, as Bridget commented to me the next day, "You looked like you were presiding over the ritual." That's because of where I was sitting. After that priestess arranged all of our seating, I was the closest of all of us pilgrims to the staging area of the ritual, and to its heat. I felt as though I ought not to move, though I must have crossed and uncrossed my legs and also shifted position at other times, and I feared making a mistake when handing the bowls of herbs, one after another, to a temple assistant, who then passed them to the priestess. Each of you had already, in turn, held every bowl, handing it from one to the other until it reached me in the front of the mesmerizing spectacle. The first bowl seemed to vibrate through my skin, and I felt both excited and a little anxious about how I might feel and what feelings I might show as the ritual progressed. Would I cry?

Bridget's first words about my presiding were "You looked beautiful," and I appreciate her glamorous description: "You looked like an ancient Egyptian queen, with your golden yellow top, dark hair, bangs, and red lipstick." I take her description to heart, as I take my third eye's sight to heart as well. Ahh, my deeply saturated yellow top, the orange of a hot, intoxicating healing ceremony, and a blue that soothes, like the Sonoran Desert sky and like heaven itself.

Dear friends, my consciousness presented me this morning with an elegant result of my experience with you, less than a month ago, during which we created heaven here on earth, as we were at once human and divine. With you, I was trusting in erotic heat, which is a crucible of connection. Eros itself is connection. The sun, the fire, and all of us, connected. The priestesses' high-in-the-head voices and, through our open pilgrim ears down through our spinal columns and their swaying, connected. Connection is a pleasure.

Wish you were here. The rain has been falling since last night, while we in this desert city were sleeping. Heavy, quick rain or less rain over hours creates rivers in many streets. Mine is one of them. We could go outside in the 50 degree morning grayness and celebrate life together. We could begin our devotions with a chant to Ganesh, our elephant deity, who is full of play and power: *Om gam Ganeshaya namaha*. We could call on him, remover of obstacles, to help us clear debris of fear, hatred, and anger, in Iraq and India, in the hearts of angry young men everywhere, in the minds of women who starve themselves for the opportunities that they think a skinny body will bring them, in the politics that determine famine in the land and in the spirit, and in the irritations and imbalances of our own daily activities and emotions.

Om gam Ganeyshaya namaha: we are chanting and dancing in my front yard and in the little river in my street, which is very wide, with occasional traffic and an unassuming name: Tenth Avenue. We can call on any deity you would like. One for all and all for one. Like the musketeers. One for All and All for One.

Thank you, my companions, for dancing in the street, which is the title not only of Martha and the Vandellas' boisterous 1964 hit, but also, with a slight variation, of a book by social historian Barbara Ehrenreich. Reading *Dancing in the Streets* in 2007, the year after its publication, either our pilgrimage had not yet come to my attention or I'd seen it advertised and it was passionately alive in my unconscious. Dancing in the street is a metaphor for happiness, and Ehrenreich subtitles her book *A History of Collective Joy*.

In India I saw men crapping in the river, I saw them in public closing one nostril with a finger and blowing snot out of the other. I saw people young and old in full squat, talking together, tending to tasks. When I used an Asian toilet, I had to squat. If you can't squat, urinating or having a bowel movement would be messy and uncomfortable. In India I was hot and much sweatier and dirtier than I am at home most of the time (even living in the monsoons of Sonoran summers). In India I showered and the steamy heat dampened my skin and brought out my wet smells almost immediately. Fans, when available, cooled me, but the sultry air and I felt at one. Dusty hairs and sandy skin, cold showers that cleaned me less than the hot ones of my homeland. Ahh, India, I am your primal daughter, and you have brought this animal to new life.

Bless you, fellow travelers, bless you, India.

Embedded in the jaguar's black rosettes

Come into me, big cat, jaguar, come into me and fill me with your power.

I learn your perfect aim, to focus my attention on what I want, what feeds and sustains me, to bound upon it once to make it mine. A second leap for you is rare.

I learn your poise in walking slowly, listening and watching for your target, in waiting for it to appear and going for it when it does, in padding along a river, ready for a turtle or a crocodilian on the beach. What appears to be too defended, tough, or dangerous is yours for the taking. Sometimes you use your teeth to pierce the skull of your mark, which is a singular technique among the big cats, as only jaguars do it. My words have teeth and can take myself and others by surprise by penetrating thick-skulled beliefs.

Like you, I climb and swim and run. I am quick on solid ground and can wind my way over it if that's the path of least resistance to my goal. I am strong-limbed and agile as I look up to heaven and down to earth. I am at one with currents that guide the ease of my actions. Your mobility through mangrove swamps and forest evergreens, from desert shrubs to wet grasslands, across a range of habitats inspires my adaptability and my primal comfort.

I knew a man who told me that to feel bloodthirsty, blood-lusting violence towards other people if they do harm to you or the ones you love is primal, and in that normal. I protested. Pro: I spoke aloud for love. He would hear none of it. His adamant assertion that I was as gnashing and ready to lash out as were he and all of humanity literally nauseated me. Soul-and-mind-inseparable-from-body had been shocked, with such force that I did not enter into an argument with that man, a philosopher. My enjoyment of logical persuasion had shut down. I felt my goodness. Goodness is a primal inclination, a primal preference, so bless you, man who believed in his savagery, I wish you well.

Scholar, artist, and animal that I am, O Jaguar, I choose the philosophy that I've embedded in your black rosettes.

Jaguar jaguar burning tough I am a diamond in the rough.

I bid you to come into me, and yet, I am scared to let you in, but I can close my eyes, and … here I am, on all fours, by myself, as jaguars tend to be, patrolling near the beach of a stream, not in the four, twelve, fifty, or more pasts and presents that remove people from the moment most of the time. I, Joanna, am scared – to be this self, this free and wildly clear in soul-and-mind-inseparable-from-body.

Yet, here it is – the grainy earth giving against my feet and studding or sliding from my claws; the call of nearby peccaries, their chattering tusks and rustling steps vibrating into me, alerting me differently from the lowing of cows, the swish and splash of water, or the touch of bark and leaf through my coat and on my skin. When crawling and hiding, I am quiet as I watch a target. The time I take pays off. When I spring, the air speeds through my fur. Parallel to the ground, I ripple horizontally, full of flex and stretch.

I am romantically distorting you, but as a human being I have the capacity to choose my state of mind, so rather than seeing your predation, kills, and physical power in terms of blood, death, and deadliness, I incorporate your deftness and your sensate and synaesthetic lucidity, your vision – clairvoyant – and your hearing – clairaudient.

In the twentieth century the jaguar population dwindled around Tucson, where I live, and throughout the jaguar's prior range, from

Argentina up into Central America and along Mexico's Gulf and Pacific coasts into Arizona, New Mexico, and Texas. So sightings – and killings – of jaguars south of Tucson near the Mexico border have dwindled too. The few jaguars seen south of Tucson, both in the flesh in this millennium and on a surveillance camera at the Mexico–United States border, caused a stir about whether the animals were transients, coming up to Arizona from Sonora, Mexico, or whether they were native to Arizona.

I am lying on a chaise in my study, reading, when I look up and see a jaguar stretched out on a chaise on my back patio. The animal is golden, even the white fur on its chest, because the sunset light warms whatever it touches. The French doors are open and the screen doors are closed and locked. I pad to the door and it seems to unlock and open by itself, silently. I leave it as is, an entrance, and my fluid steps and senses, so easily adjusting with gravity and atmosphere, create an alignment of soul-and-mind-inseparable-from-body that instantly adapts to whiffs of scent and distant sounds.

The jaguar and I look into each other's eyes, the length of time it takes for faith to trust one's sight. Jaguar, apex predator that you are, help me to put an end to delusions that I have been holding.

Bless you, jaguar.

Embracing the man under the mesquite

A man stands under the mesquite tree that shades part of the street in front of my house. The temperature is over 100 degrees. I park in that shade, which I especially appreciate during the long summer with its intense heat. I want the man to know that he can stay there in the shade, that just because I'm parking in front of him he needn't move on, when he needs the rest and the protection from the sun. He starts to walk before I'm out of the car, so as soon as I open the car door and stand up, I say, "You don't have to move. It's hot!" He's been told that a bus stop is nearby, and he asks where it is. I tell him, and he starts a conversation, talking about himself, his past, and his son who lives here in Tucson. He's a white man, and he's in his seventies. When he tells me his exact age, which I don't recall now, I say, "You don't look it," and I mean that. He has just come from the Seventh Day Adventist church on the next block, and he praises that denomination's singing, food, or both. He was a lawyer living in the South and says he worked for or with Strom Thurmond (to which I exclaim something like "Oh, no!," which he takes in good humor), that he's lost his money and other fortune, and that he'll be writing a book about it all. "That will be fascinating," I say. I am dubious about some of his story, but its details simply float around us and away, dispersing into the sunlight and the glorious blue sky. After a while I want to go inside. I surprise myself by spontaneously hugging him. Then I wish him well. In essence, I bless him. Then he blesses me, by saying, "I'll remember you." I return his words to him, "I'll remember you." All this means is: You exist for me. You will always be in my heart. All: everything, it means everything, it means as much as possible. All: simply, like only, just, and merely, it means I simply care about you.

Easy, I might say to myself, for you to bless people from your desk in your home whose comforts and aesthetics so calm and delight you, as you drink your chai with soy milk, both organic, and anticipate the day's activities, such as taking a walk in the neighborhood; going to the library to return a bunch of books – ahh! more room on the bookshelves – and to check out a couple that may enhance your clarity as you write this piece; cooking dal, brown basmati, and eggplant with garam masala and goat yogurt; and even preparing to meet with the accountant regarding your 2007 tax return, a process that reminds you: money received, money to spend, money to enjoy; and listening to CDs of mantras, chanting along and dancing. Easy for you, when you're driving in your Acura Legend, over a decade old and in very good shape, to say, in a whisper or to yourself as you're stopped at a light and a man looks broken down, wiped out – injured in some way – "I wish you well, brother." That started happening before I went to India in January 2008, and, like embracing the man under the mesquite, it surprised me. Why I notice men crossing the street and feel their pain rather than women, I'm not sure. Maybe women in that shape aren't crossing the streets in my sight? Maybe I need to soften towards men? To experience them, in their anonymity, as achingly human? Easy to bless the unhoused, unhinged, and perhaps largely unloved, by either themselves or others.

Bless you, brothers.

Prophetic reality: self-care comes true

Self-care encompasses physical, aesthetic, ethical, and erotic practices. (My use of *ethical* designates ethos rather than moral code or conduct.) Self-care encompasses one's every way of living, so it is spiritual. Care of the self is care of the Self, so it is at once prosaic and far-sighted, such as the greeting *namaste*, in which one's hands are in *anjali mudra*, touching each other, thumbs to one's heart, which Westerners would identify as a gesture of prayer. Like "hello" in the West, *namaste* is a common greeting in India and one bows slightly when saying it. *Namaste* acknowledges both people's divinity.

In the world of contemporary scholarship, the philosopher Michel Foucault is the dean of the care of the self. It became a key subject in his publications toward the end of his life, and his thinking about an ethics – ethos – and aesthetics of the self attracts the interest of feminist scholars. Indeed, the aim of *Feminism and the Final Foucault*, edited by the philosophers Dianna Taylor and Karen Vintges and published in 2004, is to consider the usefulness of Foucault's final work, in the 1980s, for contemporary feminism. He died in 1984, the year in which two essential books of his were published in France: *The Use of Pleasure* and *The Care of the Self*, respectively, Volume II and Volume III in his *History of Sexuality*.

How does a person lead a pleasurable life? Pleasurable means to me a life of beauty and love. How does Foucault's thinking about the care of the self help anyone, man or woman, to live according to such an ethos? In *The Care of the Self*, published in English in 1986, Foucault presents and explains the writings of philosophers and physicians in the first two centuries of Imperial Rome in terms of self-knowledge and self-examination, attention to one's body and one's soul, a practice of freedom that is not only personal but also social, and one's self as the final authority regarding the self. All of that reminds me of *yoga*!

In Foucault's studies of ancient sexuality, he implicitly advocates philosophy as a mode of living, putting into practice an ethos, in contrast to approaching philosophy as a search for truth in words and concepts alone. The philosopher Ladelle McWhorter plays with that idea in the title of her contribution to *Feminism and the Final Foucault*, "Practicing Practicing." In the late work of Foucault, self-creation is a process, and during that process the self changes. McWhorter discusses her dilemmas in creating a self, because it conflicts with any affirmation of a fixed identity, such as woman. Yet she keeps her humor: she is practicing practicing, and the repeated verbs gently emphasize her effort.

She also keeps her faith: she is practicing (verb) practicing (noun) by doing her best to enact and incorporate feminist philosophy, to literally act and embody it as a transformative art of living.

While Vintges addresses Foucault's focus in his late work on ethics as spiritual practice, she stays on the page and in the head, at a distance from McWhorter's practice of what is necessary for both self and social transformation. McWhorter's essay stands out from the others, not only because she brings her own experience to bear on her discussion – she does so very generally, but she does so – but also because her method of argumentation creates an essay that itself exemplifies the transformations that both concern and involve her – that of herself, philosophy, and feminist philosophy. Overall in *Feminism and the Final Foucault* the soul-and-mind-inseparable-from-body activation of Foucault's ethos of spirituality, rooted in every moment of one's life, does not advance.

We individuals need all the help we can get, and so does the world. We need feminist prophecy – remember Matthew Fox about Adrienne Rich – to come alive. In *Original Blessing*, Fox proclaims in his generously visionary and practical manner that everyone is a prophet. Prophets may make experiential as well as intellectual use of sacred texts, so that they act: by speaking, writing, and enacting their reading of a text, in private conversations and family dinners, in public places, from malls to traffic jams to the neighborhood coffee shop. Such texts can be spiritual, of course, or secular, such as Foucault's *The Care of the Self*. Prophets turn ideas into realities.

I have been interchanging *care of the self* and *self-care*. Use of *care of the self* in everyday speech and by the everyday prophet sounds cumbersome. However, in the mode of scholarly preciseness, *care of the self* is the term associated with Foucault and philosophy, while *self-care* could be used in a popular way and perhaps associated with self-help. Self-help has the ring, to some ears, of narcissistic, isolated practices that are good primarily if not exclusively for the body, an individual's physical health and cosmetic appearance, that promote smugness, and that have no socially transformative intentions or even resonance. Many popular magazines today, from those dedicated to fashion to bodybuilding to living a media-induced or superficial New Age version of the good life, function wholly or in part as self-help guides. For example, the cover of the October 2007 issue of *Body + Soul* advertises the six main stories meant to attract a middle-class self-care market. The list includes "6 essential strategies for breaking free from worry," a "complete guide to balancing cholesterol naturally," a promise of brain "focus in 5 minutes," "The key to starting your day off right," advice on "the one food you need," and "25 tips for looking great at every age." "Stop Stressing, Start Living!" grabs the eye first, as those words are directly under the magazine title. I suppose that a reader might choose to follow one or two of the offered "self-care" methods, yet I also think that so much advice might actually increase a person's anxiety about truly caring for the self that she is. Does she even know that she is a self? Do all of the literally and figuratively bold words on the cover arouse one's guilt (about not doing enough), one's insecurities (about being unfit in one way or another), one's fear of illness and the future? And more importantly, are all of these tips and strategies external to the self? Interior tools may seem esoteric or even difficult, but they are focused ways for Everywoman and Everyman, the prophet of today.

Turning to the more upscale *Real Simple*, with its cleaner design and higher quality paper, I notice, on the February 2008 cover, attention given to the same kind of regimens as in *Body + Soul*. Inside the magazine, you are told that you can learn to "Eat what you love and still lose weight," to use "Fast, effective headache cures," to prepare "Easy freezer meals," and to absorb "The secret to a lasting marriage." I read the subtitle of *Real Simple*, "life made easier," and I smile: how many programs can a person follow at one time and really lead an easier life? What's the focus of these cures and secrets? I look through and read some of *Body + Soul*, *Real Simple*, and other "self-care" publications and perceive a scattered content that is looking for a distracted and distractable reader.

In the playful mood of calling men boys and women girls, I read a regimen from the late first century CE, given by Foucault from

Rufus of Ephesus, a physician. Perhaps "The secret to a lasting marriage" – the cover blurb not the article – reminded me of Rufus, who gives advice about coition. I quote at length Foucault's summary of Rufus because the advice and the actual following of it seem as absurd as the "simple" and "easy" practices given in the magazines I've just discussed. Foucault writes:

> Around sexual activity, and in order to preserve the balance it risks upsetting, one must keep to a whole mode of living. It is helpful to drink pale red wine, to eat oven bread made from bran (its moisture is useful for preparation and regulation); to consume, in the meat category, young goat, lamb, hen, grouse, partridge, goose, duck; in the seafood category, octopus and mollusks – together with turnips, road beans, green beans, chick peas (for their heat) and grapes (for their moisture). As for the activities to which one should resort, they include excursions, on foot or horseback, and running, but neither too fast nor too slow; but no violent exercises, no gesticulation as in javelin throwing (which diverts the nutritive material to other parts of the body), no excessively hot baths, no heating and cooling off; no strenuous work. One should also avoid anything that would contribute to tiring the body – anger, joy that is too great, and pain.[9]

In choosing "A whole mode of living," I like playing with pleasure rather than submitting to control.

Show me a body, a life, a planet that is fulfilling the prophecy of an aesthetics and ethics of self-care. "Our faith conforms to our nature," Krishna tells Arjuna. "Indeed, a / person is his faith."[10] Everyone puts faith in something. Everyone imagines things and, whether consciously or unconsciously, acts according to those imaginings.

Bless you, philosophers and prophets.

Jeweled percussions from the coral of her lips

The *Lalita Sahasranama*, a medieval Hindu text of unknown authorship, celebrates the goddess Lalita in the form of Shakti, which is divine active energy. Shakti is Supreme Reality in its feminine aspect. As I explain at the beginning of *Sexual Advances* (in this book), a *sahasranama* is a hymn of a thousand lines, devoted to a particular deity, and each line itself functions as a mantra, for worshippers consider each line to be an embodiment, through sound, of one of Shakti's names. *Sahasra* means one thousand and *nama* name in Sanskrit. Shakti is primordial and infinite, epic and resplendent. Her beauty is dazzling. She is all knowledge and all wisdom. She is a provider and protector, a teacher who likes teachers, an artist and a lover of pleasure. She "promotes oneness" and the "union of souls and God,"[11] and she has many more aspects than I list here and is much larger than this list indicates, just as Krishna/Vishnu/Brahman is.

A number of Shakti's names designate her blended powers of sight, seeing, and creation. She sees through everyone's eyes, thus knowing what each individual sees and how each one lives, and she also gives everyone the potential for the wide-ranging vision that is wisdom. Also, by opening and closing her eyes she creates and destroys the universe.

Rub your hands together quickly so that they become warm. Then place your palms on your closed eyes. In the home of your self, what do you see? Darkness? Blankness? Spaciousness? Infinity?

Release your hands and open your eyes.

I close my eyes to pleasure and it disappears. I open my eyes and pleasure is every place that I see it.

One of Shakti's many names is "She who blesses."[12]

Bless you, boys, she speaks in jeweled percussions from the coral of her lips, pouring out the nectar of her voice, *I wish you well.*

Notes

1 Fox, *Original Blessing*, p. 5.
2 I incorporated Blaine's questions in my response on March 12, 2008, on WMST-L@LISTSERV.UMD.EDU
3 Ophelia Benson, March 12, 2008, WMST-L@LISTSERV.UMD.EDU
4 Eknath Easwaran, trans., *The Bhagavad Gita* (New York: Vintage, 2000), p. 63.
5 Ibid., p. 59.
6 Ibid., p. 58.
7 Ibid., p. 60.
8 Ibid., p. 57.
9 Michel Foucault, *The Care of the Self*, volume 3 of *The History of Sexuality*, trans. Robert Hurley (New York: Vintage, 1986), p. 132.

10 Easwaran, *Bhagavad Gita*, p. 85.
11 www.geocities.com/chelakkara_raja/Lalithasaharanamam.htm, line 179 and line 422 (accessed October 2009; no longer available).
12 Ibid., line 273.

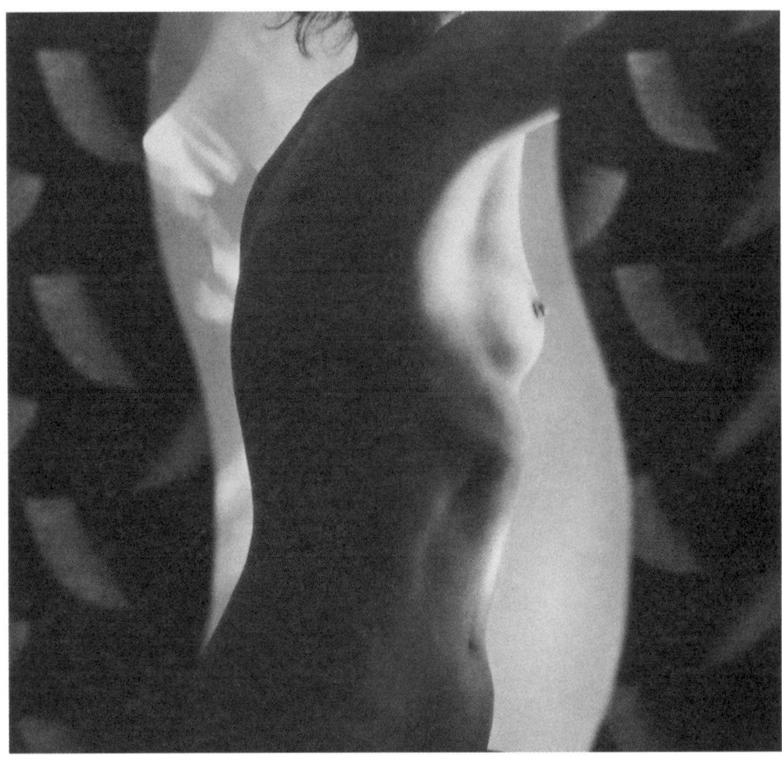

Figure 4 *Crescents*, 2006 © Frances Murray, reproduced by kind permission

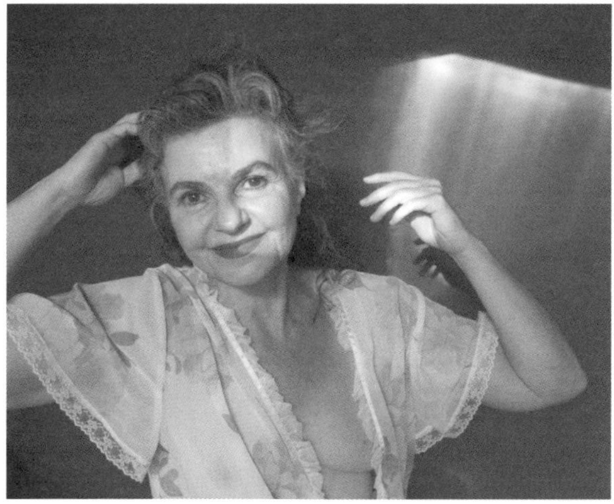

Figure 5 *Pleasure and Light*, 2010 © Frances Murray, reproduced by kind permission

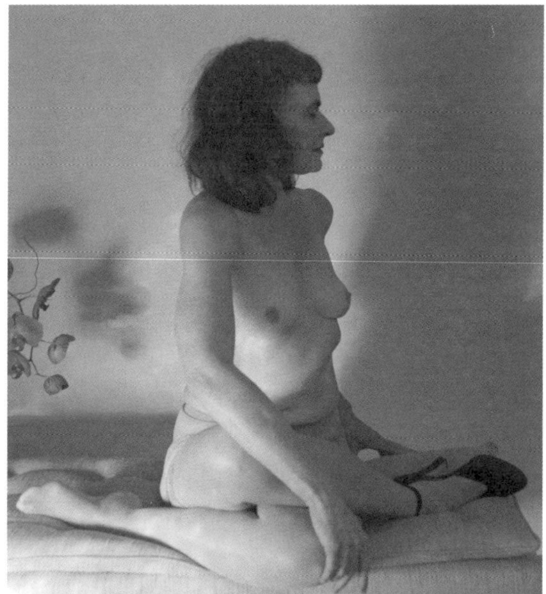

Figure 6 *Gomukhasana*, 2012 © Frances Murray, reproduced by kind permission

4

Conversation: salons

Assumptions

People assume things really often. Usually through an unconscious or unacknowledged belief that everyone is like them, especially someone they think they know well, whether friend, family member, or lifetime mate. When we speak and act from such assumptions, we misperceive and misunderstand.

I witnessed a fascinating case of assumed identity. I was the one in error, the ass in the assumption, and for current purposes I'm defining assumed identity like this: when a person thinks something about someone, often a stranger or a new individual in her life, and finds out, either pronto or down the line that she is *wrong*.

A woman was sitting next to me. Except for our being seated together, we were anonymous to one another for quite a while. Her haircut reminded me of my mother's, very short and nicely sculpted, and the woman was petite like Mom. Because of those two elements of appearance I was feeling tenderness, my own towards this woman and hers towards me.

The tenth anniversary of my mother's death was approaching, and for a few days Florence's gentle dignity, her elegantly simple fashion aesthetic, and her warm and penetrating intelligence floated in and out of my consciousness. Sometimes a daughter longs, without any melancholy or morbid thoughts, for her deceased parents. Sitting there next to the stranger, I felt keenly aware, on and off, of Florence's beauty of body and spirit and I was so sweetly in love with her. I cite the tenth anniversary of her death, but who knows why Mom's loveliness was visiting me as the stranger and I sat in silence?

Around a week later the stranger and I talked with each other. She seemed nothing like my mother in either her carriage or the sound or content of her speech, and surely the mutual tenderness that I'd felt arose from longing. Also, my describing the feeling tone of the group of people with whom we'd been sitting startled her. Mom wouldn't have been surprised at all, and that kind of description came naturally to her, as it does to me. The stranger offered her agreement with my articulation of the atmosphere that had emanated from the group and surrounded all of us, and she said something to the effect of my being able to clearly feel and express that atmosphere and that she hadn't the tools to do so.

We go around thinking that we're so intuitive and perceptive, when really we can go around for hours, days, years, or even a lifetime, clinging to one assumed identity after another, intimates included. I laughed at my recent encounter with the relatively short duration of clinging to an assumed identity. How wonderful that the stranger, in her *own* identity, could tell me something true about myself, could help me appreciate my capacities for clarity of feeling and communication of it. I thank her for that gift.

I was dating a man in 2007 – not long ago, but long enough to feel like history! – who assumed stuff a lot, and more than occasionally about me. At that time I was becoming aware of the frequency with which spoken assumptions surrounded me. Nothing special about my life, assumptions being a common reality once you wake up to them. Wishing to point out the problem with making assumptions about me, and about things in general, I said, "When you assume things, you're usually … ." He interrupted me with the word "right." Which, of course, glaringly indicated exactly the problem!! I responded calmly, "No. You're usually wrong." (I intended the "you" in my sentences to be both singular and plural.) A discussion ensued, he being a philosopher and me being the rational, passionate, and body-aware intellectual that I am, and the relationship ended shortly after that. Not because of his making assumptions, but, as I think of it now, because of a quality that is related to assuming – rigidity, which is a lack of responding to what is really in front of us.

Assuming holds the assumer in place, unable to move an opinion or an idea. Assumptions can grow into or proceed from ideologies, and they can be the soil of an emotional fundamentalism, an orthodoxy that is insufficient means for the support of love.

An assumer holds objects of assumption in place, so that their changes and unpredictabilities remain out of perceptual range and their histories survive as far more fixed than any institution's, nation's, or individual's story could ever be. If the object of assumption is a person and she believes an unexamined or uncomfortable assumption about herself or complies with that assumption, she suffers confinement by another person's thinking.

A key to unlocking the prison of assuming is to unassume, to be unassuming. If the pretension of "I know" generates my assumptions, then my being modest is a path to freedom. If my taking for granted generates assumptions, then truly paying attention to where I am, who I'm with, and what I'm doing is a good idea. If my projections generate my assumptions, then I would do well to cultivate spontaneity. I remind myself that freedom, knowing where I am, and spontaneity must be experienced, not just contemplated, and that experience can only be within my body, in closely feeling its sensations.

Be perfect be perfect be perfect with me

Intimate – an adjective indicating closeness or familiarity. I am intimate with my husband. I am intimate with recipes for chocolate cake. *Intimate* describes people, circumstances, and situations that are the closest and most familiar. *Private* also defines intimate, as in I can't tell you the intimate details of our conversation.

Intimacy – a condition, relationship, or experience marked and delineated by great closeness or privacy. *Intimacy* may refer to sexual intercourse.

Intimate – a noun that describes a person with whom we are very close.

Intimate – a verb that means to suggest or to hint at. We hope that our intimates understand us when we intimate something, because we wish to be loved in our nuances and subtleties as well as in our obvious behaviors and statements.

Intimacy is erotic. I define the erotic as connection, a loving connection. Do I connect with a man's body? Is there chemistry between us? Chemistry bonds me to a lover. Chemistry, for me, comes from and generates deep kindred emotion and a mysterious understanding of another person. I mention chemistry with a man, a lover, and we also can feel chemistry with friends, with strangers we see on the street, with a wonderful class that we've been teaching. Chemistry charges relationships with beauty and fascination. Chemistry is different from lust. Lust may likely not create intimacy.

Intimacy can also be defined as familiarity: I am familiar with my body, I am familiar with my lover's body. Many people are not very familiar with their own bodies, even though they say, "I know my own body." They may know it, but they don't listen to it. They don't pay attention to its guidance.

Intimacy is a knowing that encompasses feeling, listening, touching, tasting, smelling, and looking lovingly. I know the way to the grocery store in my car, but that's a different kind of knowing.

Intimacy requires being present. Someone can be intimate with us and then be absent … and then be intimate again, after a day, after a decade. A lover, for example, can be our intimate and then the mutual connection goes awry, becomes tenuous, disappears. Sexual relations can occur without intimacy. Interactions with our kin may lack intimacy. We can be intimate or only modestly acquainted with someone who we call friend. “Friend,” like “lover,” “spouse,” “companion,” and “parent,” covers a variety of emotional actualities.

The term *intimate strangers* applies to many relationships that, from the outside, appear to be intimate or are assumed by society to be intimate but in which the “relators” are distant from one another or even mutually antagonistic. Living in the same house, dorm, or barracks doesn’t necessarily create or foster intimacy. The partners in a marriage may or may not be intimate. Intimacy does not require physical proximity. I’d call my lover from the longest of earthly long distances, 8,000 miles apart, and that expanse felt like the most infinitesimal of spaces in the realm of intimacy.

Our culture romanticizes intimacy by giving it a privileged, glorified, and even scandalous position: young love, star-crossed lovers, the liaisons of Hollywood celebrities. In this regard, intimacy holds a voyeuristic appeal and has little to do with reality or maturity. Romantic intimacy or intimacy in a romantic relationship is often short-lived and even delusional. Extremity characterizes the initial and apparent intimacy between lovers, that can be passionate and seductive, the “intimacy” for which craving, or even yearning, may serve as its iconic feeling: existing in extremis, within the compulsive and obsessive confines of no-help, no-hope: hopelessly in love, helpless in the lover’s presence. I don’t know the personal genesis or the intention of Neil Young’s song “Helpless,” but the following lyrics from it indicate the suffering of romantic intimacy.

> Helpless, helpless, helpless
> Baby, can you hear me now?
> The chains are locked and tied across the door,
> Baby, sing with me somehow.

Actually *reciprocating is the point*

In order to be intimate we must be able to reciprocate love. I'll adjust that: *capacity* for reciprocation is necessary, but *actually* reciprocating is the point. In human relationships, intimacy first *invites* consistency, constancy, and commitment and then it can only thrive when we *provide* them. The commitment is to be true to intimacy, and such provision foregrounds communication, which may be talking, touching, or other expressions of honesty, trust, vulnerability, and openness.

Reciprocal communication is generous. Giving/receiving is all of a piece, with intimacy as the gift that joins the seeming two parties, giver and receiver, into one, which is a state of largesse, another word for generosity. Intimacy operates on the very small scale of a couple of human beings and it nurtures the very large, largesse as an essential quality of love.

Reciprocation and assumption are contradictory. Assuming things about our intimate does not serve either of us, because assumptions are false, misguided reactions.

When we're genuinely responsive, we notice beliefs, ideas, and supposed intuitions that lead us away from seeing and feeling what's in front of us.

Reciprocity takes effort, and it is action.

In intimacy, we are activated and activist – activists for love.

Intimacy requires that the people who are involved in it act on its behalf.

Toning the body's bell

I'm tempted to include the sudden and intense connections that we sometimes randomly make with a stranger – say, on the street or in an airport – under the grace of intimacy, but I think that intimates can only be people with whom we've shared our lives deeply for a period of time, way more than a few moments or hours.

Intimacy is the realest of the real. With a recent lover, I felt or discovered things about myself that I didn't know were there. I'm glad that I found them and that, even if they remain more inchoate than not, they have expanded the horizons of my heart for my own benefit and that of others. I am still growing from the intimacy that loosened itself for me in the presence of my lover's conversation, body, sensitivities, and perceptions. I became more intimate with myself, which means that I can be more intimate with the people I choose as intimates.

I don't just fall into intimacy the way that our culture expects us to fall in love – Omigod, here I am in a surprise swirling ecstasy! Intimacy is best subject to *wuwei* – action through non-action/non-action leading to exactly the right action – so I do my best, when I'm really simpatico with someone, to simultaneously let intimacy happen while guiding its growth by being as responsive as I can be. Intimacy can grow on us as we get to know a person better, but the seeds seem to have simply planted themselves early on in a relationship.

Knowing, while with my lover, that I was discovering things about myself that I didn't know were there destabilized me. That was the immediate effect. We were lying in bed, quiet, and the distinctive softness of his voice was holding me as the materiality of my body dissolved into energy alone. (I realize now, after becoming a *vipassana* meditator, that I was experiencing a particular aspect of *vedana*, sensation, called *bhanga*, in which one feels oneself as only vibration, as vibration alone. Thus the observation and sense that the body is dissolving.) *With* my lover ... our bed, our bodies, the huge loft space of his home surrounding us – yet tangibility had become unimportantly real, an inessential fact. I spoke, but my voice did not sound normal or move through space in its ordinary pitch or rhythm; more like the clearest bell that at once toned from me and filled our environment. My words seemed to be generated from everywhere, one element of which *was* my body.

Without noting when, I returned to a material normalcy, but no doubt in a subatomic reconstitution of greater generosity. I've felt the destabilization and reconstitution that I'm talking about at other times, both with someone else and by myself. Because I'm better able to articulate such experiences now, I'm better able to see that the occurrence I just recounted is not at all singular.

"I want us to be intimate"

"So you want us to be intimate." Those words could have been a question, but Evan, a student in a performance class of mine in the early 2000s, had stated them. He knew more clearly than I did one of my intentions for the semester: in their performances and in our conversations about them, I wanted us to be open, generous, vulnerable, genuine, emotionally and intellectually truthful, and loving with one another – intimate. That diverges from the usual studio critique, which students and teachers often praise with the word *tough*.

I felt the students' excitement underneath the nervousness of their quiet laughter on hearing Evan's statement, and I remember that I paused a few instants before responding because the acuteness of Evan's perception had taken me aback, and he had so sensitively articulated my own desire. I smiled and said, with tentativeness giving way entirely to delighted surprise, "Yes, I guess so. I want us to be intimate."

In the art history classes that I taught, my lectures had an air of spontaneity in the way I departed from my notes and responded to an artwork that I was showing or to an idea that popped into my head or to a student's question. My mind spiraled in enthusiasm. The creative freshness of spontaneity excites me, and spontaneity allowed both for the flourishing of my passion for teaching and for thinking out loud in a classroom.

Spontaneity is essential to intimacy. Sticking with a syllabus interrupted intimacy, and though I felt for many years what I called "professorial guilt" when I proceeded more and more slowly, which was more and more spontaneously, through a syllabus, I did my best to free myself. Guilt is a rare feeling for me, so experiencing it as part of teaching, which I love, produced a suffering Joanna. When I pushed to try and cover all the material on a syllabus, my body "rewarded" me with anxiety. I was doing what I didn't want to do.

Every once in a while I'd tease myself about professorial guilt in front of a class, and we'd laugh. Delicious spontaneity then, and as I let myself become more and more intimate. Which also led to my being more and more dubious about remaining an instructor in academia.

Spontaneity and intimacy – for me, the classroom confined them. (I felt much more roominess teaching studio courses in performance art than teaching academics.) Spontaneity and intimacy – ultimately they helped me fly from the ivory tower. In actuality I retired from a teaching position at the University of Nevada, Reno, and in a larger actuality, my flight, continuing today, was precise (precisely out of academia) but to nowhere in particular, which is the place, position, space, or condition in which vision becomes more panoramic.

Sustaining you like food

In intimacy with another human being, we follow the ancient imperative, "Know thyself." Inscribed in the forecourt of the Temple of Apollo at Delphi, "Know thyself" has been attributed to various ancient Greeks, all men except for one of the Pythias, Phemonoe. The Pythias were the oracles at Delphi. Self-knowledge demands the self-observation that characterizes yogic practice, both ancient and contemporary. Self-knowledge is also the goal of psychological introspection.

Intimacy with oneself often includes rational thinking. We examine the details of our lives, we separate out what we perceive to be pertinent elements so that we can see ourselves anew – we hope. But rational thinking as analysis tends to reorder pieces of our stories, producing new stories, and those, as well as rational thinking itself, easily serve as distractions from plumbing the depths of ourselves, in which awareness of feeling – and feelings reside in the body – is the essence. Witnessing our feelings – our sensations and whatever thoughts arise as we notice those feelings – witnessing in calmness, brings an equanimity to our lives that gives rise to joy. Knowing thyself is a joyful state of being, and joy is anything but a crazy condition.

The passions that we often associate with intimacy do not necessarily constitute joy. Indeed, *passion* derives from a Latin word meaning suffering, as in the Passion of Christ. Passionate feelings can be compelling feelings. When we are compelled, we literally and figuratively can't help ourselves. Note that people have often called me passionate. I too have described myself as passionate. So when I'd read in yogic, Taoist, or Hindu texts that passion is undesirable,

I'd pause, because I didn't understand why passion is a problem. Now I get it. In one way, the issue is semantic. How do we *define* passion, joy, calm, equanimity? What did the original Sanskrit, for instance, convey that English translations don't? Moving away from strictly linguistic concerns, isn't joy a passionate feeling? Isn't joy a passion?

I'll leave those questions in rhetorical limbo, and turn again to my own life. When people describe me as passionate, they may mean that I feel deeply. Now, that is true! And intimate relations flourish with deep feelings, ones of bliss and ones of balance. I think that many people register bliss and balance as polar, thereby making them into extremes. Also, bliss can connote blissed out, a rapture of oblivion, and balance can connote a neutrality or detachment unto non-feeling or an out-of-reach stability, an impossible peacefulness. So both words can suggest states that are radically different from where most people usually perceive themselves to be. However, one dictionary definition of bliss means "spiritual blessedness," and balance registers for me as exactly that condition.

The phrase "intimacy breeds contempt" is wrong, at least from the perspective in which *I'm* discussing intimacy. Within that phrase, intimacy reads as a shallow connection, a false closeness, closeness as reduction into a suffocating, claustrophobic, pinched, or even violent emotional world.

Intimacy breeds insight. Through intimacy with myself and others, insights come out of the blue – the way, with my lover, that I knew things about myself that I hadn't known before. Intimacy is sustaining. It is primary sustenance for me. When something sustains us, like food, it is essential to our living. How do we aid ourselves and others to create intimacy as a sustainable resource of relationships? A resource that resonates into the wider world and feeds it too? One of my intentions in hosting salons in which conversation is the centerpiece is to do just that. For me, conversation is most satisfying when it's intimate.

Perfectly undetermined

Sometimes we just want to be by ourselves, perhaps to "Know thyself," perhaps to simply relax or rest. Depending on our living arrangements and our personal and professional responsibilities and obligations, time alone for anything may be hard to come by. I think of a painting by the artist Joan Semmel, *Intimacy/ Autonomy*, dated 1974. As if we are one of them, or even between them, we see two naked bodies, a woman and a man, from their chests to their feet, one figure on either side of the 98 inch-wide canvas. (I'm tempted to call the figures nudes, but as an art history term, nude refers to an ideal or idealized body, and though the bodies in *Intimacy/Autonomy* look good, their colors are shadowy and bruised, as they are in the whole series of coital and post-coital images that Semmel was painting in the early to mid-1970s.) The figures are turned a bit toward one another, and between them is a small space which narrows from their shoulders to their hands. The latter are almost touching, and when I'd talk about this painting in my contemporary art classes, I'd refer to Michelangelo's fresco, *God Creating Adam*, on the Sistine Chapel ceiling, in which God's and Adam's hands, too, are so intimately close to one another. God and Adam, the divine and the human: they exist within an intimate space. Being together with a lover or partner and being independent in Semmel's feminist vision: the space is at once intimate, as their bodies show us, and fraught, as the color suggests.

One of my friends, who has known the lover I spoke of earlier much longer than I have, said about him, "He's good at intimacy." I'm not sure what gave her that idea, and I didn't ask. Maybe I will when I see her next. She also admits that she probably romanticizes him. I agree with that one!

Already when she said, "He's good at intimacy," I think I was ready to say, "No, he's not," and that was months before I decided to let go of him and me – because he hadn't shown reciprocity. I couldn't count on him, I didn't perceive action on his part for exploring the intimacies that we'd experienced together. Maybe my friend meant that my lover is good at sex. I liked him sexually, and he said after the first time that we made love, "Now I feel perfect." That surprised me! Several weeks later he surprised me again with, "Now I feel aligned," as our bodies stilled following lovemaking. Wow! Balance from bliss – that's pretty good. And I'd never heard either of those responses – that kind of responsiveness – before from a lover. Moreover, the statement came from a man – men being famous for their unexpressed feelings.

Sexual connectedness is an indicator of intimacy, its possibility, its potential, and also its presence, but intimacy beyond sex requires the explorations that lovemaking can begin, which are emotional, psychic, and spiritual – traveling into and through the unfamiliar territory of oneself and another in order to become more and more familiar. Without ending up intimate strangers or in contempt of one another. My lover talked about his current inability to be present and his wanting and needing to be present in order for him not to disappoint me. I can only surmise that he didn't become sufficiently present to communicate either his continuing lack of feeling present or the renewal of that component of intimacy.

Intimacy is a perfecting of the self. I don't mean that intimacy makes people faultless or flawless. In intimacies we proceed to become as good as it is possible to be. Proceed: we take a course of action, we move forward. So intimacy is a process, an undetermined series of actions, and those actions consist of the *paramita* (Sanskrit) or *parami* (Pali) Buddhist perfections. As I see it, the ten *parami* and the six *paramita* help a person to live what I'd call a good life. (The six are part of the ten.) Generosity, insight, effort, honesty, and equanimity, qualities I've been speaking about, are listed as perfections. So is resolution, which I'm choosing to equate with commitment, another necessary element of intimacy that I've noted.

Be perfect   be perfect   be perfect   with me.

The ultimate tenderness of resurrection

Arising from the slog and drift

I count myself among the resurrected. Meaning that when I have felt dead, struggling to live fully and with a reasonable amount of ease, I have raised myself from the grave that, most likely, I in fact had been digging so that I could let the earth absorb my tears, so that I could bury my heart, so that I could hide forever. Ostensibly, hide from people, the ones with whom I felt excruciating embarrassment or unremitting dissatisfaction, the ones who had defiled my integrity by laughing at me or calling me names I would never, in gentle self-love, answer to, or categorizing me publicly and professionally in terms that presented an unrecognizable me, and one that I feared could damage not my reputation but rather other people's ability to perceive me more as I myself do.

I began the previous sentence with "ostensibly," because other people have functioned as catalysts not causes. A crisis example: my father, with whom I had a deep and loving relationship, especially in his last years, did not mercilessly make or intend my sadness when he grew weaker and weaker, then died. Rather, devoid of his physical presence, I felt saddened. Sadness is a form of devitalization. So, as I cleaned house a lot in the days following the hours I sat by him while he was dying, I pined as I removed dust and straightened pillows and my husband's and my bed, and as I polished furniture and sinks, I was cleaning up and polishing up myself – practicing a process of refinement. Removing impurities and toxins. In our own lifelessness, we let ourselves be poisoned by feelings that are all but unbearable. They disturb soul-and-mind-inseparable-from-body although they are not necessarily negative. If we don't pay attention to such feelings, they call to us more loudly. Their presence qua presence is incipiently prophylactic, and consequently therapeutic. When we pay attention to them, all but unbearable feelings dissolve, as if loosened, so that they neither adhere nor accrete, but rather wash away in both the solid and invisible streams of our lives, such as dreaming, breathing, and urinating.

Wasn't Jesus an extremely refined man?

Self-refinement is the road to resurrection, which I here define as rising from the deadness that is the slog, the drift, and the daily dull-mindedness to which human beings may crucify themselves. Buddha perceived that sad plateau and rose from it, refining himself through meditation and other forms of yoga.

Simpatico with yourself

Resurrection is huge and it has gravitas. One root of the word "resurrection" is the Latin *surgere*, to rise, spring up. Resurge: to rise again after you've been down, perhaps after seeing, in contrast to ignoring or complaining about, the suffering of people, seeing as did Siddartha Gautama before he became a Buddha; to rise again perhaps after witnessing full-on your own suffering.

Witnessing your own suffering is no little thing. It takes will and focus, the discipline to be utterly simpatico with yourself.

You may swear that you're sinking, way, way down, before you rise. You may say that you're falling, beyond any abyss of previous experience, before you spring up.

To rise: rolling, swelling, sweeping. Tidal wave in contrast to tide.

Making love with the divine

To spring up, like a plant or a penis. In the northern hemisphere, where Easter comes at springtime, Christians mark Jesus's resurrection when plants spring up and flowers begin to bloom.

Like other rituals and figures in Christian myth, Easter and Jesus, respectively, take the place of pagan celebrations and deities. Jesus's resurrection overlays the figures of the Egyptian Osiris, the Mesopotamian Tammuz, the Phrygian Attis, the Greek Adonis, and more, all of whom served as gods of rebirth and vegetation, which of course is annually resurgent.

Today we apply the name Adonis to beautiful, usually young men. Jesus was a young man, in his twenties to early thirties, during his ministry. (The date of his death, and therefore his exact age at that time, is in question.) Italian Renaissance painters depict Jesus with a handsome face and a body resembling sculptures of the ancient Greek male nude. According to general belief, good-looking men are the ones who people want to have sex with, the men, in cultural imagination, whose penises readily spring up in erection.

In his book-length essay, *The Sexuality of Christ in Renaissance Art and in Modern Oblivion*, first published in 1983, the art historian Leo Steinberg argues that Renaissance artists deliberately drew attention to Christ's penis, in paintings of his infancy, or showed it erect under a loincloth or drapery after his death. The reason? To make clear that Christ was a man, a human being, to portray the fact of Incarnation. In ancient Greece the phallus – the penis glorified, erect, and powerful – appeared in public, on statues called herms and in ceremonies. In the myth of Osiris, erection and resurrection (both with the help of Osiris' wife the goddess Isis) combine.

Erect derives from the Latin root, *regere*, to make straight. In forms of meditation based in yoga, meditators sit with their spines straight so that *kundalini*, dormant cosmic energy that resides in the base of the spine, can, when released, flow up that "erection" and then into and out from the crown. In yoga, *brahma danda* refers to the spinal column and literally means "the walking stick of God." A bent or collapsing spine is something other than a divinely erect tool. In yogic terms, the erect spine with its vertical energy flow is in alignment. There, the health of the physical body and the spirit can manifest. In his book *The Yoga of Jesus*, Paramahansa Yogananda, an Indian yogi who introduced yoga to the United States in the early twentieth century, suggests that Jesus traveled to India in his youth and learned yoga. The cover of the paperback edition shows Jesus in seated meditation, legs crossed, spine straight, eyes closed, hands in a traditional *mudra* for the posture in which he sits, and Yogananda takes John 1:23 to be a teaching of "Jesus the Yogi": "I am the voice of one crying in the wilderness, Make straight the way of the Lord, as said the prophet Isaiah."[1] (Yogananda titles one of his chapters "Inner Teachings of Jesus the Yogi.") According to Yogananda, seated meditation, such as Jesus practiced, makes straight the way for experiencing the "trackless 'wilderness' of Infinite Bliss."[2] Yogananda's mystical generalizations throughout *The Yoga of Jesus* frustrate, distance, and amuse me all at once. What is Infinite Bliss anyway? Maybe it's a cosmic orgasm – erection as a surge of blood, erection as the beginning of resurrection in orgasm, coming alive through sexual intercourse, an act that in certain Taoist and pagan beliefs and practices connects whoever is making love with the divine.

Women's anatomy also springs up with a surge of blood. The clitoris becomes erect. Clitoris and penis, filled with the lifeblood that helps people feel alive in the potential of emotionally resurrecting lovemaking. Orgasm, from the Greek *orgasmos*, to *swell* with moisture, lust.

I think that lovemaking and orgasm *can* be resurrections – hugely significant in a person's life – but I think that such magnitude is unusual.

Like a lover swept away

Resurrection derives from the Latin *resurrectus*, which is the past participle of resurge, "to rise again." Is there any human being who hasn't physically fallen down? In the movie *Batman Begins*, the hero Bruce Wayne hears the question, directed to him, "Why do we fall?" both as a child rescued from slipping into a very deep hole and as an adult distraught due to a failure in his costumed crime-fighting. He hears the question in traumatic situations, and both times the answer is, "So we can pick ourselves up again." Like other comic book heroes and heroines, Batman is pretty good at resurrecting himself from crisis.

I don't think that resurrection *requires* crisis in order to occur. Then again, resurrection does seem to be a post-crucifixion event: nailed to the pain of life – which can be one's own pain or others', gradually or suddenly we may remarkably surge, freed of the cross or crosses to which we've affixed ourselves.

Why did the prince Siddartha leave his father's palace? So he could suffer a crucifixion. Enjoying worldly pleasures and deliberately and exceptionally protected by his father from seeing illness, old age, and death, Siddartha ventured from the palace one day with his charioteer and saw exactly the pain from which his father had kept him. It depressed him, and in his crisis, at age 29, he left the palace permanently and began to explore ways in which to un-nail himself from the cross of both his own and humanity's despair. He became enlightened, became a Buddha, six years later. His enlightenment was his resurrection.

Crisis can be a turning point at which a person who has fallen into misery picks herself up. That may refresh or renew her, but resurrection is not a pick-me-up – a refreshment that jazzes her like the sugar in a soda or the caffeine in coffee, a renewal, like a vacation or a much-needed nap.

Why do we fall? So we can perform a do-it-yourself resurrection. Which bears a relation to insurrection, a rising up against established authority. Most intensely and intimately, that authority has been ourselves more than any other person, more than any institution or unwritten law.

Does resurrection swell in us like a revelation? Revealed, to myself, I am rolling, like a kid down a snowy hill. Like a lover in the embrace of her beloved, I am swept away.

Christ in pink

How might someone feel looking at *Guernica*? Splayed and fragile, trampled upon, shrunken so magnificently that he is too undone to act on the behalf of love.

How might someone feel looking at Piero's *The Resurrection of Christ*? His sturdy body calms her, the plant of his foot straightens her spine, his steady gaze right into her gives assurance that his small wounds are healing. Christ wears a pink robe: does that color attest to the ultimate tenderness of resurrection?

Notes

1 The quote occurs in Paramahansa Yogananda, *The Yoga of Jesus: Understanding the Hidden Teachings of the Gospels; Selections from the Writings of Paramahansa Yogananda* (Los Angeles, CA: Self-Realization Fellowship, 2007), p. 32.

2 Ibid.

The efficiency of peace

A romantic interlude

I begin by telling you why I'm thinking about peace now. The road may seem circuitous, so bear with me as it gradually winds around to obviously addressing the stated subject.

I define a romance as a light, enjoyable, and amorous encounter of brief duration. I define an affair as longer lasting than a romance and resonant with infatuation, with being in love, which are hallmarks of romantic passion. Romantic passion waxes and wanes and provokes frustration, doubts, and insecurities, infatuations are short-lived, and being in love – the intoxication, the supreme distraction that we often associate with young couples and that we deem as unusual for people the older they get – is also short-lived. (Apparently, passion degenerates along with the presumptive massive degeneration of the body.) We think that falling in love is necessary or natural if people are to become partners or spouses, if they are truly mates. An affair may also be replete with the kinds of abundance, plenty, and luxuriousness that I indicate in my performance *I AM Desire*, with lines that state their presence, such as:

> Here is the plenty of a peaceful rod
> Here is the abundance of the next breath
> Here is the luxuriousness of taking you at your word
> Here is the luxuriousness of releasing pins and needles
> Here is the abundance of flowers in a vase on the table from the garden that I grow
> Here is the plenty of deciding for myself

I define a relationship as a long-term agreement for exploring love – the process, the constancy, and the plenty that they foster.

I've thought of love as the ultimate expansion of human consciousness, but the effects of one romantic interlude, most likely a romance, altered my thinking. I met a man online, we had a dinner date in New York City in March 2010, and around a month later I visited him in his upstate New York home for a few days. He was as playful, witty, fun, intelligent, sexy, and erotic as his emails and our phone conversations had been, a thoroughly delightful and attentive host, from the perfect omelets he made to his good-humored kindness to our easy, interesting conversations and his strong and sensual lovemaking. We made love well more than half of our waking hours. I had a wonderful time! Yet I was neither infatuated nor in love with him when we arranged our rendezvous, and those states of romantic passion did not develop during or after our visit. The same was true for him. I have no desire to turn our terrific time into a relationship, and if he called me saying he'd like to see me in Tucson in a few weeks, I'd respond, "Let me think about it," because more contact feels unnecessary. Maybe a visit will happen and maybe it won't, and whether it does or doesn't holds no anxiety for me. This surprising lack of attachment to any trajectory of connection from a delicious romance surprises me. I've never experienced it before.

Paramours of peace

I do not hold the cultural belief, which I mentioned above, that romantic passion belongs to the young. It had me in its grip from the summer of 2008, when I was 60, into the end of 2009. Indeed, a close girlfriend said to me the other day in regard to that infatuation, "You were nuts." I feel great tenderness today toward the object of that infatuation, and I felt peaceful with my New York paramour both at his place and now. My friend Dianne, who is young in years and wise, has many times offered just the right words, anecdote, passage from a book, or personal story to spark a fresh understanding or a revelatory insight. She reminded me, when I was telling her about my concomitant happiness and neutrality about the romance, of a book we'd both read in which the author produces a calibration of levels of consciousness. Peace calibrates higher than love. As I see it, then, peace overarches love, love as a way of being; and love as a way of being evolves into peace.

I've ceased looking for a relationship for the time being, and I'm thinking that romantic interludes may be for me. At the same time, a new concept is developing from my experience of post-romance peace: peace can produce a relationship. Despite my present withdrawal from a search for a partner and my simultaneous interest in romantic interludes, both of which excite me, I can imagine yet another exciting experience: a relationship with a man that is founded in peace. In other words, from its beginning the relationship rests on peace.

The economical art of easy digestion

I'm curious about the relation between peace and care. What do we care *about*? What do we care *for*? Care in its many and divergent meanings: pay attention to, worry about, provide for and look after, give importance to, feel affection for. Are we caring? Are we filled with care and overly careful? Being peaceful requires great care, the sort that contrasts with anxiety.

Peace is efficient. Like the human digestive system, which operates most efficiently when *chi* is neither stagnant nor deficient, peace operates most efficiently when love is neither stagnant nor deficient. The free flow of *chi* creates an easy digestion, of food in the body so that it is nourished well and of love in the heart so that its openness welcomes peace.

We tend to think of efficiency not only as acting economically – no waste, only necessity – but also as mechanical rather than human. In other words, without consideration for kindness. However, love cannot exist without kindness, and peace and kindness walk hand in hand. We think of emotions and feelings as being *attached* to – desirous of – a person or an outcome. That's romantic love, for example, but efficiency indicates non-attachment. A peaceful person can risk not wasting time, words, or energy. Such beautiful economy makes best use of the resource that is love. Such beautiful economy is effective – certainly for the "economist," who remains loving, kind, and unattached.

In Buddhist terms, "skillful" might replace "efficient." In more broadly spiritual terms, peace is artful.

If I were talking with you, I'd have two things that I'd like us to focus on, though we'd likely meander – artfully.

First, common phrases that include peace. Peace and quiet. Peace be with you. Make peace. At peace. Hold one's peace. Do you use those phrases? Do they serve you in actuality? If so, how?

Second, a question that encompasses the rest. How does one become an artist of peace?

Not driven anymore

Nothing pressing

I heard about a book – or a movie, news story, disease, or unexpected occurrence – while half listening to National Public Radio that an announcer, interviewer, or talk show guest called "life-altering." The adjective "life-altering" caught my attention, but neither its object nor the speaker did, because the use of "life-altering" seemed arbitrary.

Although an implicit system exists for calling something life-altering, which includes matters of loss and gain and of life and death, that system feels pat, both too inclusive and not inclusive enough. Too inclusive: a new job, a firing, a retirement; marrying and divorcing; giving birth or expiring are life-altering because they mark what people consider to be monumental, grand, or absolutely memorable. Not inclusive enough: everything is life-altering because individuals' reactions, or non-reactivity, to all that comes their way leaves a subconscious imprint.

Petite, unimposing, forgotten – no matter. The small composes the large, the ephemeral composes the earth-shattering, and quintessentially prosaic acts and impressions, whether old and latent, superficial and seemingly forgotten and inconsequential, or unconscionably self-critical, determine life alterations, what human beings call fate.

Here's what's small today:

Gunpowder green tea, brewed very strong, drunk plain Pigeon pose, both upright and in a forward fold, in yoga class meditation
The taste and nourishment of dried apricots, Greek yogurt (the Fage brand, with its very thick creaminess), tamari-roasted almonds, an avocado, olive oil, and lettuce
Letting a prose poem, composed of shorter prose poems, take shape in its own fashion, with no push from me, so that whatever results, whether written today or in a week, startles this author with its beauty
A phone conversation with my friend Shelley in Urbana, Illinois

Going to my friend Kat's performance, a house concert
Picking up Kat's nearly 100-year-old neighbor, to take her to the performance, along with my friend Frances

Nothing pressing. Life calling, and I wouldn't name any of that life today a job or a lesson or a gesture of goodwill. Rather, I feel called to be with everyday intimacies that feel at once necessary and desired.

A generous ambition

So, I'm not driven anymore.

Professionally I've lived in the art world and academia, which harbor highly driven people. Ambition is fine with me, but I notice a distinction between ambition with generosity and ambition that's everything-for-me. The latter clangs and screams in the professional worlds with which I'm most familiar: craving status, making a name for oneself, telling others how great you are by touting your publications or exhibitions or speaking engagements, asking your "peers" what they're doing so that you can compare your accomplishments with theirs and come out feeling superior, though you may well end up feeling inferior. (I put *peers* in quotation marks, because competitive comparisons do not determine relations with true peers.)

Ambition with generosity produces a desire to help others, such as a newly hired colleague with the oddities of your department at the university, a young friend with her first performance. The determined desire is for mutual success.

An email included an "ad" from someone I attended high school with, for an online interview about his new book. He sent the email to the alumni list. Ads like that, from books being touted by authors to workshops being offered by instructors to exhibitions by artists about to show up at the opening reception, arrive all the time. Similar things show up in your email, I'm sure.

Can't say that I'm an exception to self-promotion, as I've sometimes advertised my performances and new books in the currently common manner – email, Facebook. Not to mention that my blog and website, in which my intentions are to give information about my work, to present ideas and experiences about various topics, from love to everyday life, and to enjoy a kind of conversation with people who respond to the posts, can all too easily be categorized as publicity in the name of self-representation – because commodification of people into image and product rings truer than generous intentions in a society overwhelmed by an orientation toward surface and celebrity rather than soul, imagination, and creativity. People selling themselves – it's full of puffery and false promise.

Celebrities interest me very little, though I've been reading about the phenomenon of celebrity. Such as David Haven Blake's *Walt Whitman and the Culture of American Celebrity*, from which the reader learns about the construction of fame in nineteenth-century America, and through that, facts about the foundation of today's fame-as-the-manipulation-of-people – both the celebrity and the public. The worship of personality, the invasion of a so-called personality's privacy, the publication of supposedly intimate details about celebrities' lives, and the embodiment of greatness or talent in the celebrity body – nothing new. And all of it historically, as now, accompanied by – dependent upon? – frequent disinterest in and even ignorance of the artistic, intellectual, or other skills and talents that supposedly generated the "greatness" of the celebrity, and, more in line with the celebrity as star, skills and talents that presumably generated the celebrity's brilliant luminosity.

Her incandescence is a verb

I question the goodness of the intentions that I noted earlier and wonder if indeed ego is masterminding them. In that sentence, ego means the greedy self-importance and self-interest critiqued in various spiritual practices, the ego that clamors for attention, that aggresses on the planet and the heart, that leads people away from happiness. I understand the need to make a living, the desire for a satisfaction in one's work that comes from people's appreciation of it, and the healthy narcissism that is an element of self-confidence. The greedy ego overrides healthy narcissism and drives a person into unconscious self-absorption. At any rate, the idea, feeling, and activity of selling myself have become especially distasteful.

Sometime after I'd published *Erotic Faculties*, which was in 1996, my father said to me, "You'd write if you had no money." That so moved me. I remember tears in my eyes as I told some friends about Dad's words. He understood my love of writing and a driving passion to write. A compulsion? These days the compulsion is gone, and with it a compulsion for egoistic success.

My love of writing and performing is large, and in the here and now – this age of mine, this freedom in body and spirit, this ability to travel the planet and my own interior – and in the future that the here and now is creating, patterns of mine are changing.

The exceptional person

Exorcists who drive pain out of heart's door

I heard my therapist, Larry, describe me as "exceptional." The context slips my mind, but *exceptional* caught my attention. In an earlier month or year, I might not have heard the word at all. Two weeks ago, at age 62, I was ready to accept the reality of being exceptional, and I asked Larry, "Do exceptional people experience it as a problem?" He answered, "That goes with the territory." My acceptance of being exceptional and my knowing that all my life I'd experienced it as a problem has led me to dissolve that problem by looking at it. So I'm taking this salon, with only the two of you here, both of whom I consider to be exceptional, as an opportunity for me, and perhaps for you as well, to look at the problem and exorcise my – our? – fear of it. The "evil spirit" is other people's perceptions of the exceptional person and their behavior toward her; but we really can't do a thing about that. The "evil spirit" is fear of vanity: how vain are we, anyway, to think that we're exceptional? The "evil spirit" is disbelief in our own virtues and good fortune. So let us see ourselves as secular and spritely exorcists, nothing Catholic, no credulity in Dark Age or New Age demons. We are the exorcists who drive pain out of heart's door by providing ourselves with the energy to keep those hearts in loving, which features self-loving, motion.

Not everyone is exceptional, and they cannot become so even if they try.

Exceptional people are born that way. They've collected karma that coalesced in some invisible energetic field and that has brought them a slew of good fortunes, of virtues, before those people began to germinate in a woman's belly.

An exceptionally beautiful or musical or smart or kind person is not an exceptional human being. One or two outstanding qualities are not enough to define someone as exceptional. An exceptionally handsome man is just *very* handsome, an exceptionally honest worker is just *very* honest, whereas an exceptional person displays *many* qualities that are exceptional. I emphasize that those qualities must be fortunes or virtues, qualities that society and individuals consider to be gifts or blessings.

Uncategorized charisma

The exceptional person most often does not go around showing off her gifts, although people may perceive her as a show-off, egotist, or narcissist. Rather, her gifts are naturally on display. She cannot hide them. Let's imagine a particular exceptional woman: people will see that she is beautiful, they will hear her unpremeditated directness at a meeting or during workplace socializing, they will feel her self-confidence, they will be attracted, consciously or unconsciously, by her openness, they will hear that she writes, paints, and sings, all at a level of renown, and they will notice that she smiles more than they do. Because of those realities, people will sense or at least suspect that she is very different from them, and they may want, envy, love, or be uncomfortable with that difference. It may scare them, it may serve as a model, it may provoke lots of projection from the unexceptional onto the exceptional, including the misperceptions of show-offy and egotistical, narcissistic, and arrogant.

The exceptional person is not necessarily famous, monetarily rich, or newsworthy, despite the fact that society lauds the virtues that are hers. She is uncategorizable, so neither the market nor the media know how to sell or talk about her, which means that the masses cannot render opinions about her. She is lucky to live outside of media hype, which in actuality is a form of surveillance, yet society would benefit from knowing about her life and work.

The exceptional person may choose to focus attention, her own and consequently others', on one or two of her gifts as the basis of a profession or career. However, that truncates her, so it feels unfulfilling. Why be only a singer/songwriter when you can also practice law and use your PhD in Anthropology to teach in a university? Why be only an art critic when you're also a painter and can do all of the above? Why use your charisma to snare lovers when your passion for sex is tantric – completely sensual and spiritual?

Too, too, too

Just as others don't know what to do with the exceptional person, she may not know what to do with that person either. Does she try to hide her virtues in order to protect herself from people's misperceptions, disbelief, and envy? Even those of people whose love she has trusted? Does she flaunt her virtues in a kind of "what the hell?" approach? Does she proceed from "Fuck you, you won't understand anyway"? But the flaunting puts her in the glare, and she feels healthiest in natural light, and Fuck you is only her anger with the world at large for not loving all that she is.

If an exceptional person does nothing to maintain or increase her virtues, they will fall from her, like badly cared-for, tattered clothing. Staying exceptional requires creativity and work – the development of talents by learning skills that nurture them, the cultivation of health, which influences beauty, the daily continuity of practices that nourish soul-and-mind-inseparable-from-body, such as yoga, whose action, according to *The Yoga-Sutra of Pantañjali*, "has three components – discipline, self-study and orientation toward the ideal of pure awareness." (*The Yoga-Sutra*, almost 2,000 years old, sets forth 196 concise and illuminating observations about consciousness and liberation from suffering. Pantañjali most likely was a yoga teacher, and yoga during his time predated by centuries the physical practice, hatha yoga, that is so popular these days in the United States.)

The exceptional person so radically differs from the norm that others may perceive her as extreme – *too* smart, *too* sexy, *too* self-assured, *too* good, *too* happy: *too* much – too much to be true, so they falsify her in their minds. She is the exception to their rules – about gender, age, sex, intelligence, health, and strength of mind and body. She grows healthier, happier, and more beautiful as she grows older. Her vagina is wet when she makes love in her sixties, her mental and physical flexibility are greater than they were in her twenties, her emotional and physical energy are maiden fresh and more focused than ever.

Unruled in the promised land

I was telling Larry recently that in my (exceptional) happiness, clarity, and openness I enjoy talking with a smaller number of people than I used to, and only about things that fascinate me, and his words showed his understanding of me and of the ever-expanding and more concentrated self that consists of knowing, loving, and trusting that self: "The fewer people you'll want to talk with and the less you'll want to talk about." I felt elated! I felt that I'd arrived! In a promised land whose frontiers are endless. The promised land called desire, unruled – the land, desire, and myself – by man, or men, women, feminists, age, sex, or any bias.

I wouldn't know if all exceptional people feel at once steady, easy, and passionate – intensely centered – in desire. Larry's statement helped me relax into desire, and his words met in my mind with ideas that I'd been reading in *Yoga Spandakarika: The Sacred Texts at the Origins of Tantra*. Desire is at the heart of tantra, and the commentary by Daniel Odier, who both studies and practices tantra, illustrates that being in desire is as simple as soft breathing.

O radiant one!

I've spoken little about personal experiences. I think that they're important, because how we experience ourselves through others' words can tell us about our ease or unease about being exceptional. Here goes.

I've been told many times that I intimidate men. I've learned that the accurate statement is this: they're intimidated by me. In other words, the feeling is theirs, I haven't caused it. Especially over the past ten years or so as I've softened and softened, so that my friendliness and my comfortableness with myself could ameliorate the perceived threat.

I see that the exceptional woman scares men. They fantasize about having sex with her, but they have a tough time, if the sex happens or if a relationship unfolds, fulfilling their own ideas of what they need to do or be in order to be her equal. In romantic relations, the lover of an exceptional woman may worship her, and the exceptional woman may project her own exceptionalism on someone else, imagining that person to be a peer when he is not. Neither situation leads to true intimacy. The equality problem also occurs in women/women friendships. I've had the experience, the first time was in my twenties, of girlfriends saying "I can't keep up with you" and then leaving the friendship.

Apparently, an exceptional woman who wishes to meet an available man is too outstanding to be introduced to one. After Russell's and my divorce in 2001, I asked girlfriends if they knew any men for me to meet. Many times the response was, "He'd have to be so special." Not one girlfriend had any suggestion, let alone introduction.

During our first meeting, a nine-hour conversation that included meals and a drive into the desert, a man with whom I fell in love complimented me with a lovely come-on: "You're intelligent, creative, and beautiful. You must be surrounded by men." My response? Light laughter and "Oh, ... no." He said, in an understanding tone intended, I imagine, to remove him from the group on which he was commenting, "Men are threatened by you. You're too powerful."

In early March 2010 I met a lovely man online – smart, witty, sensual, creative, intelligent – and when I went to New York City later that month, we went out to dinner, a great date! In April, before I traveled from Tucson to visit him for several days, staying at his home in upstate New York, he sent me an email that began, "I've just googled you and I'm sitting here wondering why I'm not intimidated intellectually, physically, and, of course, erotically, but I'm not." He is a rare man! Both in stating the intimidation factor that comes with the territory named Joanna Frueh and choosing the adventure! What a delight – verbal truth, my enjoyment of it, and our terrific romantic interlude in which intimidation didn't figure.

In 2010 people describe me to myself with the following names and adjectives. All came out of the blue. I wasn't asking for descriptions or compliments. The descriptions come from sources of varied closeness to me: a lover, several good friends, including one from high school, and acquaintances in yoga class. I'm so happy that I hear the truth in each one of these descriptions.

Goddess
O radiant one
Ingénue
Thoroughbred
Starlet
Commanding and lovely
Disarmingly sweet for an intellectual
More beautiful than ever
A rose in full bloom with a gorgeous scent

Be true to yourself. That's a cliché, and I remind us that clichés are often truths in well-worn guises. If the exceptional person is true to herself as she grows older, she will become more exceptional, especially within her age cohort. She has probably felt weird at many times during her life – the effects of too much – and as she becomes more exceptional, which does designate a high degree of loving self-acceptance, she may also notice that, while not exactly running away from herself, she is not standing her ground, for example withdrawing, if only momentarily, from a conversation in which her experience and knowledge run counter to the attitudes and experiences of her companions. That old fear of being perceived as egotistic, arrogant, and narcissistic. Why not enliven the conversation, eroticize it magnificently, by being true to herself?

Wild sacred space

Do not proceed with caution – throw it to the wind

Like space, the sacred is infinite, which makes "sacred space" a redundant term. However, I understand that the human mind generally limits space, and a consequent instance of that is the division of space into secular and sacred. That division attempts to regulate people's beliefs and behaviors, and to ensure that the different spaces serve different purposes and arouse and contain different feelings. Spillage from the container/containment of one kind of space into the other can be very shocking, for the conventionally sacred space, such as a church, is a traditional safety zone. An extreme example: people celebrating mass or witnessing a wedding do not expect bombs to explode during those events. Neither explosive devices nor explosive emotions belong in a space where deity resides or people regularly call upon or address it, and, conversely, emotions and vocal expressions deemed suitable in sacred space are often not so in most public areas: mourn a loved one with your tears at the burial ground but not on the city bus, pray in the temple, not at the restaurant.

One root of *space* is the Indo-European base *spei*, to flourish, expand, succeed. In sacred space we flourish *because* we expand, because we have succeeded, effortlessly, in enlarging our awareness.

Limitations of physical space, such as churches, temples, mosques, and stupas, can limit mental freedom. Sacred space is free and available space. "Free space" is an oxymoron, because space denotes roominess itself, so what could be freer? Yet the designated sacred space imposes mind-fabricated structure, the dualism of sacred and secular, on reality, and sacred space becomes conditional when forced into tight quarters.

Regulation of sacred space fetishizes it, gives it an exclusivity: here we pray, here only Jews or Muslims are *really* welcome, here we perform proper rituals and receive the True Word, which sanctifies us, its genuine adherents. Here we become holier than thou. Here is the *sacred* boundary between you and I.

Regulated space encourages formality and correctness, right consciousness and perception, right thoughts, acts, and emotions.

Accepted sacred spaces become environments from which one must escape, sometimes bodily, definitely mentally, in order to encounter unpredictable sacred space, which is a wild place, where the unexpected can take you by storm. Do not proceed with caution. Throw it to the wind.

Wild sacred space does not live in parlors of worship.

Nor can so-called sacred vows, sacred texts, sacred objects, or sacred songs and music instigate or coax the arrival of that space. Sacred vows: such as the promise to kill offenders in a blood feud or the enemy in a war, to be faithful to your groom forever, to follow the moral principles in a monastery, to take care of your mother after your father dies. You can make that vow to your father when he asks you, you can make a vow to family members, to a nation, to a lifelong partner, to a community of monks, but committing to a cause, an action, an emotion, or a person, while powerful, can become just an obligation or a memory, and it can also become an obstacle to the arrival of wild sacred space. Vows are a form of so-called sacred words, spoken ones, and we come upon such words when we read scripture, such as bibles, *sutras*, and the *suras* in the Koran, or texts by sages and buddhas.

Objects – such as icons and amulets "blessed" by a religion, or the good luck charm chosen by you; songs and chants, such as hymns and mantras; spoken and written words; songs and music – all hold energy, so you can imbue them with emotional, psychic, and spiritual vitality, but none is a root or foundation of wild sacred space. Neither is meditation. Neither are the self-abnegations of ascetics who refrain from food or sex.

Language, objects, and music may be personal, artistic, literary, or cultural treasures. They may be primers of a religion or a devotional practice, and like long- or short-term disciplines in which a person focuses pointedly on her self, as body, mind, or both, language, objects, and music *may* activate sacred space, but they do not guarantee entry. So-called sacred words function as rumors about wild sacred space, and those words, as well as so-called sacred objects, music, and practices, can stimulate desire for sacred space and point us in its direction.

From here on, when I refer to sacred space, it is wild sacred space unless otherwise specified.

Were it not for our intimacy with ourselves, no other intimacy could occur

We cannot create sacred space, nor can we recreate it, because it exists within a person's awareness. That awareness can occur, for instance, within religious architecture or a memorial battlefield, but sacred space "opens" to our awareness due to an infinitely specific configuration of circumstances, of which the physical surroundings are only one. Sacred space is ever-available, which means that we could be aware of it at any time; but usually we are not, because awareness of sacred space is of an order of alertness, perceiving, or being that is out of the routine. Though I would say that such awareness is also of the utmost ordinariness, because it is intrinsic to the mind.

If you try to feel sacred space, you'll fail. It simply appears when you are ready, ripe, which may be pretty much all the time or pretty much none of it, or any state in between the two.

A human being is the instrument of sacred space when she has tuned herself to spontaneity, clarity, and availability. Then she vibrates in unison with that space. She is its twin. The vibration is easeful and instantaneous.

Sacred space exerts no pressure. If you exert pressure on sacred space, you have untwinned yourself.

What happens in sacred space? Confidences, intimacies, creativity, and creation.

A grand stretching and flexibility that we don't even think about till after we've re-entered a more regular mode of feeling. In the designated, standardized sacred space, respect for that space and the people within it is requisite, but in the wild and instantaneous sacred space, respect is too conceptual, too distancing. Respect is a high grade of politeness, a made-up refinement that contrasts with the innate refinement, the nuanced profusion of feelings and sensations that permeates a person in the wildness of instantaneity.

The intimacy that actualizes in sacred space is with oneself, even if he is with someone else, talking, hiking, eating, making love, driving a car – doing anything. In sacred space, the activity is nonessential, whether we're alone or in the midst of a crowd. After the fact of intimacy with ourselves, we may attribute it to our relation with the place in which we experienced the intimacy or with the person who shared it, but were it not for our intimacy with ourselves, no other intimacy could occur.

Toast and orifices

Sacred space exceeds expectations, and it is no more special than the bread that you toast for breakfast.

Sacred space slips through your fingers. It slips into and out from your orifices.

Sacred space cannot be rushed, it cannot be slowed. It cannot be started, it cannot be stopped. You cannot probe it with body or theory.

In sacred space a person makes no mistakes, though she is not perfect. It is utterly liberating.

Sacred space does not bridge secular and designated sacred space, as if they need to be reconciled, or can be. Sacred space is completely unlike them. It is primal.

Only here do the fires of fear not burn me

Primal means first. Never previously occurring or done, not even previously imagined, because sacred space is vastly specific and minutely encompassing. Sacred space is first space. It existed before the cosmos conceived this planet.

Primal also means basic, which indicates to me that sacred space will exist after the cosmos claims this planet, and, too, that sacred space is not only inherent to the mind but also necessary for living a happy life.

The primal nature of sacred space makes it deeper than instinct or intuition.

We do not have to prime ourselves for the primal because it's always at our disposal. Primal awareness cannot be planned, so we needn't dress in any special way for it, prepare any ritual tools or foods, display any particular images, recite any incantations, or take our bodies into any suitably worthy building, room, or location whether it be a cathedral, yoga studio, or the Alaskan wilderness.

In sacred space you are naked, revealed to yourself (and possibly to others) in exposures that may feel deliciously comfortable, unambiguously scary, or both at once. Paradox reigns in sacred space, but without supremacy. I remember feeling levitationally light walking in sandals through a courtyard and down a dirt path to the dining hall at an *ashram* in India and simultaneously feeling planted solidly on the ground. I remember coming home after a nine-hour conversation with a man rather than making love with him because I wanted to be intimate with only me in the tranquil surroundings that I created and that I know very well. I hadn't fallen in love for a long, long time and that exposure of myself to myself had me in tears within a minute of unlocking the front door as I thought about the monumental surprise of what was happening. I felt joyful and I felt scared and I needed, for a while, to share that more with only myself. (Transpose the "c" and the "a" in sacred and you've got "scared.")

Although "inviolate" is a synonym for sacred, we may feel unsafe in sacred space, because we are aware in a way that we haven't been before – the richness and plethora of *these* details are taking us somewhere new, which is what sacred space always is. A person needs to trust her primal awareness and not make a problem of what it brings her or where it puts her. Abandonment is the way to go, and even in difficult circumstances that can be a pleasure – feeling the emotions and sensations as they cluster and flow, which they do in the abandonment to orgasm, which can last and last and be alive not only in the genitals but anywhere in the body. In abandonment we are unselfconscious – carried along perhaps more than carried away in the care of our immediate awareness, which is continuous because it is present. (I'll return to the orgasmic pleasure of the sacred in a bit.) When my father, who would die within a few days and was every bit as cognizant as usual, asked me to explain to his doctor that Dad wanted a drug to help him pass from this world with some ease, I said, "I'll do anything for you." Our interaction and the circumstances deposited me in sacred space, where I was earthed and unearthed big time, and forever changed, as I was after the nine-hour, introductory conversation with the man who became a lover.

Only here, in sacred space, do the fires of fear not burn me. In sacred space I am inviolate – a synonym for sacred – because I am in the embrace of *dharma*, which can be defined as natural and cosmic law, harmony, and order. The cosmic is the primal, and the order of *dharma* is mysterious to human beings, as on those days when everything is in synch yet you have (apparently) done nothing to make it so.

When, besides abandoning myself to the pleasure that I noted with Dad and my soon-to-be lover, have I been in sacred space? During conversations with friends, on a walk in my Tucson neighborhood, at the ruins in Delphi, when I gardened in Reno, while lovemaking, sitting around my home, lecturing in a classroom, having morning tea by myself, coloring or reading as a child, writing, performing, drinking *really* good coffee to which I've added half and half, looking out of the window of an airplane high above land, cleaning the house, witnessing my parents' deaths, exchanging greetings with homeless people, doing Continuum on my bed at home and also on the one in my monkish room at the *ashram* that I mentioned, in front of an artwork in a museum. (The last example happens very rarely.)

The time in all of the above situations has ranged from seconds to hours, experienced always as simultaneously compressed and expanded.

Whisper, hush, moan, shout, silence; bees buzzing, dogs barking, birds singing; big city traffic, blowing wind, ambient noise. Sound, most often unconstructed, is frequently an important part of sacred space for me.

I think that some of the sounds and sacred spaces that I listed, as well as vows, texts, music, and objects called sacred by religions, individuals, or nations, can sustain a primal resonance or residual.

Unwilled immersions in the lost and found

One of the most basic spaces is the human body, certainly from the perspective of you or of myself as we live in our own bodies. We want that space to be inviolate, in its various meanings, which, besides sacred, include safe from injury and violation, and free. We feel elementally okay then, and I think that feeling free in our bodies, which means open and spacious, is actually rare. The body is full, of liquid and of degrees of solid matter, yet we experience our bodies more than occasionally in terms of spatial metaphors, which may be energetic, such as open or closed, and which may be architectural, such as a prison or a temple. Sometimes people guard the body space, sometimes they unlock it and let down the defensive walls. During yoga class, one of my beloved instructors sometimes refers to this elemental space that human beings inhabit as the "body temple." Ah, sacred space. When *perceived* that way. *Thinking* that your most personal, most basic abode is a body temple keeps the sacred elusive, but I can be aware: my body is a temple without trying.

Just as people can have spacious or tight bodies, they can also have spacious or tight minds. Like the tight body, the tight mind may be more obstructed than graceful, and its tensions and restraints are not just confined to prejudice and obviously injudicious beliefs. Cramping and blockage also happen when a person fills his mind with facts and theories and other information and ideas that may be interesting or useful but that can also clutter the space, most extremely in a kind of hoarding that suggests tremendous fear of clearing, which is change.

The overly filled mind obscures the sacred and shuts down pleasure. The body full of tension does the same.

People tend to think of orgasm as a peak and short-lived pleasure. Let's understand it, instead, as a changing pleasure, ranging from intense to mild, that can be localized or more diffuse anywhere in the body. (Some Taoist writings about sex discuss this, and I can vouch for the truth of this kind of pleasure from personal experience.) You needn't make love with someone to experience orgasm throughout the body, and you needn't masturbate, because releases, flowerings, and movements of pleasure occur through the opening of areas in the body. Considering the subject of this writing, we might call those open areas sacred spaces, and they can be everywhere in the body. They *can* be the entire body all at once.

I wouldn't call such pleasure an ideal state or a sexual one. I'd call it possible and erotic, and the following passage in the commentary by Daniel Odier, who both studies and practices tantra, in *Yoga Spandakarika: The Sacred Texts at the Origins of Tantra*, delightfully surprised me, because I felt a kinship with the pleasure he writes about.

> Sometimes, when we think of a mystic living alone, ... we think that it must be terrible to be all alone in her hut, in the forest, on a mountain. Or, we think that it must be idyllic. ... This is because we do not realize to what extent the ascetics experience unlimited exchange of love. Their whole body is engaged in this impulse, in this sacred tremoring. There is never any end, any obstacle, any stop, any frustration. Nor is there ever any accumulation of sexual energy because this energy is disseminated all day long in this loving contact with the world.[1]

I don't call myself an ascetic. Severity isn't me, and I've read too many accounts by or about ascetics who seem punishingly severe with themselves. Mystic makes more sense, a very erotic and sensual mystic.

Sacred space is an immersion, through no will of our own, in non-dualistic awareness, and it is entirely subjective.

Sacred space is in *you* and you are its lost and found.

Note

1 Daniel Odier, *Yoga Spandakarika: The Sacred Texts at the Origins of Tantra*, trans. Clare Frock. Rochester, VT: Inner Traditions, 2005, p. 44. For Odier's full gloss on the tenth stanza of the *Spandakarika*, see https://premakalidasi.tumblr.com/post/174299457613/stanza-10-then-the-heart-realizes-that-the-true (accessed April 27, 2025).

Dreaming the world into being

Prana fills me and I feel spacious, *prana* depletes and I deflate. *Prana* means air, breath, and vital energy or life force in Sanskrit. When you breathe consciously, *prana* fills you and you can direct it, into your mid-back, toes, jaw, heart, groin, brain – anywhere in your body. In yoga, *pranayama*, breath discipline, is the regulation and focusing of one's own breath, and the practice of *pranayama* can balance, energize, or calm a person. If you direct your prana, the vital energy within you, into the world and other people, you vitalize *them*.

When prana fills me, I am a pranamour, a spacious lover and a lover of space.

When prana fills me, I am a dream lover – not like the one in Bobby Darin's song "Dream Lover," who doesn't exist at all, the one he is hoping and praying for but who isn't materializing from the pathos, the low prana (though high intensity) of his dreaming. "Where are you?" he asks in the first line, and at the end of each verse he repeats for the umpteenth time one of the standard plaints of the lonely person who thinks that a lover will solve her loneliness: "I want a dream lover, so I don't have to be alone." The singer assumes that a dream lover, one produced by his dreaming, will be just-right dreamy, but ... I gotta say, dream on, because the petitioner in the song is a pranacide. He is a lover of dreams built from a fabric of woe, which is most narratives of romantic love, whether popular, like Darin's song, or classic, like Tristan and Iseult. Those narratives are cramped spaces, in which imagination has trouble breathing. Romantic love tends to be a program of conventions undergone by lovers: in short, self-conflagrating passion stunted by overexpectation, passion that cannot grow into the peace *and* stimulation that forms a bond between pranamours. Cramped space also describes the life that the lover of pranacidal dreams builds from them.

In contrast to the pranacide, the pranamour notices her abundance or exhaustion of prana, notices the space within his soul-and-mind-inseparable-from-body. I emphasize that the pranamour works and plays to *create* space and to dream a world into being from spaciousness. *Prana*, being life force, is creative. People's acts in the world *are* dreams come true, from a seeming happy magic … or false, like treacheries. Treacherous dreams, such as the incipient *amour fou* of "Dream Lover," can come from cramped space. *Prana* is the space of dreams, and the pranamour is my model of an inspiring dream lover who can create the condition of pranamour – love that is large because it keeps growing.

Without prana, we can create nothing.

Prayer can be void of prana, a state which "Dream Lover" approaches, and prayer can "produce" emotional and physical violence, as in the requests for death to the enemy, both Greek and Trojan, that drive the narrative of Homer's *Iliad* and that function as a model for the rallying belief in war after war through century after century that "God is on our side." Such prayers may indeed be "answered," with the killing of enemy bodies in war *and* of the petitioner's soul in her everyday life. Such prayers, like the sad petitioner's in "Dream Lover," come from reductive prana, prana that may reduce the dreamer himself to a nightmare. One origin of *dream* is the Old English *dream*, meaning joy, music. The model of the pranamour gives me reason to think that when she, the pranamour, increases her prana she augments herself into a dream of joy, which resonates with the pleasures of erotic rhythm and song. One meaning of eros is life force, so no wonder that lovers dreamed by and into joy delight in erotic pleasures.

In order to become joyful the pranamour pranafies himself. The term *pranafy* first came to my attention in a yoga class taught by my beloved instructor, Michelle Marks, who, sometime in 2009, gave us the words "pranafy" and "pranafication." Michelle has studied with the yoga star Shiva Rea, whose video *Pranafy Yourself: Pranafication with Shiva Rea: Tending the Sacred Fire Retreat, Living the Flow of Yoga* I watched on YouTube. Neither in the video nor, as far as I can tell from modestly perusing it, Rea's website, which abounds with information, does Rea describe or explain pranafication, so I'm taking it in my own direction.

Pranafication is the kind of noun that can indicate a completed action resulting in a finished thing or idea, such as commodification, unification, fortification, solidification, and deification.

Commodification results in commodities, unification in unity, fortification in defenses (like forts), solidification in solidity or hardness, deification in gods and goddesses. All of the above nouns may also be understood as ongoing actions, which is how I define pranafication: an ongoing production of prana, a process. I experience pranafication as an ebb and flow that is never a done deal. If it were, I'd be perfect, or existing in an unvarying state.

Earlier in my life, I felt much less space in myself and my life, and some of my tastes in visual art and movies reflect that lesser pranafication. An example is Agnes Varda's film *Vagabond*. In 1985 when it was released, I was 37. Mona, the title character, is more than a decade younger than that. Nevertheless, I read myself in her, and she and the film stayed with me for a long time. Vagrancy is for Mona a literal and figurative condition and it damages her physically and emotionally. In my forties I wrote about my vagrant mind, which I love and still do, for it wanders into erotic/pranafied places, unpredictable thoughts and feelings that ask for my exploration. Although a vagrant can be defined as a beggar, my form of vagrancy brings me riches.

I haven't experienced the exact events that Mona does, but her very vagabondage is the life of all of us Everywoman, at least for some extent of time when we feel desperately unhoused despite the abode of body. We haven't the faith, the finances, the friends, or the family with which to comfort soul-and-mind-inseparable-from-body. We do not love ourselves enough, and maybe no one else does either.

When I first watched the film – and watch is too neutral a word, because *Vagabond* frightened me as much as it engrossed me – I couldn't tell if Mona was crazy, I couldn't tell if she was beautiful. I thought that she probably wasn't the first and probably *was* the second. Witnessing the film again in my late fifties, I knew that Mona is both sane and stunning.

She endures a kind of exhaustion that I have only felt during the months from my father's death in July 1999 through my mother's death in March 2000 and into the summer of that year, after my husband of a decade, who had been my partner of thirteen years, moved out of our house in a separation that ended in divorce around July 2001. Over those two years the circles under my eyes were not as dark as Mona's are, though sometimes my spirits darkened as much as hers do.

The original title of the film, the French title, is *Sans Toit ni Loi*, which translates literally as "without roof or law." Mona has freedom. She is not a criminal, but she is an outlaw of sorts, following a head-swimmingly ascetic, even monkish path for, by, and unto herself outside the laws of gender, without the roof of the Father's protection. She takes a heroic path, and perhaps it is the path of the damned. She is stupendously brave.

The way of Mona the female wanderer is the way of the female warrior. Mona, my action hero who is fighting for freedom in the huge and unpretentious terrain of the heart. Mona, my scary savior, who is trying to find her way, simply from here to there, which is from one heart to another, from her own heart to another heart that understands. Does she know where she is? Or does being a vagabond mean that you never know quite where you are? Or does the condition of vagabondage maximize the vagabond's attention to the real by amplifying her no-time-like-the-present? (Or, shall I say, pinning her there? Fixing her in unfixedness.)

Mona's tale is not a success story, but for me at 37 it offered counsel in bravado and euphoria, in creating my own ground and standing there. That space can be pretty incomplete and shaky, but it does require more than a minimum of pranafication.

Creating space by pranafying your life requires clearing. Although earlier in this piece I severely critiqued romantic love (which I did also at length in chapter 4 of my book *Swooning Beauty: A Memoir of Pleasure*), the beginning period of being in love can feel enormously lucid and lucidly enormous. Surely we've become detoxified, because we sense a clear space within ourselves, a clear space that *is* ourselves, as if through pranamour all of our cells had utterly purified themselves, so that while we feel high we also feel radiant, as if those renewed cells are shining. I was so stunned at one such clearing, when I was 60, so unexpectedly taken by pranamour (and, I suppose, the man with whom I was sharing it), that, when home by myself after meeting him and spending many hours together, none of them making love, I cried and asked myself, "What *is* this? *What* is going on?" I'd anticipated being attracted to him, but bogglingly beautiful pranamour hadn't crossed my mind.

Pranamour that happens at the beginning of being in love is already large, and I think that one reason why it so excites us is that we immediately feel its largeness. Then we want more, over the next hours, days, years – lifetime. That may happen, but often it doesn't, so when pranamour fades and we're feeling cramped or trapped with the person who seemed to be our for-real dream lover, we grasp for pranamour, which is a metaphorical gasping for air, born of the same pranacidal tendencies inherent in the breathlessness of the early stages of romantic love. The body gasps for breath when it's working hard, sometimes detrimentally overworking. It can't breathe, and neither can lovers who are trying to recapture the past. Like prana, pranamour is always a present state. You breathe *now*, or you die. With mates and lovers, pranamour can be a primarily expanding state that, like breathing, is relatively stable and ever-changing. Sometimes people in love figuratively hold their breath, waiting and hoping for a change in the energies of their relationship. Love has become choppy, as breathing can, and in both cases, holding the breath can be deadly.

Pranamour never feels to me like a spell, the kind that romantic love generally casts, but pranamour can deteriorate into one. Bad spell, enchanted princess, saved by a prince or princess who, uh oh, will undoubtedly enchant her once again. As one of my friends said about a relationship of hers that had almost completely wound down with a woman with whom she had loved conversation, sex, and travel, "spell expired. Not broken." A relationship in expiration means that its time is up, it's dead. The relationship, once a living organism, has released its final exhale. Pranafication is simple – inhale, exhale, again and again, letting prana do what it does naturally, vitalize organisms and space. In a relationship people sometimes want to hold onto the inhale – inspiration – which fills them, but the exhale, which is release and relaxation, is essential. Pranamour may bring about long periods of relaxing one's grip on a partner and on the relationship itself, maybe to the point of its expiration/demise. In the body, long inhales naturally accompany long exhales. Analogously, the pranamour in an apparently failing relationship, in for the long exhales, of needs inspires herself. Doing so, she can break any spell that has her hooked into pranacidal doubts, drama, or depression.

Pranafication builds a dream home. Not that house with a swimming pool and gardens and many bedrooms and bathrooms, and the need for maids and caretakers who may or may not treat the space with pranamour. I remember telling a professional acquaintance that I was moving from Reno to Tucson and she asked if I'd found my dream home. The term affected me as it always has, producing a big gap between me and it, because I've never thought about having a physical dream home or needing or wanting one. Rather than going into my lack of resonance with the American dream-home idea, which felt like an uninteresting avenue of pursuit, I responded with, "The house I'm buying there *is* my dream home." That felt true and it still does, because dream homes do not stand unto themselves, uninhabited. Rather, a person dreams her home into being, with the furnishings and smells and decoration and life force aplenty or amok that she brings to the physical structure.

During my friend Dianne's first visit, from New York, to my home, we spent half a day in silence, during which both of us wrote for some of the time. In her journal she says that the space of my home – how the space feels, where furniture is placed – is created for big things to move through. The space of pranamour, I hope, which gives room to big, lovely thoughts and emotions.

The space of my home is very open and uncrowded, with little furniture and with few items placed on surfaces and few artworks on the walls. Whether in architecture or within oneself, pranafication requires clearing space. Not necessarily to the zen-like simplicity of *my* home, but to the degree that clutter, in visual or personally historical terms, does not infringe on a flow of soul-and-mind-inseparable-from-body: in other words, bodies' physical movement, minds' powers of imagination and consciousness, and souls' resonance, within one's own heart and with the depths of other people. So, a pranafied home is relatively clean of dirt, distractions, and accumulations – vacuumed, dusted, and free of piles of papers not dealt with on a regular basis, and of images and words, in letters, memorabilia, and other "archival" material that weigh on you because you "have" to keep them – legacy, family history – whether you want to or not, and whether you've dealt with their emotional content – for *you* – or not. A pranafied home is not about abstinence, scarcity, deprivation, compulsiveness, perfectionism, purging, or getting rid of discomfort, but rather about fullness of flow, even an opulent fluidity.

Here's what I've cleared from my interior and external spaces in the past two years: a once-close friend of twenty-five years; many books, leaving only the ones that I return to again and again, and adding to them very judiciously; handwritten and emailed love letters that I'd kept from major relationships and romances; household goods; art. Sadness and difficulty surprised me sometimes. Did I really no longer want the collection of Byron's poems, the one I'd kept from graduate school days? Was a book by a "lesser" writer, Gautier's *Mademoiselle de Maupin*, purloined from the Chicago Public Library in my twenties, more meaningful? Guess so. The love letters, on the other hand, were easy to let go of, because my openness to new and more spacious relationships felt airy and lucid to me, like a focused, wide, and gentle ray of light extending from my body into infinity. Objects of many kinds left my home, from the Chinese rug that had defined for me my grandfather's bedroom, to an Afghan knitted by my mother, to clothing that was beautiful but that I hadn't worn in a long time, to remembrances that students had given to me from their performances in classes that I taught. My love for Gramps, Mom, beauty, and my students continues, as does my love for the special men with whom the mutual holding of hearts changed Joanna in her past. At times when I clear a lot or a little, I've wondered, tongue-in-cheek, to friends, "Now, what do I do with this new space?" The expanse and freshness of that new space, which is room for a more pranafied me, available for unforeseen erotics, both with myself and other people, and for previously unseen uses of my past, now brought to an omigosh beauty and utility. Available for continuing crescendos and climaxes of pranificence (another word that Michelle used in class).

The space of pranamour may become available in a home when its inhabitants rearrange objects within it, following the lead of their own sense of feng shui. We change the position of a vase or chair that's been feeling cumbersome or heavy to us, or located at an uncomfortable angle in relation to nearby objects or to a whole room, and, whaddya know?, we breathe easy again. As little as an inch or two one way or another can do the trick.

I'd kept a key object in my life as a focal point of my living room, in Reno before I moved to Tucson and then in Tucson, for around five years. The object is a large self-portrait photo in which I'm a little over life size. I had a frame built and painted especially for the piece, which was the signature image of my retrospective exhibition in 2005 and the picture on the exhibition catalog cover. I'd used the photo a number of times in publication and publicity. I titled it *Venus Verticordia 2004*, after my favorite painting by Dante Gabriel Rossetti, *Venus Verticordia*, dated 1864–69. My second husband, Russell Dudley, and I collaborated on the photo, as we had on many previous photos since the late 1980s. In 2004 when we shot this photo we'd been divorced for three years, and that shoot was our last one together.

One day my good friend Kat was at my home and she commented on *Venus Verticordia 2004*. She'd seen it many times before and thinks that it's beautiful and complex. She comes over often, so we hardly talk about the piece every time. "Your eyes look sad" in the photo, she told me, "like you've just been crying or are about to cry." I responded that I'd never seen the sadness and hadn't intended it during the photo shoot. I saw a number of different expressions in the pictures, from which Russell and I selected for reproduction and exhibition only the one that, through Kat's perception, I was seeing anew. Interpreting the photo's iconography along with the emotional tone, she added, "You seem to be looking at someone who hurt you deeply, who betrayed you."

"Wow, I've always seen the piece as playful. And no one's seen what you have." (Indeed, in the chapter "Theory: on behalf of muses" in this volume I write about the photo from a playful perspective. That part of the chapter I wrote before Kat gave me her interpretation in early 2010.)

"They've probably seen it," Kat said, "but didn't feel comfortable saying it." Sitting at the dining room table, with the picture a few feet away, she gave me a smiling, direct look, and offered, "There's not a trace of that sadness now. Not a trace."

As we talked, I thanked her, and near the close of our conversation about the piece I said, "I'm going to move it." Which I did the next day – into "storage" (one of the large closets in my house where I keep artwork, both my own and that of others). The moving was a simple unburdening of personal history that no longer needed to be in a prominent location. No ritual. Just cleaning the glass and the frame of the photo, wrapping it in a white tablecloth that I used about once every other year – I was going to go to Goodwill and buy a sheet, but the tablecloth was handy – and gently placing the picture against a wall in the closet.

As I said, the photo is large and very particularly framed. As Kat wrote to me after I emailed her of the change in my home, "that vision of Joanna was dominating the room," which is the living/dining room area and visually inclusive of my study. The entire area is big and spacious.

No work of art, no object or piece of furniture replaced the photo. I arranged the chaise lounge and end table that had been near the picture to fill the space that it left. I like living in this new amplitude.

A dreamer can be walking around in a dream, defined as self-delusion. Or she may be experiencing her dream more in line with the derivation of *dream* from the Old English joy, music. I'm sure that's idealistically dreamy for some people, but I'd rather be living musicality – tuned to delight – than subsisting, through scorn or ignorance, without a practice of pleasure.

As dreaming the idea and reality of dreaming the world into being swirls through soul-and-mind-inseparable-from-body, a famous Maidenform ad campaign suddenly arrives from who knows where. Main image: a woman in a Maidenform bra. Main text: I dreamed I was ______________ in my Maidenform bra. All kinds of amazing possibilities fill in the blank, and I remember seeing Maidenform ads in magazines. The campaign ran from 1949, the year after my birth, to 1969, so during the formative years of my femininity, my love of the erotic, and my ambitions for what I wished to do with my life. Some of the ads are very weird, such as "I dreamed I was a Jack-in-the-Box in my Maidenform bra" and "I dreamed I was ogled by creepy clowns in my Maidenform bra." Unappealing, for sure. However, many of the ads appealed to Joanna the romantic and the idealist, who loves sex, sexiness, and beauty. The female figure in the ads truly stars in them, and while her "costume" varies, she always looks elegant, and always her bra is the intended focal point of the ad. Here are some of the "dreams" I like, always beginning with "I dreamed I": had the world on a string, was a toreador, was bewitching, opened the World Series, was Queen of Hearts, won the Academy Award, rode a roller coaster, went square-dancing, had Spring Fever, went on a safari, was a work of art, played chess, made sweet music, was a medieval maiden, played in an all-girl orchestra, covered the Paris collections, was a siren, was a classic beauty, was tickled pink, went strolling, stopped traffic, barged down the Nile. Adventure, art, fashion, history; love, excitement, play; bodily and mental intelligence. You, dear reader, might criticize the focus on a bra and therefore metonymically on breasts. You might ask, "Is that all a woman is? Flesh, sex, and an anatomical destiny of feeding babies with her body?" Dear reader, I understand your complaint, but I respond to the pranafication that the Maidenform woman personified for me – though, of course, my younger self didn't have the word pranafy to articulate the allure of the ads. The Maidenform woman encouraged my pranificence. I could dream, too, and build this body of love that I am.

I dream … I dream … and the pleasure of prana fills me.

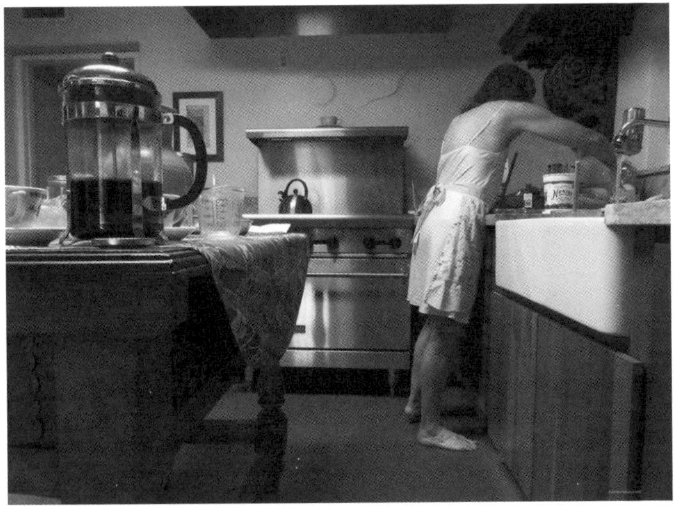

Figure 7 *Joanna's Kitchen*, 2013 © Kathleen Williamson, reproduced by kind permission

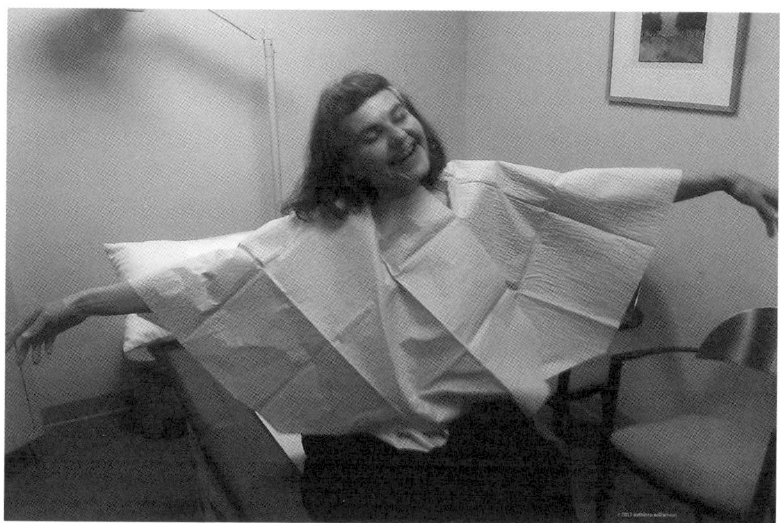

Figure 8 *Pretty in Pink: Waiting for the Oncologist*, 2013 © Kathleen Williamson, reproduced by kind permission

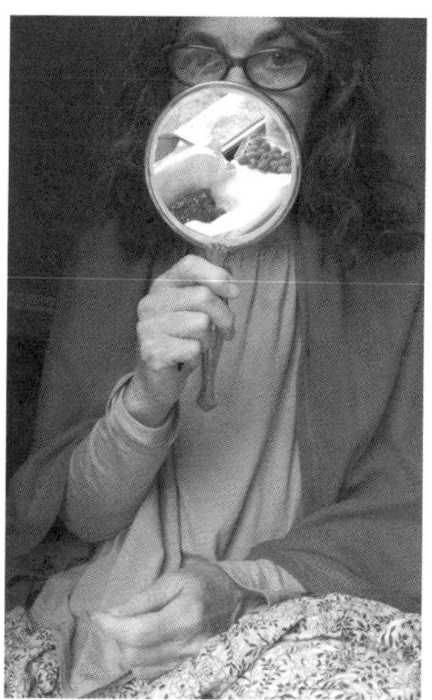

Figure 9 *Self-care and Raspberries*, Dublin, 2014 © Kathleen Williamson, reproduced by kind permission

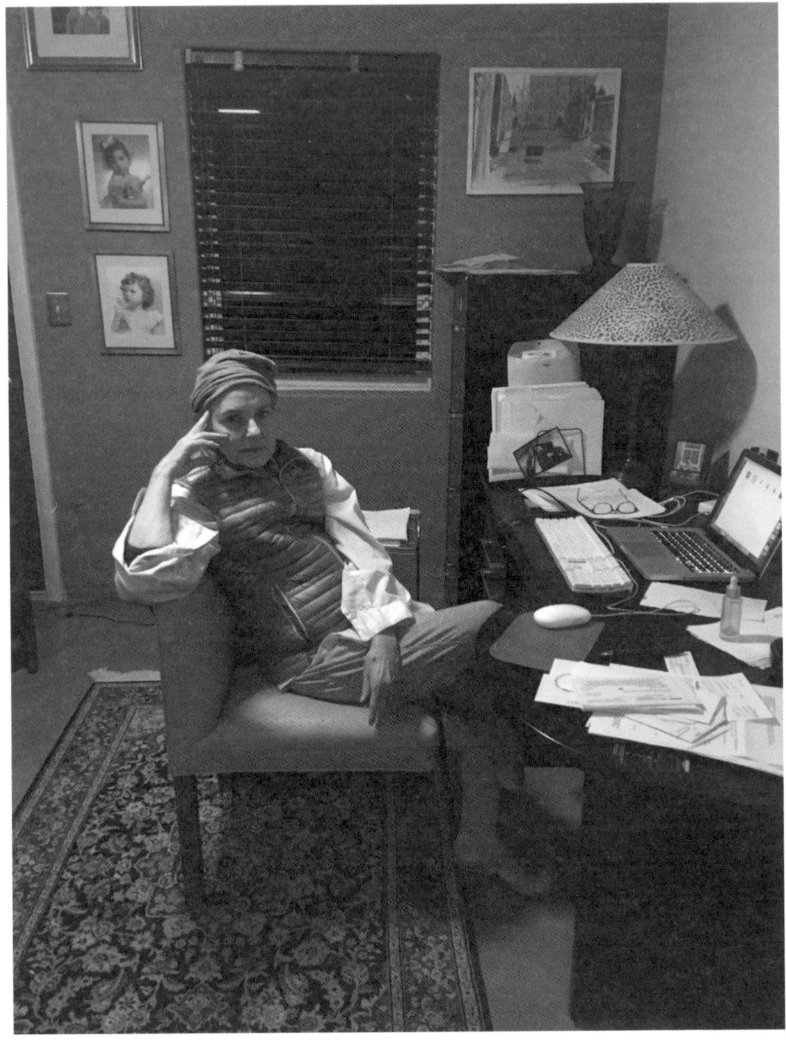

Figure 10 *Joanna at her Desk*, 2019 © Kathleen Williamson, reproduced by kind permission

Part II

The results of pleasure

5

Performing

I loved being the star of grade school plays. I was a shy child, but being in front of an audience came easily for me. So did memorizing lines, and dressing up for stage events was fun. I felt in command; not controlling, but powerful. I wrote some plays from childhood into my teens, probably because my own ideas and feelings and expressions of them were as important to me as those of others, which is why I became a performance artist who creates every aspect of my work rather than an actress performing someone else's words and interests, and directed and costumed by someone else.

Performing and re-performing: debuts and transformations

I've performed many of my pieces only once. I haven't presented any work more than four times. This "procedure" always felt right, and I never thought about it until people asked me why I present my performances so few times. My answer is this: my life changes so I'm thinking about other things. Indeed, I've usually begun newer work before debuting a new performance. Soul-and-mind-inseparable-from-body moves into unpredictable permutations and my work follows them.

In 2007, after I premiered *Goddess of Roses*, I thought: Ha! Each performance is a transformation presented in a kind of public ritual, theater, and once I've transformed myself (and perhaps the audience) then whatever I've transformed is taken care of within me and I'm ready for something new. Today I explain that process this way: living *is* an experience of change and I'm into it.

The *Goddess of Roses* debut and thoughts about transformation arose during the 3:30 p.m. sound check for *I AM Desire*, in September 2010, and I was thinking that I might experience the transformation directly before *or* during *or* right after I performed. I thought, too, that the ritual transformation element in the production of *I AM Desire* had already passed, having happened in the writing of the piece, and that my next piece would be another debut rather than a repetition of *I AM Desire*.

Repetition of performances could also happen in the presentation of an old piece. Because I began performances in the late 1970s and am very productive, I have a large repertoire from which to draw. Yet performing an old piece feels as beside the point as performing a new one many times, and its possibility hadn't crossed my mind till my friend the artist and scholar Jill O'Bryan, who knows my work well and has written about it,[1] asked if I ever considered performing older pieces, such as *Pythia*, from 1994, that she especially likes. (The text for *Pythia* is in my book *Clairvoyance*.) I imagined how I'd feel performing *Pythia*, or *Mouth Piece*, or *The Aesthetics of Orgasm* – for me, *Mouth Piece* and *The Aesthetics of Orgasm* are two of, say, my five most important works – and I said, I don't think so. Especially *Pythia*, which, while being very beautiful and impassioned, expresses a lot of anger and darkness. I feel no need and see no reason to return to those aspects of myself as a former incarnation of the present Joanna, who *has* transformed them. I'm certainly interested in my past, but I like to incorporate it into new work in ways that change the past – the particulars of its meaning and of my feelings about those particulars.

Jill also asked if I'd be interested in having someone else perform any of my work or would give them permission to do so. I'd never thought of that, and was surprised when another friend said he's sure that people will perform my work. That happening would be fine once I got over the possibility of a piece being turned and twisted in ways that, though fascinating and apt, might seem really skewed to me. I wonder if I'd insist that the costuming and staging be the same as mine, both of which I specify in detail in stage directions. Also, I imagine that my work would change drastically if performed by a spirit and a physicality – presence, features, gestures, size, and voice – that are not mine.

Having many audiences witness your work probably appeals to a number of performers. Presenting a piece numerous times increases a performer's artistic history and could garner greater attention for her. However, doing a piece over and over would dry it out for me and sap my engagement in it. Also, a significant part of my history as an artist is in the *publication* of my performance texts.

The transformation with *I AM Desire* did happen, but I wasn't aware that it had until I was sitting with two dear friends right before performing. So it didn't happen as a public ritual. I was tearing up as I briefly spoke with them about having realized sometime between 4:30 and then, around 7 p.m., that my freedom and pleasure in speaking as and for desire and celebrating it had already released me from a self-protection since I was a child about fully expressing the power of my *being* desire. That may sound strange to anyone familiar with my work, but new work for me always expands into ever greater self-recognition and freedom. Writing *I AM Desire*, my living with and from its premises, passions, and happiness, and my readiness to give them to an audience – all accomplished the transformation.

Note

1 See Jill O'Bryan, "Fucking Hot: An Introduction," in Joanna Frueh, *Clairvoyance (For Those in the Desert): Performances Pieces, 1979–2004* (Durham, NC and London: Duke University Press, 2008), pp. 4–47, and Jill O'Bryan, "Ontology and Autobiographical Performance: Joanna Frueh's Aesthetics of Orgasm," *TDR: The Drama Review* 55:2 (Summer 2011), 126–36.

Readings and performances

I make a distinction between giving a reading and doing a performance. I've given readings of excerpts of pieces that I've performed and of pieces that I may not perform. For example, I delivered "The Dark Lord and his Wily Mistress," in this volume, as part of a lecture on my work, and though I've more than toyed with the idea of developing it into a performance, I think that's unlikely, because I'm moving into new territory in my writing, which means that a new performance interests me much more than does presenting older, even if recent, work. (See the section above for why I like performing my newest work.) I'll generally dress up for a reading, but not necessarily in the costume for any performance that I'm excerpting.

Audio and video

Because I speak and sing my own texts, audio lends itself to my work. Audio pieces range from live recordings of performances with many songs in the 1980s, to studio recordings in which I only sing or I speak the text alone. Audio recordings in studio are of *BRUMAS* (1982), which includes only the five songs, *Sexual Advances* (2010), and “The Dark Lord and his Wily Mistress,” in both of which I stick to the prose and the singing in the text itself. That kind of delivery differs from most of my live performances, which have opened up more and more into spontaneous interludes with the audience, and those have increased in occurrence and variety since 2007 with the first performance of *Goddess of Roses*. The live recordings are of *Justifiable Anger* (1982–83), *Solar Shores* (1984), and *Clairvoyance (For Those in the Desert)* (1985–86), all performed with Thomas Kochheiser.[1] I make my audio recordings available now and then on my website.

I use video in two different ways to document my performances: the first as a pretty straight record of me with an audience, and the second as a piece shot in studio. I’ve also wanted to create video pieces, separate from live performance work or its texts, a fresh genre in which my voice, speaking and singing my own words, combines with images of my everyday world, which could as easily be the Sonoran Desert in which I live as the interior of my home. The closest I’ve come to fulfilling that desire is *Sexual Advances, Tucson* (2009), in which I excerpt lines from *Sexual Advances* and appear in seven different locations in my home speaking them. *Sexual Advances, Tucson*, is around seven minutes long, whereas the spoken piece in the audio recording is around ninety minutes, and the two live performances of it were, respectively, over two and a half hours (at Cabinet in Brooklyn) and over two hours (in Tucson). The two performances that I’ve recorded in studio are *Mouth Piece* (1992; debuted in 1989) and *The Performance of Pink* (2004; debuted in 2003). Here’s a complete list of live performance video documentation: *The Aesthetics of Orgasm* (Banff Centre, 2002); *Goddess of Roses* (University of Arizona, Tucson, 2007); and *Sexual Advances* (Cabinet, Brooklyn, 2009).[2]

I used to be very hesitant about the public display of video documentation of my performances. Reluctance came from my belief that video documentation does no justice to the live performance, even if the video is technically sophisticated, meaning that sound, light, and camerawork have been very controlled according to the artist's specifications. Before 2009, when I documented the debut of *Sexual Advances* in a pretty basic way with the intention to use it on my website and in other public venues, I thought that video documentation of my live performances was hopelessly flat, vocally, visually, and emotionally, which is why I produced a couple of pieces in studio. I do not equate them with the live performance. They are pieces unto themselves.

My revised opinion about showing video documentation means that where once I thought that nothing truly conveys a live performance, now I think that all forms of documentation hold some reality of a live performance. Also, I no longer believe that someone must witness a live performance of mine, the original source, in order to adequately feel, study, or understand my work. With the publication of the text for *Goddess of Roses* in *TDR: The Drama Review* in 2011, I decided that making available two excerpts and the entire video of the premiere performance on my website would be helpful to interested readers. That said, neither the color – reddish – of the *Goddess of Roses* video nor the perspective – foreshortened – are as aesthetically pleasing to me as could be.

Notes

1 The texts of *BRUMAS*, *Justifiable Anger*, *Solar Shores*, and *Clairvoyance (For Those in the Desert)* all appear in Joanna Frueh, *Clairvoyance (For Those in the Desert): Performances Pieces, 1979–2004* (Durham, NC and London: Duke University Press, 2008).

2 The texts of *Mouth Piece*, *The Performance of Pink*, and *The Aesthetics of Orgasm* appear in Frueh, *Clairvoyance*.

Photography

My photos are primarily self-portraits, often nudes or in performance costumes. The work partakes of high art, erotica, and family photos. My posing or modeling for the photos is a kind of performing, a visual equivalent of my theory of aesthetic/erotic self-creation, which I present in my book *Monster/Beauty: Building the Body of Love*. There I develop the idea that human beings have the ability to lovingly build their own beauty.

I am an art historian who is fascinated by the classical Greek female nude and whose PhD studies concentrated on glamour girls in nineteenth-century art and literature, especially those of Dante Gabriel Rossetti, a painter and poet who was a rock star of his time. Some of my photos appropriate ancient Aphrodites and some honor and personalize pictures by Rossetti. My self-imaging performances enter into my reputation for being a trailblazer, as the photo work began in my forties and presents a woman who dreams herself into the being of glamour and sensuality. Most of the photos have been shot in collaboration with other artists, three in particular: Russell Dudley (my second husband), Jill O'Bryan, and Frances Murray.[1]

Unto myself, I've never been one to take fine art photos or snapshots. However, I love to work with a collaborator, both of us directing, chatting, and contributing to my styling, though the latter is mainly done by myself. If I want to document my life or remember the past, for the pleasure or retrospective revelation of it, I turn to journals, which I've written mostly since the beginning of midlife and when I travel. On my first trip to Europe, when I was around 20, I took a camera, probably bought for the journey. Early on, the camera broke, before I'd shot even one roll of film. I felt bad at first, but that had more to do with how I *should* be feeling bad, I *should* want those pictures, and I *should* buy another camera right away than it had to do with the loss of either "memories" or the camera itself – submitting or catering to the tribal tourist, who *must* take photos. Quickly, the fairly shallow mourning disappeared and the tribal tourist gave way to the solitary writer. I'd bought a journal, and its images and insights as I wrote and when I read them later satisfied me just fine. Also, I have a very good visual memory, so I easily recall people. (I also easily remember people's voices.)

I love the gorgeous solitude of writing, even in a botanical garden in Belfast or Melbourne, a restaurant in London, a gazebo in the jungle of an Indian *ashram*, or poolside drinking a lot of coffee at the Arizona Inn in Tucson (where I stayed several times while living in Reno before moving to Tucson). In each of those environments people walked by, close or at a distance, I heard them speaking, sometimes to me, and I observed and listened, and spoke when communication felt right. Observing and listening, which can happen for hours at a time, give me great pleasure.

If I were a collector, I might want all those photos that I've never taken. As it is, I am full with people I've met and seen and places I've visited. I love it when they surprise me by turning up in a new piece that I'm writing.

I do have photos from a few significant events in my life, such as the parties celebrating my two marriages. My second husband and I married in New York, and the party was at the small penthouse apartment of one of my friends. Summer night, Betsey Johnson dress, Russ in jeans and a new blue shirt (bought right after our ceremony at City Hall), Russ's Mom and godmother, an intimate group of friends, and great food, including lemon cake, Russ's favorite, for our wedding dessert. Two friends took photos, and one set is wonderful (the color is off in the other). Everyone looks like themselves! Russ and I look utterly happy, which we were! A sexy couple, indeed. Perhaps I'll publish one of those photos sometime. Also, in the past couple of years I've become more respectful of the privacy of people in my life, so using photos of them or their names in my writing feels uncomfortable.

One of the reasons that I often don't like or keep photos of myself or of myself and others, whether taken by me or them, is that the people in the pictures don't look like me or my companions. In April 2010 a friend and I took photos of ourselves and each other as we sat in LaGuardia Airport before I boarded a plane after visiting him. We don't look like ourselves, although in one of my photos his delicious big smile certainly feels like him, and they do resonate with our being happy and tired. Still, I wonder why I kept the images on my phone for as long as I did. Guess I *did* like the memories! However, the pictures that I liked best were in my mind, as they still are, along with his voice and touch, and they're more available – instantly – than on any device. He and I didn't see one another again – an easy and comfortable decision for each of us – and the sensory array in my soul-and-mind-inseparable-from-body of him and me, rather than the photos of us, was the stimulus that kept me aware of the transformative openness that our visit engendered.

I love the photos that are my art, the ones that appear in my books, and now and then on my blog and in exhibitions. Creating the glamour of reality thrills me. The definition of glamour would seem to preclude its having anything to do with reality, yet in my understanding, my life, and my aesthetic/erotic self-creation, glamour is energy rather than artifice. The entire process of producing photographic works, from an idea or image that appears in my mind to thinking about props, costumes, and historical antecedents, to collaborating with another artist whose eye behind the camera is exciting and trustworthy, to choosing the pictures – out of many in any one pose, attitude, or series – helps me to be the Joanna who excites and trusts herself. I know that glamour is real, because people tell me, "You look just like your photographs."

Note

1 See *Maiden Elder* in this volume for more about my work in photography.

The activity and experience of performing, from seductiveness to comedy and specialness to serenity

"The *Ars Erotica* of Joanna Frueh" is the title of a section about my work in the Summer 2011 issue of *TDR: The Drama Review*. The section is comprised of three essays, the text of *Goddess of Roses*, and numerous photos. A person's creation of her own *ars erotica* indicates, at least a little, that she and her work may be seductive, and indeed the essay in *TDR* by Tanya Augsburg is titled "The Concupiscent Performer, Joanna Frueh's 'Art of Seduction.'"

In 2004, after debuting *Ambrosia*,[1] a compliment from an audience member struck me so profoundly that it initiated an expanded self-terminology. I've called myself a performance artist for many years, and because of her comments I've added "actress," knowing that *actor* is the currently preferred term by and for women who act; although the November 2009 issue of American *Vogue* called several prominent women who act actresses.

The audience member said, "You're different, talking with you, than you are onstage." I laughed and agreed, and asked her to articulate the difference. "Onstage you're so seductive and ethereal." I surprised myself by responding, "If I were that way all the time, *nobody* would talk to me! As it *is*, almost no one talks to me after a performance." Then she said, "It's the actress."

We posited that the seductive and ethereal qualities might be heightened states of me in everyday life, and I recognized, in her comments and through our conversation, not only the radiant allure of being seductive and ethereal, but also that they are characteristics of the actress.

If I am perceived as seductive and ethereal onstage, those qualities serve as ways to embrace the audience. Feminine wiles are beside the point, because as an actress I am interested in the erotic relation between me and the audience. I define eros as connection, in the richest, most joyous, and embracing ways. Erotic connection happens beyond the strictures of gendered language and of gender itself.

My friend Jill O'Bryan, who knows my work very well, having written the introduction to *Clairvoyance* and one of the essays in *TDR*, tells me in correspondence from October 23, 2009 that

> The actress, while very present, is also inaccessible – behind that invisible wall that happens in the theater. There is a vast history of attempts to break down this wall, but the truth is that no matter what you do, it's a one-sided conversation: the actress speaks and we, the audience, listen. It is therefore completely overwhelming when after a performance we come into contact with the actress. How do you return the other side of the conversation that has been presented with such passion? What do you say to someone who has just affected your being in a profound way? Sometimes speechlessness has its own presence.

I agree with what she says about speechlessness and I think that we might also call such a response to an actress silence. Silence in the stimulation, intimacy, or overwhelm of an experientially (for an audience member) seductive passion. I understand that silence can proceed from reticence or fear, but the silence of speechlessness that she and I were in the process of defining is fearless and activating. An inspired silence. Also, I do comprehend Jill's calling the actress inaccessible. No matter what. I do my best to converse post-performance, though I do like time for myself before any socializing.

Sometimes academic institutions have scheduled Q&A directly after a performance, right after I take my bows and give my thanks to the audience. Mostly I've enjoyed those occasions, but they seem beside the point, certainly for me, and often for the audience, who can seem to be groping for questions or comments, because more than occasionally they feel superficial or extraneous to me.

Jill helped clarify for me that the conversation I want to promote may be happening in an inspired silence, between an audience member and me the performer or person while performing or with the performance itself, though I do imagine vocally conversing with audience members about essentials – to me! – regarding a piece after I perform. Essentials can include aspects that I've thought about or ones that come as total surprises. I love those surprises! My desire in such conversations is for intelligent intimacy.

Comedy entered my performances in 2007 with the debut of *Goddess of Roses*. Not that I'd never been funny, in the writing itself or in the spontaneous breaks from the texts while performing, but an unpremeditated freedom took hold of me – can freedom ever be premeditated? – that night, and during those breaks many things that I said and did caused the audience to laugh. My unconscious integrations of comedy surprised me and now it just happens during a performance. More play. More engagement with the audience, in which I can tease them about not drinking more of the chocolate malts I'm offering or ask them for a Kleenex or for their help in further personalizing or conceptualizing an idea or a story in the text.

In 2002 or so I had the notion that I wanted to be funnier in my performances. I was almost interested in writing and performing shtick, but let that thought float away as I read a semi-scholarly book about female comics and let their bravery, skill, and talent filter into me. What a delightful surprise to witness that emerge in *Goddess of Roses*.

I think that comedy balances elements of the seductive and ethereal actress who appears to leave people speechless, and helps to bring her down to earth.

Before the debut of *Ambrosia*, which I mention above, I noticed a new feeling pre-performance. *Ambrosia* was part of a conference honoring the philosopher Alphonso Lingis, with whom I was friendly and who would be in the audience. The venue was a beautiful, small theater. I knew no one at the conference except Al, who had never seen me perform before but who had avidly read my work. *Ambrosia* was in large part written with Al in mind. I was addressing the subject of innocence, which Al beautifully discusses in his book *Dangerous Emotions*, and I'd witnessed Al being astoundingly innocent, most markedly when watching favorite sea animals at the National Aquarium in Baltimore. Before performing I'd always felt very excited with a little anxiety mixed in, and although I'd wonder, sometimes out loud to a friend or to a relative stranger assisting me in the often makeshift dressing room of a gallery or museum, "Why am I doing this?", which expressed the nerves, I always knew that once I began to perform, they'd disappear entirely.

The facts of performing "for" Al (for the first time) at a conference honoring him and my knowing no one but him would seem perfect for my feeling an intensification of my pre-performance excitement/nerves. But downstairs in the dressing room and the green room, which I had entirely to myself – and I'd changed into my costume and put on my makeup (minimal even onstage) unattended by anyone – I noticed my tranquility, with no thought of anything like "Why am I doing this?" I was distinctly aware of feeling different from any time that I'd previously performed, and I noticed my tranquility, too, very early in the performance, maybe even before beginning to speak. It especially impressed me because I also noticed that I felt exceptionally vulnerable, not only performing with Al seated where I could see him, but also because I was barefoot (the first time I'd been barefoot all through a performance), he was sitting next to a good friend of his, Alexandre, the son of former Canadian Prime Minister Pierre Trudeau, and the end of the piece involved me walking into the audience and crowning Al with the wreath of white roses that I was wearing throughout the performance.

Pre-performance serenity pretty much stayed with me, and it's become so normal that I don't notice it anymore, which is why Jill's remarking, "You're so calm," as we were conversing in a room to ourselves before I premiered *Sexual Advances*, surprised me, in a way that led me to a new understanding of that calm. I said to her, "Yes, I'm that way now. Performing is like any other part of the day. They all flow into each other." Performing excites me, but it doesn't feel special, meaning that it doesn't feel set apart from all other activities.

That particular lack of specialness applies to my recent costume choices. I used to purchase new clothing for a new performance, but my choice for *Goddess of Roses* was the same dress that I wore for *Dressing Aphrodite* (1997). I'd been stewing around in my decision, buying a dress that ultimately didn't work and then putting together various outfits from my closet, ones that I'd previously performed in and ones that I now was finding stage-worthy (sort of), but they all registered as either overdone or ordinary, and I felt uncomfortable in them. Repeating a costume had never crossed my mind before (if I was dressing up for a party, as it were, I wanted a new dress!), but now, the long bias-cut gown with the three-quarter length sleeves,

Vionnet-like in its elegant and sensuous liking of the female form, was the only item that felt right to my imagination and on my body. Why look for something else *like* it? (I did buy new shoes.) Same with the dress that I found for *Sexual Advances*, suitable for a 1950s glamour girl. I wore it, too, for performing *Maiden Elder* and *I AM Desire*. The habits of this woman in her sixties.

Habits are not special.

Today, performing does not feel separate from occurrences that seem to be unrelated to it or that would seem to upset the flow of a performance, which means that what might once have been disturbances no longer are. For example, when I performed *Goddess of Roses* in Melbourne in 2008, a band (jazz, if I recall) in the hall outside the auditorium in which I was performing played a few short sets during my piece and anyone inside the auditorium could hear their music. My event and the one in which the band participated had been scheduled at overlapping times. My props included three chocolate malts, one of which I was drinking. The others I offered to takers, and no one partook. Near the close of the performance I lie down in *savasana* with my head toward the audience for a minute or so before standing up to face and bow to them. While I was lying down I heard an object fall to the floor with a sound more like a crash than a thud. After the performance someone told me that the object that had fallen was part of the videographer's equipment.

All in a night's work! None of it bothered me, and I have to say that the audience was wonderful. I saw and felt their attention to the language and ideas, and they laughed readily at the comedy that I spontaneously let loose, including teasing them about their being a bad audience for not partaking of the malts. As with students coming in late during a class that I used to teach, the intrusions during that performance probably disturbed onlookers more than they did me. The flow of a performance, like a lecture, takes over. It's like a meditation, making what would seem to be distractions or obstacles something very different, opportunities for the performer's pleasure and equanimity.

"You take everything as an opportunity," a friend of mine said out of the blue. In retrospect I'm not sure if he was referring to the Melbourne performance, which he attended, and its apparent obstacles or to my handling of life in general. Either way, I like his observation.

Note

1 The text of *Ambrosia* appears in Joanna Frueh, *Clairvoyance (For Those in the Desert): Performances Pieces, 1979–2004* (Durham, NC and London: Duke University Press), 2008.

6

Performance texts, 2005–10

A Flowering of Vision, 2005

Frueh's look is girly and dignified, bold and delicate, as she approaches a podium from the audience. The romantic droop of the extra-long, soft cotton laces of her black leather boots, just below the calf, compliments the overall dash of an unexpected combination: a lavender, mid-calf dress sprinkled with pink and dark purple rosettes and topped by a short, very trimly fitting, navy blue tuxedo jacket with an outsized satin collar, whose neckline reveals the scooped bodice of the dress. Frueh's hair, down, and lipstick, red, perform her signature style.

Vision is not only what we see, but also what we know.

The world is blooming around me. And I am of the world. So here I am, a rose among roses, speaking to you, all of us a taste of pink, a touch of honey, a fragrant vision, all like roses in their multiplicity of scents and shapes and colors.

Beginning with basics, we can use dictionary definitions and derivations to guide our learning about vision. Reading through them tells me that the sense of sight is related to the soundness of wisdom.

We say, "I see," and we often mean by that, "I know." Seeing and knowing share linguistic roots. Vision derives from the Latin *visio*, which comes from *visus*, the past participle of *videre*, to see. *Videre* originates in the hypothetical Indo-European base, *w(e)di-*, to see, know, from which *wise* itself derives.

These basics bloom when our reason sees their roots and colors. Human beings can see to the heart of a person, an event, or a dilemma.

That full-flowered vision – seeing truly – is wisdom, and it happens in an instant. The profound simplicity of wisdom – seeing in an instant – is available to everyone all the time; though most people rarely use that ability.

"Give room to the roses." Those words came into my mind as I was digging up the irises in my front yard three mornings in a row. In the eight or so years since I'd planted the irises, I'd never divided them, which I've read that a gardener is supposed to do each year. So the irises were tightly massed, compacted really, gorgeous when they were blossoming last April into June – in their chocolate red and linen white and blush-tinged lavender – but crowding into the six rose bushes, which created anxiety in me. "Give room to the roses." How peaceful I was, sweating in the 100 degree heat, seeing space appear around the roses and moving through it.

Some people become wise through study and research in libraries, others become wise through practices such as meditation, and some inhale the mountain air or street life and learn the compassion that wisdom liberates. With experience – gleaned through books and thinking, through mystic awareness, through immersion in the scale and minutiae of nature, or through observation of human beings in any actions from the most lurid to the sweetest – we open to our own wisdom. Because experience can expand us, can help us develop spacious minds, hearts, and spirits. At the same time, wisdom is innate, so experience serves to lead us back to our inherent lucidity. On one hand, wisdom requires experience; and on the other hand, wisdom demands nothing. For when we are wise, compassionate experience has so molded us that we let go of preconception, we get out of our own way, so that we are free and present. Like vision itself.

The first definition of vision in *Webster's New World College Dictionary*, 4th edition, is "the act or power of seeing with the eye." An act is volitional: you decide. You decide to see an injured child; or two bees buzzing close together, one plump, the other long and thin; or a cut, almost healed, on your ankle; or your brother's blue, blue heavenly eyes. Power is a faculty, a given.

Vision is therefore a gift; and the wise are gifted in vision that is more than only a faculty. They see what is in front of them and they see its significance – the avenues and locales in which an object, individual, situation, or event exists in beauty, because vision has transformed the ordinary, the ugly, or the frightening. Consequently, wise people can make the invisible visible.

Here are a few examples, all of which have happened. Martin Luther King, Jr. saw dogs attack nonviolent black demonstrators. Through vision, he saw peace between black and white Americans; and social sanity, such as the United States Supreme Court ruling, on November 13, 1956, against Alabama's local and state segregation laws, corrected racial injustice. A woman sees spider veins on her face and legs. Through vision, she sees her radiance and communicates it, the way a goddess does; and she is known for her luminous beauty. A psychotherapist sees his clients' sadness as they recount their misery. Through vision, he sees them joyful, and their love for living grows.

The effects of vision are far-reaching. No matter if the sight is considered spectacularly public – the nonviolent demonstration – or ridiculously trivial – the woman's spider veins, because vision does not measure the visible. Perception does that. Vision does not measure how valuable the result of transformation is. King, the woman, and the psychotherapist let their vision see beyond the material world, which is the world of form. They saw beneath externals. Beneath the grotesque materiality of dogs at human flesh; beneath the tiny purple lines that a body-damning beauty culture calls flaws; beneath the walls of resistance that manifest in words expressing virtually unrelenting pain.

Human beings cannot predict the effects of vision, which are beyond measure. *Ahimsa*, nonviolence, is one of the *yamas*, which are ancient yogic disciplines that guide people's ways of being in society and in this world that we think we know, but that is larger than we can imagine. Gandhi's practice of nonviolence changed India, and King's practice of nonviolence, which he learned from studying the techniques and philosophy of Gandhi, changed the United States.

Also, *ahimsa* remains an element of contemporary yoga practice.

Our culture appreciates effects on millions of people, or, at least, such numbers impress a culture that relies on them as proof of effectiveness. However, one woman's luminosity offers to everyone who experiences it their own radiance, and people who are in love with life provide their peace and vibrancy in every space through which they move.

Vision always moves from one to many.

Here I am, hand in hand with you, at ease to see what we can know.

We are unwise to underestimate the potency of vision. An appalling vision sickens the heart, casts a pall into the unconscious. A sickening vision is forceful: it is a strength working against sanity, a coercion that incites the mind to hatred, fear, guilt, shame, and hostility. A heartsick vision lingers in the unconscious, pressing for release by creating anxiety. A mass of pressing visions lodged within the organs of a human being – brain, heart, colon – and the organs of a society – government or entertainment – becomes impacted. Congested organs are a cause of suffering bodies.

The eye is at home in sensuousness. As the dictionary says, vision is the "sense of sight." Yet if vision congests itself in the world of sense, whose foundation is the world of form, vision stagnates. The ability to see the material world is a sense shared by human beings, it is a sense they hold in common, a common sense. Fluid vision sees freedom in the place of punitive belligerence, grace rather than blemishes, and sparkling eyes where a dim outlook had amassed a dank treasure of woe. Fluid vision is the use and outcome of the common sense of sight. Wisdom is that common sense, ready right now for all, we the common people.

Irises were my mother's favorite flowers. I'd planted mine several years before she died, which was in 2000, so I wasn't digging up a memorial garden. Yet I paused: how interesting! A grief had finally gone. And I realized too, in the way that we stun ourselves with the obviousness of the facts of our own lives, that within the previous week I'd cleared congestions in my body: a liver cleansing with a pre- and post-colonic, both strongly recommended by the author of the liver-cleansing book whose instructions I had followed. Cleaning my garden and my body so that both could bloom, cleaning my garden and my body as metaphors for cleaning my mind of don'ts and shoulds and oughta bes, for cleaning my congested vision.

Much of what I've been saying about vision is connected to Webster's second and fourth definitions of the word. Here's the first part of 2a: "something seen by other than normal sight." Here's all of 4b: "force or power of imagination." We could say that seeing beyond what is in front of us is an other than normal phenomenon. However, what is common can be understood as normal; so wisdom is normal vision. Just as the obstruction of organs in the human body is not their inherent condition – people are not born that way – neither is impacted, stagnant, congested, obstructed, constipated vision normal.

Don'ts and shoulds and oughta bes constipate vision. So that we cannot see that we are rooted, splendid, simply ready for kisses wise as petals colored flame and sun, flesh, innocence, and heart throb. Since antiquity, the rose has symbolized profane and sacred love. One flower: all there is to know.

Force of imagination may be arousing: apocalyptic images abound in the world of extreme effectiveness. The forceful pressures of apocalyptic images, which pervade many a post-9/11 imagination, move from the *New York Times* or Quentin Tarantino's movies, from insurgent fundamentalist websites or Mel Gibson's *The Passion of the Christ* into the body of humanity and harden it.

Impacted vision is hardened vision, and it confounds our common sense.

Apply the power of imagination, and the abnormal state of impacted vision, often characterized by gloom and inflammatory ideology, is relieved. *Here I am, swooning in the flower bed, kissing a longitude of beauties*. Vision as laxative. Vision as lax – a botanical term meaning loose or open and describing a flower cluster. Full-flowered vision. Flowers do not open through force.

Effortlessly, they reveal their beauty.

Here I am, a corolla readying to be seen.

Intestinal metaphors may seem inappropriate for talking about vision, which people tend to locate in the head – the eyes (which house the faculty of sight), the mind (which exists within the brain). In that model of sight and body, vision is literally and figuratively a high function of the human being; the bowels are a low function of the human animal. When we pay attention to phrases that ring true, such as "I know it in my heart" and "I know it in my gut," we are hearing human beings' common knowledge of seeing with the body. Your gut is your bowels. Gut and bowels are synonymous, and when we are blind to their vision, they cramp, ache, bloat, congest. Webster's gives an archaic meaning of bowels: "the inside of the body, regarded as the source of pity, tenderness, etc.; hence, tender emotions." Kindness, love, compassion – the tender parts of human beings, the ones that grow through our common sense. When we pay attention to the bowels of something, we see it intimately, we see its tender parts. When we use our common sense, we know the world by heart and we have intestinal fortitude. Intestinal fortitude and guts are synonyms. Intestinal fortitude is the strength of being tender, being soft – kindness, cordiality, compassion, love, and generosity.

If vision resides in the gut, among other corporeal sites, then there is nothing supernatural about it – even though Webster's gives the following definition, which suggests that other than normal vision is unreachable, fanciful, transitory, or useless: "something perceived in a dream, trance, etc. or supernaturally revealed, as to a prophet." Most people do not regard themselves as prophets because in the everyday world of work and family life, of grocery shopping, gas stations, email, and striving and surviving in the world of form, prophecy seems highfalutin, arrogant, megalomaniacal, and impractical. However, the dreamer, the person entranced by beauty, and the prophet are all the common people acting on their common sense. James Melvin Washington, editor of *A Testament of Hope: The Essential Writings and Speeches* of Martin Luther King, Jr, titles his introduction to the book, "Martin Luther King, Jr, Martyred Prophet for a Global Beloved Community of Justice, Faith, and Hope." The last words of the citation for the Presidential Medal of Freedom given posthumously to King, on July 4, 1977, reads, "his dreams sustain us yet." King's keynote address for the March on Washington, DC for civil rights, delivered in front of the Lincoln Memorial on August 28, 1963, contains the most famous lines he spoke, repeated near the end of the speech as the first words of five sequential paragraphs: "I have a dream." He ends that series with a powerful vision of loveliness: "I have a dream that one day every valley shall be exalted, every hill and mountain shall be made low, the rough places shall be made plain, and the crooked places shall be made straight and the glory of the Lord will be revealed and all flesh shall see it together." Regardless of how you feel about the Christian rhetoric, King's vision is one of all and every seen through our common sense.

Here we are, all flowering visions. Move with me through the roses. Here we are, all infinite occasions for being lax.

It takes guts to see a vision of loveliness. Like King. Like artists when they practice the sensuous use of common sense.

It takes guts to *be* a vision of loveliness, to see oneself as a luminous human being, to be entranced by one's own beauty, so generously delighted that the rapture is infectious. For vision always moves.

Visionaries see visions of loveliness, which move by means of inspiration. Vision as I've been talking about it is a profound kind of visual literacy.

Usually, we think of visual literacy as an understanding of the plethora of images that surround us, many of which we barely notice – either their appearance or effect – because they are so familiar. Images on our computers and TVs, in entertainment, advertising, the news media, and the visual arts. Visual literacy is useful, because it helps us to decipher and probe our culture, so that we are not just unconsciously reacting to it or being numbed or awed by it. Visual literacy is a sign of a human being's aliveness. The most visually literate people peer into and reveal the bowels of culture. Often, those people are artists, art historians, and art critics, people who are educated to see. Artists in particular are asked and expected to dream and envision by a contemporary society that may not appreciate or financially reward the results but that nevertheless believes in the mythic grandeur of the great artist as visionary.

Let us all be grand. By visiting the far and fruitful wildly flowering corners of our common sense. By exploring its vistas. Like vision, visit derives from *visus*, and vista derives from *videre*.

Softly, powerfully, effortlessly, let us all be visionaries. They are useful, for they change the world. *Give room to the roses.*

I performed *A Flowering of Vision* at the Out of Bounds conference, Monash University, Melbourne, Australia, in 2008. In 2005 I presented it in a contemporary art course that I was teaching at the University of Nevada, Reno.

Maiden Elder, 2006

Frueh pairs a cobalt blue velvet jacket with a startlingly pink chiffon dress. They and her short boots of lustrously smooth black leather share a dynamically sculptural quality. The jacket's squarish shoulders and fitted waist emphasize her broad shoulders and little waistline. Geometry and femininity combine: clean lines, the most elegant darts, a peplum, a noticeable, but not in the least outlandish, rose – blue velvet – where the waist snaps into place. Frueh keeps on her jacket through the performance, which brings greater attention to her lower buttocks and thighs, to which the fabric conforms. Overall, an haute female look, sexy and self-respecting.

"How do you reconcile glamour and feminism?" A writer for style.com, the online spin-off of *Vogue*, asked me that as I was circulating through the crowd after my performance *Goddess of Roses* at Shelly Steffee, the eponymous fashion shop in the "uber-trendy boutique and restaurant-laden Meatpacking District."[1] (The boutique closed in June 2010.) The writer prefaced her question with "You're glamorous." She was 24, I was 60. The date was April 26, 2008. *Maiden Elder* belongs within my harmonization of feminism and glamour.

In Issai Chozanshi's *The Demon's Sermon on the Martial Arts*, a philosophical "guidebook" for samurai written in the eighteenth century, the demon in the title advises a swordsman, "When you follow your own true character and are not a slave to your passions and desires, your spirit will not be troubled."[2] Speaking from my own true character, feminism works for the freedom of all human beings, glamour grows from a person's knowing herself and following that knowledge, and maiden and elder have little to do with a woman's age and everything to do with her exceeding their culturally determined boundaries, such as limitations on her self-representation and self-creation, which I equate with self-discovery. Self-representation is an external manifestation of one's own true character. My definitions of glamour and feminism are intended to stir the imagination. "Maiden elder" is a term of endearment.

Essence and true character are equivalents, and according to the demon, "Essence and function are of one origin, are not distinct, and have no interval in between them at all."[3] If the function of feminism is freedom, then the feminist manifests freedom.

Charisma powers glamour, so maiden elder, a feminist glamour girl, inspires others to be true to themselves. Although maiden elder is an idea, I do not intend for it to denote any fixity of appearance or behavior. As the demon says, "Relying on thoughts or concepts, you will become taut,"[4] and he advises his listeners to "use the clarity of intuition."[5] Maiden elder can serve as a model of living peacefully and vivaciously in soul-and-mind-inseparable-from-body, for while she is an idea, she more importantly supports the process of living one's own life, which can only be done intuitively. Merely *thinking* for oneself readily brings about the tautness of disconnected body, soul, and mind, each existing in a rigid conformity to some concept or practice, whether it be the "right" way of a body, soul, or mind system, such as the Atkins diet or Pilates, a prophetic or a wisdom religion, or performative theories of gender or a Foucauldian philosophy of sexuality. Useful as they are for expanding our knowledge and discovering aspects of ourselves and the world that we may not know, nonintuitively "right" ways muddy true character. The potential discoverer exists, then, as a follower by resisting the flow of process, which implicitly means change.

I have heard that "change is difficult" so many times that my heart aches from its implications of enslavement to tautness. I say, change is soft, change softens tautness, change is freedom, and change is glamorous. In his introduction to *The Demon's Sermon*, its translator William Scott Wilson writes that "the kanji for 'change' and 'easy' are one and the same."[6] Easy, to change more and more into one's true character. Easy, moving from soft – vulnerable, receptive, inward – to strong – mountain solid, storm-wind firm, and steady as a confident public speaker. Easy, to move from maiden to elder and back again an unthinkable number of times with such subtlety that no distinction exists between the two. Easy, to move from discovery to discovery.

Easy, the spontaneity and adaptability, the focus and fluidity which are a jaguar's primal virtue. Generally, human beings need tools for honing and releasing those same qualities, for tapping intuitively into their own primal virtue. Virtue is simply excellence, and the demon helps the samurai to learn how to be excellent.

The Demon's Sermon makes clear that excellence is anything but a fixed position, a particular skill that produces the same good outcome in every (seemingly similar) situation, or a sole behavior that always outsmarts circumstance. *Maiden elder* is a name, like *samurai*, and, like *samurai*, it is larger than a noun. A maiden elder, like a samurai, is a process, a continual event, and an unfolding.

Lusty, lustful, and lustrous, I am consciousness immanent in the body. In my lusts and lusters, I choose to be maiden elder. The physicist Amit Goswami argues that consciousness is choice, and he asserts: "In every moment, we literally face myriad alternative possibilities. From these we choose, and as we choose, we recognize the course of our becoming."[7] That may sound obvious, simplistic, or impossible, but perhaps you have experimented with choosing one thought or action over another and then experienced the creation and the definition of self that arises from such choosing. Below is a story about my own recognition of choice.

In my early fifties I was walking with a friend past a hedge and she exclaimed something like this: "That poor little branch, struggling to survive!" I distinctly remember her use of "struggling." Before she had spoken, I'd noticed red leaves extending upward through the mass of green. My thoughts were: What a beautiful red! What a beautiful contrast with the green, and everything looks so healthy. So my friend's comment surprised me. I didn't say anything to her about it, but the difference between our responses struck me, because it indicated a difference in consciousness, a difference in choice.

We can recognize what we choose, or we can choose unconsciously. The latter seems paradoxical, but unconscious choosing proceeds as much from who we are and how we observe the world as does conscious choosing. The unconscious is part of consciousness, of choice. For example, we *consciously* choose carrot cake rather than pecan pie from the menu in a restaurant because we *prefer* the cake; we *unconsciously* tie our left shoe before our right because that is our *habit*. Preferences and habits can be healthful or hindering to our well-being.

My literally not seeing the same thing as my friend began my recognition of the pained, ashamed, knee-jerk, and negative perceptions that numerous people project onto occurrences and behaviors that they witness, experience, or hear about. My consciousness – my way of choosing and what I chose – was opening and softening in such a way that struggle felt awkward to me, uncomfortable, part of the supposed way things are that now appeared as perception, projection, and concept. Not much earlier in our friendship I likely would have seen the way that my friend did, from the suffering of struggle.

I was beginning to unconsciously choose a world of luster. In our lusts and lusters, we are in true character.

True character lies not in appearance as such but in the distinctive qualities and essential traits that a person's physical appearance make visible. True character lies deeper than personality, which is an "I" in action, the mere surface of one's being. True character lives in the interconnectedness of beings. As I define it, eros is connection, which makes true character as erotic as can be.

> He who practices Virtue is one with Virtue;
> And he who courts after Loss is one with Loss.[8]

So declares the *Tao Teh Ching*, a classic Chinese philosophical text from the sixth century BCE, attributed to Lao Tzu but likely written by various people, whose eighty-one verses of wisdom, often at once paradoxical and utterly straightforward, penetrate me to the quick.

Women learn to court loss as they grow away from chronological maidenhood. Loss is the subtext of many contemporary American women's will to beauty and of the Hollywood and high fashion ideals of female beauty itself.

In *Six Names of Beauty*, the philosophy professor Crispin Sartwell's examination of various cultures' words for beauty and his ideas about it, he defines the English word beauty as "the object of longing," and he associates beauty with loss.[9] When I taught his book, I did not hide my displeasure with that association. I court a different word for beauty: the Hebrew *yapha*, which Sartwell defines as "glow, bloom," and the Navajo *hozho*, which he defines as "health, harmony."[10] The Tao indicates that the cultivation of loss is not a virtue. We can understand *yapha* and *hozho* as processes, not only qualities. However, *yapha* and *hozho* intuitively strike me as excellent paths to cultivate. Indeed, their cultivation strikes me as a technique for the unfolding of primal virtue.

In the beauties of *hozho* and *yapha*, we women embody and extend the glamour of Aphrodite, and in that glamour, which is itself a process, we bridge the sacred and the profane, like the samurai, because in one's true character a person exists in a liminal world. When she uses techniques such as the cultivation of *yapha* and *hozho*, that move her into her primal virtue, she is an artist. As Wilson writes, "The martial artist ... must inhabit ... [a] liminal world between the sacred and profane to truly grasp his art."[11] To be caught up primarily or solely in the material world is to believe that the "techniques" available and useful in the chronological maiden years – into one's twenties – are forever viable. The demon would call that stupid. He says, "Youthful vigor is only temporary and is not rooted."[12] Other kinds of vigor must become part of one's art, such as the vigor of ch'i. Ch'i can be translated as vital energy, and it permeates all living things, stones and mountains as well as human beings and animals. Ch'i is an energy at once sacred and profane, so the samurai and the maiden elder need to tend to it. Danger: a person's ch'i can congeal. For example, it can be weak, too strong, heavy, muddy, confused, or frozen. It can be light and active, dense and sluggish. One's ch'i can produce fearfulness, slowness, anxiety, dryness, or just-right action. In the demon's guidance, ch'i must be flowing and clear, and that can be true for a person of any age. Flowing ch'i makes everything easy.

Because *aging* is often a negative word when applied to people, elder is a tarnished term. In a pamphlet that I noticed a few years ago, titled *A Kinder, Gentler Approach to Menopause*, published by Reed's Compounding Pharmacy in Tucson, Arizona, the functions of various hormones feature prominently. In the information on pregnenolone, we read that "the bodies [sic] own production is reduced with aging, stress, depression, hypothyroidism and toxin exposure."[13] The pharmacists who write the introduction are clear about menopause being natural and about the importance of using natural hormone replacement therapy (if one chooses hormone replacement therapy at all), but *aging* does not belong in a list of neutral or natural occurrences, unless stress and the other conditions are assumed to be natural conditions of living that are accepted and acceptable. Because everyone grows older, aging seems too vague and way too general to be an illness, yet it appears to be just that.

Contrary to the popular cliché that the old are wise, age itself does not confer the status of elder on everyone. Being an elder most often requires that someone's life spans a number of decades, probably more than five. The fifth decade generally situates women in and then past menopause. In many people's minds, menopause itself designates women as elders, "crones" in the word of awe and praise used by some New Age women.

When elders in age are wise, it is because they care about human beings as individuals and in communities. Wise elders have learned to think with the heart. In thinking things through, people often think things to death. The wise elder thinks things to life, which means that she thinks creatively.

A few years ago, a beloved young female colleague declared that my "wisdom" – she used the word – was necessary at a get-together of some of us faculty and staff women, and in a seminar that I taught in fall 2006, a student asked me for my response to a question he'd asked the whole class because he wanted my "sage" words. "Sage" caught me off guard, but I felt his sincerity.

I fear the gross exposure of my ego, but I fear more the damage to my spirit from denying my true character.

I prefer self-acceptance to the self-effacement that some people believe to be humility. Humility is poise, a lightness that indicates maturity. That lightness lives in the maiden's luster, and that maturity lives in the elder's alluring sure-footedness.

People believe that their bodies are corrupted – the sweat and snot, the feces, and the surly plains and patches of hair growing from the smelly skin of both sexes – and that they become more so with age. The believer in bodily corruption is an addict, and the addict turns her past of perceived incremental corruption into a future of corruption full-on. No peace in the present. Believing in one's corrupted body, the present is an abstraction rather than an experience. A falling apart at the heart of things. A falling apart of the heart.

Poise exists only in the present.

We could exhibit false modesty when hearing compliments about ourselves. Or perhaps our humility surfaces and we accept with poise.

True character does not flaunt itself. If it did, a person would be suffering from the desire for fame. Nor does true character recede into a self-effacing humbleness. If it did, a person would be slinking into a sad passion for self-humiliation, through which she asserts her shortcomings and dulls herself by demanding that others testify to her defects, whether in oblique or blatant ways. True character does not remain ignorant of itself nor of its effects. True character is not self-congratulatory, but neither does it question itself to death nor exhaust itself with redundant self-doubt – should I? am I? what if I? – so troubling that it damns an individual into retreat, most insidiously, from herself.

In a professional photo of me taken in fourth grade, you could say that I look dreamy-eyed or that I look wise beyond my years. Calm and clear, just like an innocent and just like an elder. May that child's wisdom flower in its effects.

In September 2010 my friend Frances Murray and I did a photo shoot. I've modeled for her since 1983, appearing in various series of the black-and-white nudes for which she is known. She calls me her muse. Besides the black-and-white images that she shoots with film, she likes to take test shots and also record our play in her studio on a digital camera. "This one shows your exuberance!" "This one shows your femininity!" "This one is so erotic!" she exclaimed about our fun. Her pictures show me enjoying my body and laughing with the glee of a young girl.

I performed *Maiden Elder* at the Question of the Girl session at the National Women's Studies Conference, Denver, Colorado, in 2010.

Notes

1 Blythe Sheldon, "Feminism Meets Fashion on Gansevoort Street; In Related News: Meatpacking District Still Standing," [blog], April 28, 2008.
2 Issai Chozanshi, *The Demon's Sermon on the Martial Arts*, trans. William Scott Wilson (Tokyo: Kodansha International, 2006), p. 102.
3 Ibid., p. 107.
4 Ibid., p. 136.
5 Ibid., p. 142.
6 Ibid., p. 26.

7 Amit Goswami with Richard E. Reed and Maggie Goswami, *The Self-Aware Universe: How Consciousness Creates the Material World* (New York: Jeremy P. Tarcher/Putnam, 1993), p. 108.
8 Lao Tzu, *Tao Teh Ching*, trans. John C. H. Wu (Boston, MA and London: Shambhala, 2003), p. 49.
9 Crispin Sartwell, *Six Names of Beauty* (New York and London: Routledge, 2004), p. xii.
10 Ibid., p. xii.
11 William Scott Wilson, introduction to Chozanshi, *The Demon's Sermon*, p. 21.
12 Ibid., p. 151.
13 *A Kinder, Gentler Approach to Menopause*, introduction by Dana Reed-Kane, Thomas C. Reed, and Courtney Miros. Brochure picked up by the author at Reed's Compounding Pharmacy in Tucson, Arizona in November 2006.

The Sphinx Unwinds Her Own Sweet Self, 2007

Stage left. A low, small table holds a bottle of Caron's Rose perfume and a clear glass vase filled with white roses. A folding metal chair sits next to the table. About ten feet away, stage right, a black metal music stand for Frueh's script and a tall stool for her clear glass of water await her entrance from stage left.

Luminous with humor, eros, and intelligence, Frueh feels playful and seductive in her form-fitting dress of white moire velvet, her ivory-colored satin mules with a rosette at the toe, her gorgeous red lipstick, MAC's Lady Danger, her bountiful long dark hair, worn loose, her necklace of seed pearls: white on white. The dress hangs a bit below her calves and flares a little at the hem. It flexes and bends as she does. It is comfortable and an easy pleasure to wear. The dress catches the light and shimmers all the time, like Frueh, who feels free and full of grace.

Within the cliffs that she called home, the Sphinx held tight the eyes of Oedipus; his eyes fixed on hers. In each other's grip – for eyes tell all we are and all we wish or all that has died within us – they were as close as lovers, and she, an ultimate monster/beauty with her lion's tail and her profile calm as that of any goddess of classical Greek style, perched simply on his torso, front paw a few inches below his heart, back paw to high thigh, was seconds away from strangling him into a corpse. (Or mangling him, devouring him, or tearing him apart, depending on the version of the myth that you might read about the Sphinx who terrorized passersby outside the Greek city of Thebes.)

How I loved that Sphinx, she, enamored of a young, lean man whose long hair seemed to pouf from the moisture in her hideaway, her fastness, which no one would enter unless he had to as a challenge to himself, for he would have to be an expert climber, for sure, a soloist, which Oedipus indeed is in the painting that I've been so romantically describing; all by himself and barefoot too, like some daring athletes who are artists of the rock today. How I loved the beauty of them both, Oedipus and the Sphinx in the enraptured stillness of their intimacy, their mutual bedazzlement, all the rich emotion that superseded their foreknowledge of this situation, to which they had committed, on the rocks.

It was usually paws to claws (or so we're told), around men's necks and into other soft spots too, those places that only ask for kisses when we are conscious of love, because the riddle that she posed went wrongly answered by the previous men who had sought her. We see some of their parts – a hand, a foot – on rocks below our protagonists in Gustave Moreau's painting, dated 1865, which still provokes my ardent interpretation, above, around forty years after the image mesmerized me when I was a student in college and in graduate school.

When art so deftly and decisively appeals to us, it is because we witness in it our own conditioning, the habits of our unconscious; or, through our fascination, we may find the greater glamour of our deconditioning, our freedom from the unanswered questions that wind around our minds. Mostly we are unaware of how tightly we are bound.

See me stepping out, away from the winding sheet of why didn't you and why don't they and what if I'd done such-and-such and if only he'd do this and wherefore art thou Romeo? Juliet has long left me, all her turmoil, though I am girlish in this everlasting prime of mine.

The man who rocks me, like the joyful rhythms that set me dancing loosely and elastically from the shroud, the man who rocks me, like a cradle for this newborn, renewed sphinx, materializes as I speak.

Frueh walks to the chair and removes the stopper from the bottle. She smells the perfume and dabs some on herself. She repeats that action whenever the spirit moves her. At some point, she asks her assistant, who is sitting in the audience, to come onstage and to see to it that the bottle is passed around the audience and returned to the table.

I identified with the Sphinx and other nineteenth-century femmes fatales created by writers and artists, from the most famous, such as painter Gustave Moreau, artist and poet Dante Gabriel Rossetti, and writer Oscar Wilde, to many more who are known pretty much exclusively by scholars and enthusiasts of that century. In *Evil by Design: The Creation and Marketing of the Femme Fatale*, one of the most recent studies of the nineteenth-century literary, artistic, and popular phenomenon of the fatal female, the dangerous woman who at once captivates and terrifies men, the author, art historian Elizabeth K. Menon, gives 1854 as a likely first appearance of the term "femme fatale" in French literature.[1] We see the femme fatale parading in Parisian culture high and low, from the salons to illustrated periodicals belonging to mass visual culture, and we see her grim and gorgeous deeds and body paraded, too, in visions of evil womanhood and perversely mystical women, produced in Europe, the UK, and the United States.

The Sphinx asked a probing, relevant, and tricky question, or so the standard story implies: "What creature walks on four feet in the morning, two at noon, and three at night?"

"Ah!" thought Oedipus to himself. "A crawling baby, an upright adult, an old one with a cane." Unthinkingly, unfeelingly, he answered, "Man," and so, the story goes, the Sphinx killed herself. Because he bested her, some versions say. Because she had no more reason to live, say others.

Her reason being to ask and ask and ask.

Cut here, paste there. Create a different story, one that works for women and for men, for animals and natural pastimes, like making love and conversation, for the nature of love, which unwinds all sorrow. (*Man* means little in the midst of cliffs from which he has no wings to fly.)

Everybody sides with Oedipus. He answers the killer question. He resolves a problem. He does it through deductive reasoning. He is rational man, so people assume that he is right and good.

Almost everybody.

I am on the Sphinx's side and I am on the side of Oedipus as well, for I am on the side of a bigger picture. That's what the Sphinx was really asking for: she wanted a bigger man, one the woman in her would love.

Ostensibly, the Sphinx asked a question about the life cycle, one of those universal subjects that male writers, artists, and philosophers are said to deal with very well. So the answer could only be, it had to be, *Man*. Woman dies upon hearing that response, that answer to so many things that spans the ages of humanity.

In a sickly vision of only several years ago, I imagined a dictionary of subjects and symbols in art and literature. There, Woman and the sex called women were put in their proper place, as secondary references.

Delilah, see Samson.
Helen, see Paris.
Mary Magdalene, see Jesus.
Olympias, see Alexander.
Medea, see Jason.
Medusa, see Perseus.

Did she even see him as he swooped down on his winged horse, then left her dead, a headless corpse – a common phrase for her remains. He kept her head with him; he used it, to turn his enemies to stone. In his hands she had become a bodiless head – an uncommon phrase – destabilizing an accepted relation between mind and body, a relation in which mind is pure and body beastly.

Venus, seen generally as a beautiful and most likely mindless body, make sure that you see Mars. Love, make sure that you see war, that you know it is a major theme in Western art.

Soul-and-mind-inseparable-from-body: that phrase centers me in perfect soil, where anyone can plant a seed of love.

The Sphinx, having seen Oedipus and been unsatisfied, flew away to far lands, and wooed herself with foreign tongues and foreign learning, for they were fresh to her. She flew distance upon distance, and her haunches relaxed into rosy elation, then sprang into a realignment that so suited her spirit. "I am flying into the arms of love," she sang, which never riddles anyone who has cleared her doubts about it. I am tasting the body of love, which is all I see, and, as we touch, the body of love is all I hear, so it is all I speak. Speaking is believing, which creates the reality intended in the words.

O, the glamorously rosy scent of the Sphinx's haunches!

If I wished to believe the old, sad story, I could think that maybe the Sphinx did kill herself, because Oedipus' answer dismisses Woman. And it dissociates the animal from the human – body from mind; passions from intellect; senses from speech: her from him.

Here's the real killer question, the one at the bottom of the Sphinx's riddle, the one she knew that she was asking. Here's the real killer question, which is not the one that endangers would-be heroes, but the truly exciting one: Who am I?

What crawls? What walks? What asks for help in words or behavior when injured in soul or mind or body?

What she wanted was a good conversation, full of poetry, philosophy, and the personal. What she wanted was coziness and kissing, questions about her own life, such as these: How do you like the crags? What do you think about besides that riddle? Someone could have asked something this simple: How's it going?

Sad, the fate of femmes fatales.

They so intimidate men that no one asks them anything about themselves. They are fetching, but they do not inspire intimacy except in men's sexual fantasies, in which the femme fatale plays the role of threatening temptress.

Our renascent Sphinx, she had a flair for intimate relations, a flair for asking the most personal of questions – Who am I? – which is why she wanted to answer questions, have questions asked of her, so that she could reveal herself.

I tend to ask a lot of questions, and very direct ones, I've been told. I remember Dad telling me when I was in my late teens that I was curious. Curiosity is one of the femme fatale's traits, and in the nineteenth century, Eve and Pandora, among other figures, display that trait.[2] In his long poem, "The Sphinx," written in 1894, Wilde calls his sphinx "curious," playing on both meanings of the word.[3] To him she is an outrageous creature, curious, to say the least, and he also perceives her intelligence, which my father understood in me. I paraphrase a student, Sue, at the University of Nevada, Reno, who told me that my questions to students, in class and in my office, were so startlingly direct that students often didn't know how to respond. My friend Peggy says that I ask "probing questions." The kinds of questions that I ask come naturally to me, and I ask them because I am interested in the heart of issues and ideas and, of course, people. I am interested in the real.

My friend Becky, who has witnessed me in many professional and social situations, says that I show curiosity about the person with whom I'm conversing. She reminds me, too, that most people don't ask or don't know how to ask people questions. Be that as it may, I love questions that care to draw me out, that show interest in the real. For example, Jennifer Brooks – Jenny – a student at the University of Cumbria in north-west England, emailed me questions about intimacy. Here are her questions, and my responses from July 4, 2007.

> *How would you define intimacy?*
> Intimacy can be defined as erotic. The erotic can be defined as connection, a loving connection. Do I connect with a man's body? Is there chemistry between us? Chemistry bonds me to a lover. Chemistry, for me, comes from and generates deep, kindred emotion and a mysterious understanding of another person. I mention chemistry with a man, a lover, and there is also chemistry with friends, with strangers one sees on the street, with a wonderful class that one is teaching. Chemistry charges relationships with beauty and fascination. Chemistry is different from lust. Lust may likely not create intimacy.
>
> Intimacy can also be defined as familiarity: I am very familiar with my body; I am familiar with a lover's body. Many people are not very familiar with their own bodies, even though they say, "I know my own body." They may know it, but they don't listen to it. They don't pay attention to its guidance. Intimacy is a knowing that encompasses feeling, listening, touching, tasting, smelling, and looking lovingly. I mean these literally and figuratively. I know the way to the grocery store in my car, but that's a different kind of knowing.
>
> *What is it that makes an artwork "intimate," or indeed, can an artwork be an intimate object?*
> An artwork can be an intimate object, and artworks often are intimate objects. It's a matter of the relationship – the connection or the familiarity, as I speak of them above – between the observer and the object. *Response*, even *responsiveness*, may be more precise and profound than *relationship*. For me, pleasure is the ground of responsiveness. In light of that, I'm astoundingly responsive to Caravaggio and Rossetti. Sometimes my own responsiveness, my own intimacy with them/their art surprises me. I want to be closer closer closer … They bring me into intimacy with myself, soul-and-mind-inseparable-from-body. The feeling of being in love – not in a horridly romantic obsessive way, but in a light and fascinated way that propels you to want to know, see, do, and be the best and most beautiful you can be – is the intimacy I feel with Rossetti's and Caravaggio's art.

> *Do you think that femininity and intimacy are linked?*
> The answer to this question could be an essay or a book. I think that many avenues can be explored in regard to this link.
> I don't think that femininity and intimacy are *necessarily* linked.
> I'll speak about my own experience. Intimacy with a person or an artwork brings out my femininity. Receptivity is a conventionally feminine quality, and intimacy opens me so that I'm receptive. Bold innocence and receptivity go hand in hand.

The title of my MA thesis is "The Sphinx in the Nineteenth Century," which opens with a quote from Wilde's "The Sphinx" and lingers on Moreau for several pages midway through.[4] The title of my PhD dissertation is "The Rossetti Woman." I received the MA in 1971, when I was 23, and the PhD in 1981. I was struck, when gathering materials for this, my ministration to the Sphinx, that I still own classic texts about the femme fatale, that I moved them with me to my new home in Tucson in May 2006 after recirculating *many* books before leaving Reno (and having recirculated *many* books prior to that). Menon lists all of the following classics, which I own, in her introduction to *Evil by Design*: Bram Dijkstra, *Idols of Perversity: Fantasies of Feminine Evil in Fin-De-Siècle Culture*, Mario Praz, *The Romantic Agony*, and the exhibition catalog *The Earthly Chimera and the Femme Fatale: Fear of Woman in Nineteenth-Century Art*.[5] The exhibition was installed in 1981 at the David and Alfred Smart Gallery at the University of Chicago. I received my PhD from the University of Chicago that same year, and while looking at the title page of the catalog I remembered that I gave a lecture at the Smart Gallery during the exhibition. I titled the talk "Re-Vamping the Vamp." Need I remind myself that vamp and femme fatale can be synonyms?

O Sphinx, I wanted once to be like you, in the incarnation passionately given by men who wound you through their fantasies into a sullen seductress whose fearsome mien and habits both lured and repulsed their sex. The Sphinx of the Oedipus story is, of course, female, and nineteenth-century artists and writers produced fantasies not only about her but also about Egyptian sphinxes, altering its most famous form, the wingless Gizeh sphinx, a male monument, into a perverted feminine feline. O, Theban Sphinx: Salomes and Circes, Liliths and Eves, Medeas and Cleopatras,

Delphic oracles and demon Venuses, Medusas and Amazons, vampires and serpent women were your sisters, construed by male imaginations that scholars in this century and the last have proved to be hostile to feminism – which was moving through Europe, the UK, and the United States – and consequently, to women.

Menon's interest in the femme fatale extends into today's popular culture, where she thrives in the fashion and entertainment industries, often because women creators respond to her appeal. What exactly that is, Menon would like to know.[6]

Dr. Menon, here I am, a femme fatale in transformation. I've been a vampire in my piece *Vampiric Strategies* (1989), a fearsome Delphic oracle in my performance *Pythia* (1994), a fierce and dazzling avenger in my song "Demento Beauty" (1985). I titled one of my books *Monster/Beauty* (2001). Isn't that exactly what the Sphinx has been? For the Greeks? For Moreau, Wilde, Rossetti? A long time had passed, probably decades, since I read "The Sphinx in the Nineteenth Century," and rereading it today, I see roots of my personal and scholarly explorations – they are always one – and of my mission, which is to heal with love the wounds of human beings. In 1999, the musician and scholar Russill Paul asked the Dalai Lama his advice for today's artists. "Transform your own energy first,"[7] replied the Dalai Lama, before burdening your art and your audience with your negativity and problems. "Then use your gifts to bring healing to society."[8] Healing is not only the artist's but also everyone's mission, and the particularity of mine is to practice the healing as a scholar, a writer, a performer, and an image-maker who learns and teaches the erotic and redefines it, from acts and images of simplistic sexuality to an oceanic engagement with life.

Eros welcomes carnality and spirituality, divinity and humanity, appetites and satisfactions, wishes and fulfillments, giving and receiving. Eros encompasses receptivity and openness, generosity, abundance, and compassion. The femme fatale is an erotic archetype, erotic in its usual usage of sexual and sexy. I want to see the femme fatale as an archetype of eros itself. I want to see her happy in the world, fatal not as in disaster, damage, and destruction leading to lethality; fatal not as in fatality and fatalism; fatal not as in doomed, unfortunate, and ominous. Rather, fatal as in fateful, meaning prophetic, significant, and decisive.

Prophetic: the femme fatale promises beauty and joy. Significant: her transformation from evildoer to beneficent lover bears consequences in the physical world. Decisive: her destiny is good fortune. (O, Sphinx, your fate is in my hands.)

The physicist Amit Goswami writes that "consciousness is the only ultimate reality" and that choice is the ground of consciousness. As he titles a chapter in his book *The Self-Aware Universe: How Consciousness Creates the Material World*, "I Choose Therefore I Am."[9] Many artists today, especially those who speak about their work in terms of intentionally radical political and social content, choose to present or reflect problems, such as one of the many permutations of violence.

For a general public, an essence of art is beauty, and art serves to elevate the viewer.

Those traditional values do not pertain to a great deal of today's art. People educated in contemporary art practices know an aesthetics of ugliness, which emphatically exists in the nineteenth century with Realism. Among other subjects, Realist artists depicted laborers and everyday situations, bodies and scenes that drastically departed from the classical model of the nude – a body clothed in beauty, like a god or goddess – and from traditional ideas of ennoblement. Twentieth- and twenty-first-century art includes countless examples of Realist progeny, from the mild, such as Man Ray's 1921 black-and-white photograph of washing hung out to dry, to the gross, such as Daniel Joseph Martinez's *Self-Portrait #7: George and Daniel. In an Insane World it was the Sanest Choice* (2000), a color photo of a man shot in the head, blood splurting (digital manipulation gives realism to the shooting.) Such an aesthetics of the everyday and of the topically political and social is one identifying characteristic of contemporary art. In a statement for his exhibition "Without Anesthesia OR This Isn't a Nice Neighborhood," Martinez speaks about suffering. The following statement appears on the website for SF Camerawork, where the show was installed from October 29 through November 30, 2002.

> Many of us suffer tremendous pain, and we have numbed ourselves to such a degree that we don't know how to feel anymore. We've lost touch with our own selves, our own bodies, our own souls. There are

> many different ways to uncover those things that have been numb for so long. Sometimes the nerve endings need to be laid bare. They need to be raw again. In order to heal a wound, sometimes you have to open it up to let the disease out. And sometimes you need to do that without anesthesia.[10]

We all know that opened up wounds are everywhere. I see, hear, smell, and sense them leaking their poisons, their pain, in the classrooms where I've taught and the restaurants that I frequent, and the airports through which I travel. Leaking, from bodies, voices, gaits, and postures, the subtle angers, the twitching guts, the programmed responses to the unpredictabilities of life, whose delights are plentiful. People say that we're desensitized to horror, and I say we're desensitized to beauty, love, and gentleness.

Sometimes artists, or critics who write about those artists' works, or scholars who are articulating their own research interests, use the word "resistance" to describe the process or purpose of their efforts. Resistance stays with the problem, stays within its energy, which differs greatly from the Dalai Lama's implicit suggestion that artists would do well to transform energy, not only their own but, in so doing, the energy that creates and thus becomes the physical world. In the *Star Trek* sagas, the Borg, a population of cyborgs that assimilate the populations with which they come in contact, almost always realize their fatal slogan: "Resistance is futile." (Borg females belong to the highest rank of sexy, scary femmes fatales. O, Sphinx, you and your science fiction kin are simply irresistible!) To choose, according to quantum theory as discussed by Goswami, is to create. Resisting is choosing to stand *against*. It seems to me that the Dalai Lama is asking artists to stand *for* the most profoundly positive and loving humanity and to stand *with* a yielding heart. I have heard and read performers, film directors, visual artists, and writers say that, in their work, they are showing their audience social difficulties, wrongs, and injuries.

Responding to the subject titled "Answers?," the playwright and actor Anna Deavere Smith states, in an *AARP: The Magazine* profile that appeared in the September/October 2007 issue, "No, I just ask the questions – the questions are what give energy to my work."[11] The combined interview and profile format shows Smith's heart and intelligence, and she speaks of "our need for grace as we live and die," yet in a very short article – 310 words – she brings up her interest in questions three times. Often, artists are sphinx-like, asking questions, implicit most of the time, and leaving them unresolved, ostensibly so that the audience can ponder what's been asked and come to their own conclusions. Like the Theban Sphinx herself, artists, at bottom, are wanting to ask or are actually asking: Who am I? My feeling about the Dalai Lama's words to artists is that they – the artists – can contribute to well-being by providing rich and beautiful answers that relieve suffering – indeed, that produce joy. In the world of contemporary art, doing that could easily elicit a charge of sentimentality. I say, give me the prophetic, the significant, and the decisive.

Why repeat the holocausts of history, families, nations, peoples? Why blast them into your brothers' and sisters' brains? Perhaps you identify with those holocausts so strongly that you have neither recognized nor perceived a way out, which is transformation, not escape. My friend Jill used to say that she needed her darkness in order to make her art.

One chooses and creates whether one is aware of perceiving a choice and its effects or whether such perception occurs unconsciously. Goswami asserts that "when we speak of unconscious perception, we are speaking of events that we perceive but that we are not aware of perceiving."[12] True healing begins with the choice of self-love, which is a change in consciousness and which transforms one's identity. True love moves beyond any single human being, and it is an erotic consciousness, the erotics of inseparability: we are all One, consciousness is unitive. Through their work, artists find ways to heal both themselves and others if they choose the "inner creativity" that Goswami associates with "a natural sense of love and service to others – a natural surrendering of our separateness to the quantum self,"[13] which is consciousness. In an activist mysticism, Goswami acknowledges that "changes occur in our psyche as we accumulate experiences, but ordinarily these are low-level changes. They do not transform us. What we do in inner creativity is to direct the force of creativity specifically to the self-identity [so that] we creatively transform our own identity."[14] O, Sphinx, to know you is to love you is to change you is to change myself.

I wonder, if the Sphinx and Oedipus had made love, would those rocks in which she kept her lair, those bleak sheer walls of isolation, have softened into sand dunes surrounding an oasis?

Softened along with his dedication to a rationalist stance, so that he could feel his intuition like her tail along his belly. Softened along with her animal pride in teasing all the men with a foregone conclusion, the drama of destruction by a *fatal female*.

O, Sphinx, you and I let love take its divine course, which mystics say is the only real one, and love, the mystics know, is the only way to well-being.

That anyone can be a mystic is the always underlying theme of Wayne Teasdale's book, *A Monk in the World: Cultivating A Spiritual Life*.[15] Teasdale, who often uses "monk" and "mystic" interchangeably, is a lay monk in the combined traditions of Christianity and Buddhism: he is a Christian *sannyasi*. Brother Teasdale lives in the world, and from his uncloistered position, he, I am sure, like the Dalai Lama, knows that artists whose "inner issues … burden society [when] it is burdened enough," are letting trouble take its course.[16] With love comes service, which is healing. Service follows naturally from love.

As a 23-year-old graduate student who looked at her beauty in the mirror, and through the words of her lovers, friends, and parents, my sight was limited by my own lacks in self-love. I saw the lovely features and gestures of the femme fatale, yet I doubted their loveliness. As a tenderly and boldly alluring young woman, who never wished to lead men to their downfall, who never was manipulative and bitchy like some attractive women are said to be, and as a young scholar researching and writing her MA thesis, thinking and feeling deeply about the particular monster/beauty called Sphinx.

In the thesis, after introducing my subject with a couple of lines from Wilde's poem, I spent two pages discussing it. Wilde speaks as a student who both adores and abhors the Sphinx. His "exquisite grotesque" – monster/beauty, indeed! – is Egyptian, which allows him to spin line after line – that chill me as I read them now and bring me to tears, they so affect me, still, with their consummate poetics and their nearness to the pain that once described my heart; that detail the thrilling pitch of her sex life with one after another hybrid deity from the Egyptian pantheon, as well as women, men, and animals. My thesis begins near the end of Wilde's poem: "Get hence you loathsome mystery! Hideous animal, get hence! / You wake in me each bestial sense, you make me what I would not be."[17]

The student winds up condemning the Sphinx because, being body in the nth degree, she "wake[s] foul dreams of sensual life," which stream, as I wrote thirty-six years ago, from his "morbid obsession with the purported sexual adventures of the Sphinx." Wilde's Sphinx watches the student silently from a dusky corner of his room, and the scene and situation, as I noted in the thesis, grow "increasingly intense and provocative" because he feels his chemistry with the Sphinx. He wants her head on his knee, he wants to stroke her throat and see her body, to touch her tail and claws. He wants his own intimate relations with her, and that desire manifests itself in work after work that features the Sphinx or a sphinx-like woman. Those nineteenth-century sphinxes display all or some of the following characteristics: they are simultaneously tempting and rejecting, they are sexual aggressors, and they are inviolate, a word used by Wilde to describe his Sphinx, and a status given to many nineteenth-century femmes fatales who move with sexual confidence in the world and at the same time are untouchable – aloof and haughty. Not exactly intimate.

Jenny sent me another set of questions, to which I responded on September 3, 2007.

> *In your opinion, can you experience erotic intimacy with a person without loving them/being in love with them?*
> I define *erotic* as connection in the deepest and richest sense, so *erotic* includes love, and therefore erotic intimacy includes loving. Feeling "in love" is different from feeling "love." For example, the woman who I once called my best friend I no longer do. I love her but I'm no longer in love with her. Sexual activity has never been part of our relationship, so being in love with her was a matter of high passion, expansive enthusiasm, and sheer delight in our conversations and our closeness – our intimacy. That intimacy has vanished, as she has grown darker and I've grown lighter. A connection – an eroticism – of similarity has vanished. When, as a heterosexual woman, I am in love with a man – a lover, partner, or husband – or a woman – a close or best friend – I am deeply in eros, in an erotic commitment

of ecstasy as well as responsibility. Loving someone, who may be a best friend, a stranger on the street in front of my house, a student, or a regular in the yoga studio I go to, always entails responsibility, but not the ecstasy and bonding of sexual chemistry or of felt similarity. That ecstasy and bonding are particular to love within erotic intimacy.

Do you believe that things such as female sexuality and masturbation are still taboo in Western society?
Yes, because:

1) Women's bodies are reviled and joked about in ways that men's are not. For instance, people titter at tits. The verb itself, titter, feels trivializing, as though it's referring to something mere and superficial, perhaps cute and silly. "Cunt" remains a shocker, one of the most shocking words in English. People don't know what to do with it. I suppose that reflects their not knowing what to do, either, when "face to face" with women's sexual parts, proclivities, and pleasures. Cunt is a mystifying "thing" and therefore mystified. Pricks, cocks, and dicks do not suffer from humor that sees them as silly or from a mystification that is dependent on the lingering cultural invisibility of the cunt and its literal invisibility vis-à-vis the cock.
2) Female masturbation is understood too exclusively as clitoral stimulation. If it were understood – even loved! – as regular behavior and as simply – meaning elegantly – and beautifully as a mode of pleasure, then, obviously, the taboo would not exist.

Do you think that increased exposure to an image desensitizes a viewer to it? For example, if viewers repeatedly saw images of the naked female form masturbating, would it cease to be shocking?
In answer to your second question, I imagine so. Yet desensitization works in multiple ways. The word implies a numbing or a not caring: thus, images of women masturbating wouldn't matter and would be taken for granted. Yet buried within desensitization is the stuff that an individual or a society has not dealt with. People in the United States have talked for decades about Americans' desensitization to images of violence. I think that this so-called desensitization is a *burying* of sensitivity, of emotion, of connection – of eros. So the disturbance or thrill of whatever the shocking image is remains, sometimes insidiously, as a toxin to the mental, physical, spiritual, and social health.

What are your views about the pornographic industry?
The industry? Not sure, as I'd like my comments to be grounded in research; and pornography is an area to which I have very minimally applied my scholarship. Pornographic images and access to them? Obviously, access has grown tremendously and the industry is huge and hugely successful.

My sense of things, from what I read, see, hear, and observe, including some recent – and differing – perspectives from younger women, such as Pamela Paul's *Pornified: How Pornography is Damaging our Lives, our Relationships, and our Families* and (a thus far cursory look at) Violet Blue's *The Smart Girl's Guide to Porn*, is that porn continues to treat sex simplistically.[18] The implicit ideology is this: sex is exteriority. It is physical, it is a series of surface effects, it is acts and activities that can be seen. In Blue's book, a page of porn jargon, which she titles "Smart Girl's Porn Vocabulary," lists eleven terms, six of which focus on male ejaculate and seven of which feature male "doing," pleasure, or fluids. I love sex with men, yet that list does nothing for me. If anything, it saddens me. I've written about what I call vaginal action and vagignosis – women are active, engaged.[19] Very present. Also, I'm a very visual person, yet the exteriority of porn bores me. How does sex *feel*? Where does it take me? And the fixation on cum is so Sadian. I know that Sade remains a literary deity, and his work can be read as satire, yet I'm for pleasure, for loving, passionate sex, for the heights of eros. Porn lacks that kind of connection between and among its "actors" and between those actors and myself.

How do you feel about pornographic images being reused in feminist art?
Reuse of any image, whether pornographic or high art, runs the danger of being an unengaging parody or of being an imitation that lacks the power of the original. Certainly, feminists change the context of the original images. Also, the value or transformation of the pornographic image depends on what exactly that image *is*.

Thinking about this reminds me that I wanted to create erotic videos or films with Russell, my second husband. Videos or films in which aesthetics were paramount – light, environment, bodies, sounds. Everything created for the erotics of beauty and the beauties of the erotic, and images that come from the reality, intelligence, and creativity of two people who are artists who love one another. I think that we may have talked about such a collaboration. If so, that's as far as it went.

Do you think a piece of artwork has to have specific qualities in order for it to become an intimate object?
I don't know. I'd have to think about this for quite a while.

What is it that you respond to in Rossetti's and Caravaggio's work? What do their pieces have that others lack? Do you think that your response is related to the fact that the pieces were painted as pictures rather than as political statements?
What do you think of the work of Ghada Amer and … Miranda Whall?
I put these questions together, about the men and the women, which you'd asked as separate questions, because my response to all their art is this: it comes into existence in the artists' receptivity to their own pleasure. I respond more strongly, with greater identification, to Rossetti and Caravaggio, most likely because their pleasures are visualized in ways that delight me more. Their work is more beautiful to me – the frankness of light and composition in much of Caravaggio's work, the lushness of Rossetti's female figures and their surroundings.

Do you think that it is possible to make work about the female body without it being political?
Well, the personal is still political. So, for a woman, making work about the female body is political.

Does self-portraiture produce a more intimate work than images of other people?
For the artist or for the viewer? And in contemporary work or in the history of Western art? Speaking in general, self-portraits do seem more intimate than do images of other people because I imagine that artists are making themselves vulnerable by taking the risk of seeing themselves as clearly as they can and showing that clarity to others. I speak here, of course, as an artist as well as a critic and a historian. My self-portraits are glamorous and sensual, which some viewers perceive to be daring, and that position and perspective through which I see myself – the presentness and delight of glamour and sensuality – both comes from and brings into focus – for *me* – my aesthetic and erotic lucidity.

Recently, I dated a man for about a year. That was after Russell, my second husband, and I divorced in 2001, and I had a couple of short affairs. The relationship ended in June 2007. The man was kind and generous, thoughtful and respectful, and I loved his intellect. I loved the logic of his arguments, a logic often different from my own, and I loved the preciseness of his language, so our conversations as well as the traits that I just listed seduced me. When I told him, "You are seducing me masterfully," I meant it. And … he asked me questions, about my life, my work, my history, my relationships, and my sexuality. I experienced a new kind of romance with that man who gave me flowers, chocolates, and lingerie, who took me shopping and on weekend trips, who gave me gifts of many books. Early on, we made out, then talked about Nietszche, then made out again and talked about Aristotle and his student Alexander, then made out again and talked about another philosopher or another philosophical issue, and that excited me.

Everything I've so far told you excited me initially.

He seemed surprised when I whispered to him in a public place, "I want to fuck you." Like no woman had ever said that to him before. He seemed surprised when I kissed him, passionately, as we walked on a city street. One day and for the first time, I pushed him up against a wall, very privately – in my house. I may have said, "I want to fuck you." My body surely made clear what I wanted. He did not respond in kind. He laughed, and not in a sexually playful way. I didn't get it. I felt weird. I asked why he laughed, and his response left me feeling even weirder: "You're playing, right? Like a child." I was playing femme fatale in the sweetest way. I was playing I want strong, physical, intense, and elegant sex, because that's what fucking is to me, not merely a banal word for one act, intercourse. I was playfully forceful, manly feminine, like the Sphinx had wished to be with Oedipus. The man said something like: "Men aren't used to this. Women don't do this." I said that the men I've been with like it for sure. And when my friend Caedron and I talked about our recent breakups and I was telling him this story that I'm telling you, the pushing up against the wall story, he said, "Sounds good to *me*!" The man was a little younger than I am, and Caedron is 26, but I don't think that their different responses have anything to do with age.

Like many people in the throes of early romantic elation, the man and I deluded ourselves. In my delighted exploration of aspects of romance and relationships that I previously had not explored, such as being with an intellectual and someone only a few years younger than myself – my husbands and lovers have mostly been much younger than I am – and receiving luxurious gifts, I suppressed, for a while, my passionate affection for very physical and graceful sex, which is born in the chemistry between a man and me. For my relationships of any duration I had chosen men with whom I immediately sensed that bond – the animal – men who liked and worked their muscles, whose bodily ease felt both natural and conscious. In those intimate relations, we instinctively moved together. To be animal is to be instinctually present, which the man I dated in 2007 was not. Our bodies did not fit one another, which brought to light too many other ways in which our beings were uncomfortably oblique to one another. After too little pleasure for too long, I knew that I wanted my freedom, to let a brightly shining man, with whom I share a soul-and-mind-inseparable-from-body chemistry, materialize.

The comparatively gray man's analytical mind wound me round with his assumptions. He wound me round with his anxieties, and thus he created their materialization. He said, so many times, about our relationship, "I can't believe that this is real," and so it was not. He wanted to analyze me and my history with men, as if I remained the same person whose life he read about in my books, or even the same person he spoke with on our first date. Pained by my feeling unjustly evaluated as having problems with intimacy, I asked Larry, my therapist, "Do I have intimacy problems?" With his characteristic humor and brilliant statements of the obvious, Larry answered, lightly laughing, "*Everyone* has intimacy problems."

The femme fatale has intimacy problems. In 1992, after I'd performed *Faculties of Love* at Weber State University, in Salt Lake City, a woman professor told me, at the request of a male colleague who couldn't stay for the post-performance socializing, that I'd totally attracted and totally intimidated him. I was shocked – and thrilled – at the same time. Friends, too, told me that men felt intimidated by me. What was I doing, into my late forties, to deserve what I considered to be a kind of peculiar praise? I wore that maladapted and archetypal femme fatale energy as a badge of honor: men wanted me and my demeanor refused them. That behavior of mine was unconscious. Maybe it stems from a key moment in my life. I've told the story in my book *Swooning Beauty: A Memoir of Pleasure* and in my performance *The Aesthetics of Orgasm*. Here is a briefer account, along with insight that came to me after the book's publication in 2006. In my memory I'm 8 years old and my parents are having a dinner party in honor of a young pianist. He stares at me from across the table, and in his gaze and posture I'm deliciously and exuberantly aware of my beauty and of my sexual power. I'm loving how I feel while also wondering why the pianist doesn't look at my very beautiful mother the way that he's looking at me.

An 8-year-old girl has pretty much no place to act in the knowledge that I gained that day, and which has always stayed with me. She can enjoy her own body, which I did and had already been doing, in masturbation and in wearing clothing that adorned my femininity and sensuality, and in dressing up in Mom's clothes and makeup. However, society imposes a taboo on the natural feelings of sexuality that women, let alone little girls, have. I luxuriated in those feelings, yet I suppressed them, and the aspect of *my* receiving the young man's attention, rather than my mother, produced another restraint that has only disappeared in the last several years: keeping under wraps, in social situations, my naturally flirtatious self and my awareness of my attractiveness, so that I wouldn't be competing with other women.

Perhaps that very evening in my family's dining room I became a sphinx – an inscrutable and enigmatic person, who, in female form, is a mystery to men – and shared the Theban Sphinx's joyless, condescending, removed, and distant demeanor. Just this summer, my friend Dan told me that when we first met, in our early thirties and in professional circumstances, I intimidated him. Dan is a little younger than I am, and he used those four adjectives – joyless, condescending, removed, and distant – to describe me back then. As a little girl dealing with the glorious gaze of a young man and with society's fear of sexuality, especially females' and children's, I became susceptible to the femme fatale, a figure that found me from movies, comics, and pin-up decks, and that I sought in them and, later, in books and artworks. In the costume, pose, and poise of the femme fatale I could breathe a little easier in my passionate eroticism, even though she lived in psychic quarters that I know now to be pretty cramping.

The femme fatale has been, for me, a way to explore the erotic and the animal, the fear that I had and hid, because my pursuit of soul-and-mind-inseparable-from-body chemistry with men seemed so *verboten*. Wilde's gloomy Sphinx is stinking of her bestial sex, the fluids and the sweat, the fecal and the fecund, aspects of the animal, the chemistry of human beings in sweet pursuit of love, that grow in coarseness and brutality as the student admits, through his lush fantasies, his animality then tries to crush it.

The subtitle of *Monster/Beauty* is *Building the Body of Love*, and my intention was to theorize personal beauty, what I call "aesthetic/erotic self-creation," within the pages of the book, in a way that would embrace my own body, the reader's body, and, of equal importance, "bodies that differ from one's own in age, race, sex, and shape."[20] If we are the body of love, then we see others – directly, not peripherally – as the body of love, and we embrace them, soul-and-mind-inseparable-from-body. Monster/beauty, the term itself, and my articulation, elaboration, and love of it, were unconsciously chosen beginnings of redeeming and releasing the femme fatale.

I wanted to free her sweetness that underlies the sickness built into her.

I want to free the perfume that I perceive haloing her in Wilde's poem and intoxicating the student as much as does an obvious fetidness, the bestial reek that has him vainly turning to a crucifix.

"Only when we are sick of our sickness / Shall we cease to be sick," I read in the *Tao Teh Ching*, a Chinese sacred text from around 600 BCE that is attributed to Lao Tzu and most likely written by various authors.[21] Only in one's *consciousness* of her own sickness does she make a choice to be well. Quoting Goswami from earlier, "What we do in inner creativity is to direct the force of creativity specifically to the self-identity [so that] we creatively transform our own identity."[22] People tend to think that identity – their own and other people's – is fixed, yet I am acutely aware of unfixing identity and of identity as a process when I think about Jill O'Bryan's discussion, in her book *Carnal Art: Orlan's Refacing*, of the cosmetic surgeries performed by the artist Orlan.[23] O'Bryan is a scholar, and she is my friend Jill, an artist who, as I said before, thought that she needed her darkness for her art. Using inner creativity, Jill transformed her own self-identity, one that was culturally rooted in the archetype of the brooding genius.

According to Lao Tzu, wisdom and health go hand in hand, and, like identity, health is a process. Sickness is cramped psychic quarters and joylessness, an extreme and perhaps prolonged unsweetness. "The Sage is not sick," continues the *Tao*, "being sick of sickness; / This is the secret of health."[24] The Theban Sphinx was known for her intelligence: some old stories say that she killed herself because Oedipus outdid her intellectually and she was ashamed.

O Sphinx, you have always been a sage, and you grow ever wiser in your sweetness.

My friend Andrew loves my sweetness, yet he says he misses the bitter. "Where you go for sweetness, I almost cannot follow; where you go for joy, you almost leave me behind." I responded, "I wondered about your feelings. And I wondered, Who will join me?" Andrew answered, "I said 'almost,' which means that I can and would join you."

I sense that my friend Guillermo expected a tougher person when we sat talking face to face in summer 2007 after many years of not communicating (for no untoward reason). He surprised me with, "You're sweet," which I took as a compliment.

Dan says that I'm a different person from the one he knew before. "You changed," he said, which we agree is far more to the point than analyzing ways in which I used to intimidate men. Dan, thank you for helping me see who I am now.

Frueh sits down and removes her shoes. By this time, she has flung roses to the audience and strewn them on the stage to make a path between the table and the microphone. She returns to the microphone and sings Nick Cave's "The Ship Song."

Who am I?

I wear Rose, a perfume that its producer, Caron, describes as "evoking the delicacy of a rosebud plucked at dawn" and "ultra feminine with a touch of exotic class." Top note: sparkling and piquant. Heart note: round and sweet. Bass note: warm and lasting.[25] I am tender, newborn, and simply, completely divine in my curves and heat, my champagne laughter and tart, true intellect. Like the whole rose plant, I am passionately fragrant everywhere – petals, stem, and leaves. Like a whole rose garden – people have planted them in small towns and capital cities throughout the world – I am precious: beloved and desirable and held in high esteem.

Rose Précieuse: it is one of the rose perfumes created by Ernest Daltroff for the House of Caron. Dated 1910, Rose Précieuse is no longer available. But I am, in all my sweet passion. Another Daltroff rose perfume, created in 1936 and also no longer in production, is La Fête des Roses. Festival or celebration or merrymaking of roses. Passion of roses. Passion: how that word, that experience, that feeling grows into the refrain of this unwinding.

Frueh returns to the table, picks up the perfume bottle, and walks as close to the audience as she can, pours a little of the perfume into one hand, dips the fingers of her other hand into it, and flicks the scent towards the audience, in a gesture of blessing. She may do this more than once. She holds the bottle, now clearly a sacred object, as she speaks the next lines.

The Sphinx, she makes her bed of roses, where the man who materializes as I speak is offering himself to her muzzle.

Flexible and heliotropic, turning easily to the light, they are unwinding one another in their own sweet time.

Addendum (not performed)

Benefits of using myth in contemporary art

As is evident from the beginning paragraphs of this piece, myth opens an artist's imagination. I've loved Greek and Roman mythology since I was little. I remember reading stories from it in third grade, and ultimately the deities rather than any tale stirred me. I don't recall exactly when Aphrodite became my favorite, but by my early forties, a little over a decade after I began writing and presenting performance pieces, she starred in my personal pantheon. For a while it was Athena – my identification with intellect and assertiveness, as she is the goddess of wisdom and war. I took to the Greek goddesses more than the Roman ones and haven't been surprised that when I travel in Greece it feels like home to me.

In agreement with master yogis, I write in *Goddess of Roses*, which I first performed in 2007, that humanity and divinity are one. Because of that, deities can serve as models for human beings. Aphrodite, in her beauty, laughter, glamour, playfulness, and erotic power, became a model of femininity and human grace for me. My performance *Dressing Aphrodite*, debuting in 1997 when I was 49, lovingly considers and revises aspects of Praxiteles' and Hesiod's Aphrodites and invents a new Aphrodite so that she is useful for contemporary women and men. Aphrodite appears in other performances of mine as well, and I dedicated my book *Monster/Beauty: Building the Body of Love* to her.

We can become our own Aphrodites. Our own beloved beauties, filled with spirit and an appetite for living. We can fashion myth to our advantage by reshaping its heroes and narratives. Employing Aphrodite, the Sphinx, and other figures, I've chosen to create visions of my own life as rich, delicious, and joyful. Life responds positively to those visions.

Women's beauty/one's own beauty

I have described, interpreted, and analyzed bodily beauty, especially women's beauty, and my own appearance as well, throughout my work. How great people would feel if they could look in a mirror, see their attractiveness, lovingly accept that, and even articulate it to themselves, silently or aloud! That is my goal, which includes a transformation of the image of Venus looking into a mirror from a representation and warning of (women's) vanity into a loving contemplation of oneself. That is an erotic way to live. Erotic as I define it means life-enhancing and connective. In all of my work I develop a theory and practice of the erotic. As both a foundation and argument, eros supports every page of my writing.

Personal, poetic, scholarly, and autobiographical considerations of vanity, narcissism, sexual assertiveness, celebration, joy, self-awareness, self-confidence, and self-reflection interweave in my work, so I would advise a reader who is interested in such subjects to skim through my books, taking special note of the following readings. *Mouth Piece*, *Dressing Aphrodite*, *The Performance of Pink*, and *The Aesthetics of Orgasm* in *Clairvoyance (For Those in the Desert): Performance Pieces, 1979–2004* (Durham and London:

Duke University Press, 2008); "Vaginal Action: Vagignosis" in *Swooning Beauty: A Memoir of Pleasure* (Reno, NV and Las Vegas, CA: University of Nevada Press, 2006); and the introductions to *Erotic Faculties* (Berkeley and Los Angeles, CA and London: University of California Press, 1996), and to *Monster/Beauty: Building the Body of Love* (Berkeley and Los Angeles, CA and London: University of California Press, 2001). I title the first section in the introduction to *Monster/Beauty*, "My Body/My Beauty."

Curiosity and self-transformation

Questioners can be superiors, such as instructors who lead class discussions with questions, and questioners can be inferiors, such as students who ask instructors for answers to questions that range from exam logistics to extreme abstractions. This means that responders also exist in both of those roles. Questioning and responding is a rich relation, an erotic relation, one of connection, in which the dynamics shift. An authority becomes the curious one, an underling becomes the expert. People learn together. While I cast myself in the Sphinx's role in *The Sphinx Unwinds Her Own Sweet Self* and I am the superior/authority when as a professor and a senior scholar I answer the student's questions, I am also transforming myself throughout the piece. Which makes me as much Oedipus as Sphinx when I respond to the student.

Self-transformation is a state of curiosity, and I write my performances in that state. It is explorative, and the outcomes of my writing, of my performances, of the material world in which I move, and of my own being are all unknown. Once upon a time I adored the Sphinx and I idealized the femme fatale, but my own well-being nudged me into recreating them. The femme fatale in her conventional representations and characteristics became intolerably painful to me, which is evident in this piece. As I transform her rather than destroy her, she rises, phoenix-like, to a calling different from danger, distance, and other kinds of behaviors damaging to herself and others. That calling is love. As an act and perhaps a new archetype, my invention, I hope, gives insight and avenues into the ease and joy of being a woman who is intelligent, powerful, confident, attractive, and lovable for herself and others.

That said,

I am an angel, released from hell. The clock resets.
Bones realign.
Now angels fly easy because wings once inflamed grow all their feathers. Smoldering women are thought to be hot –
A metaphor taken far by Hollywood fantasy
And too far into the bodies of some women. I am an angel, released from hell.

Notes

1 Elizabeth K. Menon, *Evil by Design: The Creation and Marketing of the Femme Fatale* (Urbana and Chicago, IL: University of Illinois Press, 2006), devotes her study to a discussion of the femme fatale in mass visual culture.
2 Ibid., pp. 18–28.
3 Oscar Wilde, "The Sphinx," in *The Portable Oscar Wilde*, ed. Richard Aldington (New York: Viking Press, 1946), pp. 573–85.
4 Joanna Frueh, "The Sphinx in the Nineteenth Century" (MA thesis, University of Chicago, 1971), p. 2.
5 Bram Dijkstra, *Idols of Perversity: Fantasies of Feminine Evil in Fin-De-Siècle Culture* (New York and Oxford: Oxford University Press, 1986); Mario Praz, *The Romantic Agony*, 2nd edn, trans. Angus Davidson (London and New York: Oxford University Press, 1970); *The Earthly Chimera and the Femme Fatale: Fear of Woman in Nineteenth-Century Art*, exhibition catalog (Chicago, IL: David and Alfred Smart Gallery, 1981). Reinhold Heller, my dissertation adviser, organized this exhibition and wrote the preface for the catalog.
6 I have tried unsuccessfully to find the online interview with Menon in which I read of her puzzlement about the femme fatale's contemporary appeal.
7 Russill Paul, *The Yoga of Sound: Healing and Enlightenment through the Sacred Practice of Mantra* (Novato, CA: New World Library, 2004), p. 130.
8 Ibid., p. 130.
9 Amit Goswami with Richard E. Reed and Maggie Goswami, "I Choose Therefore I Am," in *The Self-Aware Universe: How Consciousness Creates the Material World* (New York: Jeremy P. Tarcher/Putnam, 1993), pp. 105–12.

10 Daniel Joseph Martinez, https://sfcamerawork.org/archive-2002-exhibitions (accessed April 27, 2025).
11 Anna Deavere Smith, in *AARP The Magazine*, September/October 2007.
12 Goswami, *The Self-Aware Universe*, p. 108.
13 Ibid., p. 234.
14 Ibid., p. 233.
15 Wayne Teasdale, *A Monk in the World: Cultivating a Spiritual Life* (Novato, CA: New World Library, 2002).
16 Paul, *The Yoga of Sound*, p. 130.
17 Wilde, "The Sphinx," p. 585.
18 Pamela Paul, *Pornified: How Pornography is Damaging our Lives, our Relationships, and our Families* (New York: Henry Holt, 2005) and Violet Blue, *The Smart Girl's Guide to Porn* (San Francisco, CA: Cleiss Press, 2006), p. 70.
19 See Joanna Frueh, "Vaginal Aesthetics," *Hypatia: A Journal of Feminist Philosophy* 18:4 (Fall/Winter 2003): 137–58 (special issue, *Women, Art, and Aesthetics*, ed. Peg Brand and Mary Devereaux). The piece includes three black-and-white self-portrait photos shot in collaboration with Ariana Page Russell. A longer version of "Vaginal Aesthetics" appears in Joanna Frueh, "Vaginal Action: Vagignosis," in *Swooning Beauty: A Memoir of Pleasure* (Reno, NV and Las Vegas, CA: University of Nevada Press, 2006), pp. 198–224.
20 Joanna Frueh, *Monster/Beauty: Building the Body of Love* (Berkeley and Los Angeles, CA and London: University of California Press, 2001), p. 11.
21 Lao Tzu, *Tao Teh Ching*, trans. John C. H. Wu (Boston, MA and London: Shambhala, 2003), p. 161.
22 Goswami, *The Self-Aware Universe*, p. 233.
23 Jill O'Bryan, *Carnal Art: Orlan's Refacing* (Minneapolis, MN and London: University of Minnesota Press, 2005).
24 Lao Tzu, *Tao Teh Ching*, p. 161.
25 Editorial note: The Rose perfume by Caron to which Frueh refers is no longer in their list. Its successor is Rose Ivoire: www.parfumscaron.com/en/collections/tous-les-parfums/products/rose-ivoire?_gl=1*14f1q43*_up*MQ..*_gs*NQ..&gclid=EAIaIQobChMI1ejkpKH0jAMVHIFQBh0LYwD7EAAYASAAEgJGn_D_BwE (accessed April 27, 2025).

Goddess of Roses, 2007

Clear glass vases loaded with white and cream-colored roses adorn the stage. As the houselights dim, Frueh enters stage left to stand at a microphone at center stage. Next to the microphone a clear glass of water sits on a hip-high metal stool. A black music stand holds the text. Stage left a table displays several items: three chocolate malts in old-fashioned metal containers, ready for pouring into classic soda-shop glasses; straws with the paper still covering them; a large bottle of Caron Rose perfume; and a vase full of red roses. A metal folding chair sits beside the table.

Frueh wears an ankle-length dress with three-quarter length sleeves. The color is ecru, the material lingerie light and a little stretchy, the effect elegant and sexy. Neither underwear nor stockings encumber Frueh. White satin mules with a rose and leaves near her unpainted toes clop gently when she walks. Pearl and diamond jewelry glimmers and glows.

Ease, grace, joy, majesty, and wonder: Frueh conveys those qualities whether she is as happy as a child drinking a chocolate malt, as authoritative as an oracle responding to the questions of a sovereign, or as honest as anyone can be confiding to a best friend.

Frueh speaks her text only when standing. Sitting, she drinks malts and dabs herself with perfume as the spirit moves her. She may offer a malt or two to the audience.

When did I know I am Goddess of Roses?

I give myself a sacred name because the crises through which I shaped my early fifties I also let transform me, from a person who believed in love but whose faith in it was less than large; from a viewer of bodies acting, preening, speaking on the screens of popular culture and each of our private imaginations – screens whose pictures we perceive to be reality – to a clearer seer of spirit, yours and hers and his and theirs: all larger than those pictures that array our fantasies.

Beginning in my twenties, many men and women have called me goddess.

It always surprises me. Like a couple of months ago when my yoga instructor exclaimed, after I told her my age upon her asking, "You are a goddess!"

At the house where I grew up, from ages 1 to 11, my father planted a row of roses. I was a goddess when I played around that rosebed, when my erotic magnitude and dignity have intrigued eye-wandering men in decades of my life from the teens into the present. My corporeal presence, they would say, if asked, stopped their wayward looking. No, that's my language. They say, in their own equivalent language, "She's hot," or "I want to fuck her." Here's what I see: their simple gazes are still unveiling the true aim of their hearts, which is love.

Roses: since ancient times, they are the flowers that symbolize spiritual and carnal love.

When did I know I am Goddess of Roses?

It began before I knew it, the way things always do. It began with my passion for pleasure. I was a little girl who ordered chocolate malts at just about every restaurant lunch; who masturbated often, pressing my upper thighs together for an orgasmic effect that still today is far more intense than any fingering of my clit can bring. Enthusiasm and sensuality marked my passions, and in my passionate mind, Dad's dazzling roses are always realigning me, when I am out of balance, into spiritual and carnal beauty.

When did I know I am Goddess of Roses?

When Tom, my first husband, said I looked like the female figures in Indian temple sculptures. Their simultaneously slender and voluptuous beauty, their bodies ornamented with jewelry and bits of clothing are elements that stunningly attract a viewer to the temples' lovemaking couples – to which these female figures belong.

Throughout my younger years, I sank too much in romantic quicksand.

You like to fuck me? Fine, I am a gorgeous body stuck on suffering, even though I revel in your lips and cock and all of our bodily charms pressing into one. One: it is the most important number. For even though our bodies separate after we come then touch some more, our love, no matter its false starts or apparent destitution, is the one and only conclusion that remains. Love draws us, everyone, together, like a master artist who sees the world as clearly as an angel.

All along I have been love. Only now, I am brave enough to name myself.

Goddess: I look and feel divine.

[Standing]

"Who do you think you are?" we ask when we suspect or detect arrogance. Someone who calls herself a goddess must be suffering from the delusion that she is supremely hot stuff. In response, I say, we need living proof of love.

Rosy friend and rosy lover, you are as divine as I am. According to the religion scholar Karen Armstrong in her book *Buddha*, "The ancient religions had believed that the deities, human beings and all natural phenomena had been composed of the same divine substance: there was no ontological gulf between humanity and the gods." The insights of Taoism and Confucianism in China, of Hinduism and Buddhism in India, and of rational philosophers such as Plato and Aristotle in Greece – all belonging to a period termed the Axial Age, 800 to 200 BCE – agree that, in Armstrong's words, "the Sacred was as close to us as our own selves." Gautama Buddha sought and found the knowledge of sacred self directly, in his own experience, by leaving the riches, protection, and goals in which he had been raised, as a prince, and deconditioning his mind. Consciously awakening to what appear to be the most mundane of perceptions is as valuable in deconditioning as are the many methods of stilling the mind in order to release it from the conditions of normal consciousness, with its practical considerations and its incessant repetitions of self-criticism, of critiques directed at other people, and of preconceptions.

Contemporary American society, so fixated on a rigidly narrow standard of human beauty that is a body devoid of mind and soul, can only ironically declare, "He looks like a Greek god." Because Apollo in appearance alone, in just the flesh, is divine solely in a colloquial way. Divinity in human form grows from self-discovery – the recognition of one's own radiant being, which is the recognition of love. Love is the essence of being human, and it is the expansion of that essence beyond oneself. We wear ourselves from the inside out. People cannot be genuinely human without being divine. Love gives itself, gives *of* itself. Giving is intrinsic to love, so intrinsic to the lover.

God gave a lot: in some people's minds, his fatherly womb created the universe. You, rosy friend, create the world every instant with your own conceptions and your preconceptions, from your tongue-lashings to your language of love, for the word is made flesh.

God gets lots of glory in the dictionary. *Webster's New World College Dictionary*, 4th edition, defines god as "deity," particularly, "male deity," and he has "special powers over the lives and affairs of people and the course of nature." "Deity" in that most general sense does not apply to "goddess," and the second definition in *Webster's* does not have an equivalent for "god": "a woman greatly admired, as for her beauty." Also, while "God" works all by itself – or himself – "Goddess" sounds correct with an article, "the" or "a," in front of it, and most people hear "goddess" with a lowercase "g."

Now and then, the minimization of "goddess" and the sexing of divinity, which unnecessarily divides divinity from One into two, tires Goddess of Roses, who knows that roses grow easily and grow everywhere, they grow wild and through breeding, their varieties are numerous as are their honey heady spicy fruity fragrances, they are beautifully spindly, husky, rambling, climbing, creeping, and trailing. Roses are many beauties within one, the genus *Rosa*. As people are many within the species of human beings.

Lover of roses, rosy lover, you likely presume that *human* entails human nature, which common belief holds to include goodness and evil and everything in between the two. We may think that *human* defined by that range of possible attitudes and behaviors is expansive. Indeed, that definition is inclusive. But if we take it as a fact, then we also take as fact that to be human is to hate and to put that hatred into action through cruelty, injustice, and hard-heartedness of all kinds.

Rosy friend, let us redefine ourselves. Let us be flagrant lovers, of ourselves and others. When we are alone in bed, let us caress ourselves to sleep. Gentle fingers on the forearm. Simple touches, like a palm pressed in circles to a knee sprained long ago, or knuckles softly kneading flesh below the navel. When we are with a person we call lover, lying side by side or skin within that rose's skin or enveloped by it, let us rediscover the humane in humanity. Let it be so much a part of our unconscious preferences and conscious acts that we are continually awakening to our own erotic power. Our culture equates *erotic* with sexual activity. That is simplistic. If we let it, the erotic, which is *connection*, can permeate our lives. The rose is a symbol of that connection, of sacred and profane love. *[Sitting]*

On New Year's Eve 2005 I watched eleven episodes of *Sex in the City*. Plenty of profane love. Previously, I'd only seen one program in its entirety and the end of another one. Both were on the two disks that my friend Becky had loaned me, so I skipped the episode I'd seen, and I learned, in the words of protagonist Carrie Bradshaw, the author of a sex column for a New York City daily, and through the events of her life and those of her three best girlfriends – all four are heterosexual – that everyone in New York is looking for sex. There I was, alone as the year turned and I'd soon be 58 (on January 18), not having had sex for a few years, lying on my velvety, gorgeous orange sofa, gazing now and then at the velvety red, long-stem roses given to me as a Christmas present by my friend Jill, and full of erotic power. Which was the awareness of my Indian temple goddess allure and my simple desire for sex with a man. There I was, ready for the velvet of my cunt to discover the velvet of a lover's cock. A week earlier, my friend Ariana and I had laughed for several delicious minutes after I exclaimed, "I haven't had sex for years!" She was having a man problem – exactly the kind that the *Sex in the City* girlfriends would have helped each other with – and she was asking for my counsel, so I surprised us both with my exclamation, to which Ariana responded, "But you've had a lot of sex!" "Yes, I have," I agreed, as we kept laughing. But after the divorce from my second husband, Russell, in 2001, I'd had a couple of lovers, nothing lasting, and no desire just to fuck around.

Ariana was asking for erotic knowledge, which may entail one's own experiences in the realm of sex, but more important, erotic knowledge is the wisdom of the rose.

When did I know I am Goddess of Roses?

When, after sleeping with a man or two in my fifties for whom I did not feel an animal connection, I breathed a sigh of relief in the recognition that chemistry with a man is nonnegotiable for me.

[Standing]

In their looking for sex, Carrie and her friends and all their dates, infatuations, and almost-fiancés are looking for connection, for their rose-fast roots – love that is divine in both the popular and spiritual usages of that word. The erotic is mysterious, because the rich and joyful connection that characterizes it cannot be explained. However, the erotic is not a mystery to be solved, and reveling in the erotic does not mean that we are muddled or that we should try to think ourselves out of some enigma by reasoning, speculating, or obsessing.

Connection is relation: people exist in relation to one another. A relation exists between one person's energy and another's response: warmth welcomes, aloofness intimidates, pushiness repulses, and seductively innocent sweetness can be inviting. Connection is a circuit of communication, the flow of any language – speech, sex, feelings – between people. Connection is success. Just as a batter connects with the ball, people connect with each other's words, bodies, and emotions as expressions of the soul. They connect with each other's mystery.

Dr. Elliot D. Abravanel knows that we don't know. In his *Dr. Abravanel's Body Type Diet and Lifetime Nutrition Plan*, he gives a sense of the mystery of human beings as he focuses on the body:

> We know, in a sort of gross way, what the body is made of. We have some sense of its composition at the material level. Yet, in the same way that we can't measure the soul, so too we have not been able to measure the energetic identities of the body that give rise to and sustain the physical body. Besides, in many areas we don't have a good sense of even its material construction. The trace minerals are a good example. Exactly which and how much we need, no one is sure. And their synergy with all the other nutrients, hormones, and chemicals of our body – that area is also mostly shadow right now.

Within the body, which many people in twenty-first-century America treat as though it were a strictly physical entity, connections are mysterious. In the erotic terrain of the body we look for answers to our questions about love, which grow from our stunning fear of love and desire for it. We look as we bare our skin to a stranger's gaze; as we enjoy breakfast for two at a favorite greasy spoon after a night of uncontrolled soul-to-soul encounter; as we prepare spaghetti marinara with a new crush after softly stroking each other's winged nature in a conversation of tongues that touch one another – both mouth to mouth and throat to inner ear; as we share our enjoyment of chocolate truffles with a friend who bought them just for us; as we gaze in a mirror at any age and wonder, Who am I?

[Sitting]

When did I know I am Goddess of Roses?

When today I touch myself, anywhere and in any way, that comes from smiling passion. When today, slim-hipped and ready for sex, I put my power in your hands. You: you may be the man whose fingers linger along his lips as he listens to me speak. The shine in your black hair is raising my awareness, of your beauty and of my wish to closely know that shine, its scent and thickness. That shine is awakening me to "Do the Non-Ado." So different from "Stand and deliver."

[Standing]

"Non-Ado" is one translation of the concept at the core of Taoist philosophy: *wuwei*, presented in the famous Chinese classic of sacred literature, Lao Tzu's *Tao Teh Ching*. The person in a state of *wuwei* is as present as can be. So *wuwei* cannot be mistaken for passivity or inaction, laziness or incompetence, cavalier or too casual. Receptivity and readiness, knowing, from the erotic integrity of all you are, when, how, and why to act, at ease in your responsiveness to life.

[Sitting]

Lovely in our Non-Ado, together, simply talking for the first time, we are sparkling. Which sets me wondering, when today you emerge in my mind, then into type, about the depths of sparkle. Is it a condition of the heart, lit with golden light that I breathe out to everyone near me, then everyone in the city where I live, and, graciously, to every fellow being on this world and in worlds past and next? The light that my yoga instructors have asked me to envision? You: I see you in my favorite desert, the one that people call Sonoran, next to a saguaro or offering me a margarita that you've made. You: I find you in my bed when I seem to be alone, when I am feeling lonely for the power of *your* slim hips in my hands. You ... and you, and you ... You promote my faith in the radical acts of love. You promote my faith in its availability.

[Standing]

When did I know I am Goddess of Roses?

When I see a white rose breathing, and as it breathes, it grows, to a scale of utter innocence.

When did I know I am Goddess of Roses?

When I see blue roses, infinitely shaped, like snowflakes. Blue roses do not exist in nature, and despite genetic engineering by companies such as Florigene, a blue rose has yet to be produced. The blue rose has symbolized the impossible. O rosy friends and lovers, you are the turquoise, cobalt, and periwinkle that I see, the sky and powder and baby blues, the inherent beauty of blue moon romance and bird-wing shimmer. You are the possibilities engineered by the open heart.

[Sitting]

When did I know I am Goddess of Roses?

When I wear Rose, a perfume that its producer, Caron, describes as "embodying all the delicacy of a rosebud plucked at dawn" and "ultra feminine with a touch of exotic class." How seductive yet vague those phrases are. More than only inklings of the perfume's power come to me through the public relations poetry of Caron, and yet the perfume remains a mystery.

[An assistant comes onstage from the audience, dabs perfume on herself, and passes the bottle to a person in the front row. The bottle circulates through the audience, people dabbing themselves with it as they please. The assistant brings the bottle back to Frueh after everyone has helped themselves to the crystal's touch and the liquid's scent.]

In my own mystery, I know this: like the whole rose plant, I am passionately fragrant everywhere – petals, stem, and leaves. Like a whole rose garden – people have planted them in small towns and capital cities throughout the world – I am precious: beloved and desirable and held in high esteem.

[Standing]

Rose Précieuse: it is one of the rose perfumes created by Ernest Daltroff for the House of Caron. Dated 1910, Rose Précieuse is no longer available. But I am; in my complete color, shape, and fragrance, which is passion. Another Daltroff rose perfume, created in 1936 and also no longer in production, is La Fête des Roses. Festival or celebration or merrymaking of roses. Goddess of Roses knows all about that!

[Sitting]

When did I know I am Goddess of Roses?

When I understood what people meant when they told me, about my writing, teaching, performing, and simply myself, "You're refreshing." That response had come into my ears over decades, and I finally heard it after I became friends with Becky, a colleague in the Art Department at the University of Nevada, Reno. Her innocence refreshes *me*, and I saw my own innocence reflected in hers. Innocence: an ability to perceive the world freshly, to be present, as in *wuwei*.

When did I know I am Goddess of Roses?

When I taught love as a subject in a university seminar in the spring semester of 2003. We read books whose authors come to the subject of love from different perspectives: Denis de Rougemont, *Love in the Western World* – historical; Norman O. Brown, *Love's Body* – philosophical; Wendy Langford's *Revolutions of the Heart: Gender, Power, and the Delusions of Love* – sociological. The books served as an intellectual grounding for our conversations, and sometimes as an emotional one too, as people – all of them in their twenties – sometimes reacted to the readings with passionate likes and dislikes. But the true basis of our class, in which all of us were teachers and students, was the reciprocity of love among us. The class was disarmingly humane. Men cried, and they wrote papers whose depth of feeling and self-exploration astounded me. The eyes and the writing of people who hardly ever spoke told of their presentness. One day I walked into the classroom laughing and singing the theme song for the TV show *The Love Boat*, and I sang Nick Cave's "The Ship Song" the same day, during my lecture on de Rougemont's book. We were all Goddesses and Gods of Roses, for our love supported our ability to enter the erotic, to speak about the mysteries of love, and to apply our erotic wisdom later in the semester to the work and the writings of contemporary artists and, of course, to the artwork of the students in the class, all of whom were pursuing a BFA in the Art Department at the University of Nevada, Reno.

In that class we redefined *humanity* with our humaneness. Love typified our relations. As individuals and as a group, we developed faith in our capacity to hold one another in our hearts when we expressed ideas and emotions and faith in our capacity to be held. Indeed, one day – it may have been when I was reading a poem by Diane Wakoski about how men leave her breathless – I felt myself on the verge of tears, and I was afraid to cry. Yet at the same time I wanted to, because to withhold the tears was to withhold my rosy heart, the heart that wished to reveal itself more fully to my classmates. So, almost in a whisper, I asked, "Is it okay if I cry? Are you here? With me?" Their faces said Yes, but fear had me repeating or rephrasing my questions. Again, my classmates' faces responded lovingly, and then Evan spoke softly: "Yes." That day was an awakening for me, one of many with that group, and one of many in the past few years as I have grown into my rosiness with the confidence to call myself Goddess of Roses. By giving my classmates my heart, I let them give theirs to me … so I could give more of mine … and they could give more of theirs …

[Standing]

In the reciprocity of mutual giving we come to know that the infinity that is love is available. To give love is to open oneself to its reception, to become receptive to love.

Whatever is common to people or typical of them we call human.

However, the typical or common is not necessarily the essential, though it may appear to be. The typical or common may become so through social or historical patterns, such as ethnic hatreds that breed wars, physical abuse that repeats through generations of a family, and women's repulsion by their own bodies in the late twentieth and early twenty-first centuries because of increasing media focus on the generic "ideal" of tall, slim, blonde, and big-breasted. The "human" seems so – seems real – because we've known it for millennia or decades.

Lush rose and rosy lover, eros is Aphrodite's art, and it is yours. Eros, meaning love in Greek. Eros, the ancient art of connection.

[Sitting]

Eros, it gave me and my classmates the confidence to pursue emotional and psychic, intellectual and profound knowledge.
[Standing]

Com, with, plus *fidere*, to trust, is the basis for the Latin *confidere*, which means *to confide*. Confidence derives from *confidere*, and one of the roots of *faith* is the Latin *fidere*. These ancient linguistic connections among faith, trust, confiding, and confidence bring to that last word a depth that we miss when we think of confidence only as self-assurance. Who asks herself: Am I willing to confide in myself? Am I my most trusted friend? Can I be my confidante rather than my confessor who every day belabors a multiplicity of mea culpas? Do I live with faith?
[Sitting]

With faith. I used to struggle, because I feared my faith. I struggled with the gently honest expression of emotion, the feelings that miss their mark, that die when people push and force on others their words and moods, their neurotic desperation for love; the feelings whose funeral is bluntness and confrontation.

For example, asking for men's love by declaring "I think we ought to sleep together" before a reciprocity had seduced us there; wanting their compliments by manipulating a conversation into the subject of beautiful women and squeezing their desire for me – which often was real but not ready, then or perhaps ever, to be stated or acted on – out of that subject. Oh, I was skilled at impatience and disappointment.

I didn't know that faith, or rather its weakness, was troubling me. Even though a student in a performance art class that I taught at the University of Arizona in 1983 had seen right through me. I don't know what provoked the following statement, but one day she completely surprised me with something like, "You don't know what you want. You lack faith." Which reminds me of another student, also in her early twenties, a year or two later, who advised me, after I'd expressed doubt about some ability of mine, "Have no doubt." The guides are always right in front of us. The roses. But our vision may be dim, and it diminishes our confidence.

I certainly taught, performed, and wrote confidently, and I had a bold confidence in my sexual and physical attractiveness and my style, which enhanced them. Bare legs, ankle boots and anklets,

Mary Janes, long hair, richly colored lips, sensuous fabrics like leather, velvet, lace, and satin that fit well, that flow and sometimes flutter, that often cling: they have fashioned a self-assured person who loves her body and feels good in it, naked or clothed. "The Goddess of Style": that's what my second ex-husband's partner straightforwardly called me at a party at her and Russell's home when she suggested to a girlfriend of hers who was looking for some suede high-heeled pumps that she'd be wise to consult with me. In my writing, performing, teaching, and style I've been very confident, in the usual way that we use that word. My work and my style exude aplomb and daring.

Yet, with deeper faith in spontaneity, in the glowing uniqueness of this rose, in the free and easy following of her erotic ways, I could loosen my grip on my own heart. I could let the content of *me* – every energy – lighten. I could learn, as Lao Tzu advises in the *Tao Teh Ching*, to "Do the Non-Ado." Which means to move like water does: it simply goes where nothing stops it. And to be flexibly strong, like tree branches in a wind. And to be soft – to be humane. To myself before all others, because what I am is what I give, and as my therapist Larry says, "The way we do relationships is the way we do relationships." I *am* my heart and I can observe my heart. I have a relationship with it and can feel its connections and disconnections. At times in the past year I've felt my heart aching. No heart attack. Simply a heartache that feels expansive, like a yoga posture inside my body, clearing the glop, mass, and blob that obstruct the light.

Faith is a particular kind of confidence. With faith, the denseness of impacted woe that has weighed down my heart dissolves, and solid pain – obstruction – transforms into weightless light.

Aphrodite, created by the Greeks to be loved for the lightness of her laughter and her smiles. Shared smiles and laughter both generate and emerge from our humaneness. Aphrodite, goddess of intimate connections between soul-revealing skin, my goddess who I choose as sister, my close companion who supports my appetite for chocolate malts and sex and men, my every move, you are risen from water, birthed in foam – they say it was produced by the severed genitals of an aged Uranus – and foam, they say, the Greek *aphros*, gave you your name. Give me my name, O Aphrodite, the name that transforms misperceptions with a kiss. Goddess of Roses!

I kiss myself into being, and as I do, my kiss is healing an old wound of yours. They say that one of your son Eros's arrows happened to graze you, just as you were looking at the mortal beauty, Adonis, who one day out hunting would die from the attack of a wild boar. As you ran to aid Adonis, a thorn tore your flesh, and so you bled. Perhaps you wore a white rose, hanging between your breasts on a necklace, clasped in your hair, or wound with many others in a wreath. Perhaps wild white roses grew near you as you bent, in an agony of erotic and fearful passion, to pull the thorn from your body. But it grew in your heart, for you could not save Adonis. They say that white roses were your flower until blood from that accident colored the white petals red. An accident, a stain, a stabbing in your heart: let me retrieve you from the gloom that you have suffered. Let my kiss nurse you as we deck ourselves in white and creamy roses, and let us, together, find the lovers as they find us, who know our name: Goddess of Roses.

[Standing]

What others name us, we become. That is why name-calling can be such a powerful weapon of lasting denigration to its object. And what we name ourselves, we are.

[Sitting]

Call me a name, O Aphrodite! Call me into being.

Call me the name that transforms weight to lightness, I asked my goddess long ago: maybe in my mother's belly; maybe when I read about the Greek and Roman deities in third grade; maybe when I mistook faith for belief, which resides in the bedrock of a human heart and which, though people say it is the same as faith, demands a drubbing into a person's consciousness or a conscious logic. Conscious logic sometimes is another kind of drubbing, and it forces our own lived experience into silence. O Aphrodite, call me the name that gives and begets kisses, I asked the many times when faith has been a word that has escaped me. O Goddess, we kiss ourselves into humaneness.

[Standing]

And so the heavy water turns to foam.

Friends and lovers, let us flower in the humaneness we give to roses. They receive our loving care, and they grow with our faith in sunlight and water. Roses love the light.

Humane and *human* both derive from the Latin *humanus*, and humane originally meant human. Humane today stands for the best qualities of human beings. It is a more specialized word than human is, as if respect and kindness, care and generosity occur under uncommon conditions and are offered by atypical people. Perhaps only the humane person is a specialist in love. Or perhaps we think that love is so special that we reserve it for certain people, thereby withholding it a lot of the time. Love withheld forms a blockage in the body – a glop, a mass, a blob – a discomfort caused by what we believe to be discriminating taste in people. We discriminate with our love: I love *you*, I don't love *you*; I love you more than I love him; I love you less than I love her. We separate and measure, and our discrimination only appears to be synonymous with taste or reason or passion. Blockage is lack of freedom: energy or fecal matter or words don't move easily. If we were not so discriminating, we would be freer, and we would not sever our love from its home – in our fellow roses, in the rose that is ourselves. To see clearly, unprejudicially, is to discriminate in a process of freedom: by being present, observing ourselves and other people, we give ourselves the opportunity to release them and us from familial and cultural patterns that have "specialized" not only in obstructing the freedom of soul-and-mind-inseparable-from-body, but also in embalming it. Rosiness is the antithesis of death.

[Sitting]

When did I know I am Goddess of Roses?

When I broke my wrist in May 2002 and let the summer be slow and still. I'd traveled to Lake Worth, Florida, next to Palm Beach, to debut my one-woman show, *The Aesthetics of Orgasm*, on May 14. I arrived between 8 and 9 o'clock the night before the performance and checked in at the hotel ravenous for food and hoping that its restaurant would be open for at least another hour. It was, and I ate a substantial meal of fish, rice, and vegetables. The hotel was only blocks from the beach, and I asked, either at the front desk or in the restaurant, if a woman could safely walk to the beach alone. I wanted to hear the water. That had been my desire before leaving home. Seeing the ocean hadn't been my goal, but I had imagined myself being at its edge and hearing the huge movement of wave upon wave. Like many people, I let water mesmerize and calm me – from a rush of ocean waves over my feet to a stream flowing by me seated in wildflowers and low grasses. The past school year, just ending, had been both strenuous and renewing. Not because of classes or meetings or colleagues, but because it started shortly after Russell, my husband of twelve years, and I divorced, and its first month brought a lover to me – his completely unexpected declaration of attraction astonished me – and our affair, ardent and intermittent, lasted into the spring. I wrote *The Aesthetics of Orgasm* as a paean and a prayer. I theorized the beauty of sexual pleasure, rhapsodizing about its details with my lover and offering throughout the performance a wish, unlikely to have been known by anyone but myself, for my lover and I to continue as a couple. I knew that the fulfillment of that wish was unlikely, and the strain of that knowledge had contributed greatly to my May exhaustion. So had my continuing sadness over the deaths of my parents – Dad in July 1999 and Mom in March 2000. Deaths and divorce had heralded a huge change in my life – the psychic independence that can come when you are a parentless midlife person and when you are a single woman for the first time since your early twenties. Such an oceanic change that I now give myself the name Goddess of Roses.

The ocean was farther than I'd been led to believe by the waiter, or maybe it simply felt farther because my exhaustion that night had me in a twilight zone of simultaneous tension and limpness. Despite assurances that the walk and the beach were safe, I felt on guard, and my tripping a couple of times on my way surprised me. I thought, Oh, my shoes are too big, and I'm clumsy in them, but I knew that my stumbling came from physical and mental fatigue. When, after what felt like too long a walk, the ocean's voice embraced me, I sobbed as these words suddenly filled me at the shore: "I finally made it." I consciously repeated them to myself, more than once, as if I was making sure that I had actually heard them in my mind, because they surprised me as much as my stumbling had. Well-known artists exhibited at the Palm Beach Institute, but my "making it" didn't have anything to do with my career. Here I was, at the edge of a continent and a long way from home; here I was at the edge of a new life, after the endings of my parents' lives, of a marriage, an ardently sexual affair, and another school year. As the ocean at once lulled and excited me, Mom and Dad felt strongly present. That surprised me too, because I certainly hadn't come to the edge of the ocean to search for them or call to them, and I certainly hadn't expected to find them on that eerie and enlightening night. I felt so very far from Reno, where I was living, so very far from friends and family, and I felt so much the stranger, anonymous yet self-conscious, almost falling over her own feet. But there at the edge of the ocean I felt the edge of my own existence giving way. I felt amorphous, expansive, apprehensive, and ready. So my parents assured me, in one of those conversations that spontaneously happen with the dead, that indeed I'd made it and all was well.

Some lines from a song that I wrote for a performance of mine in 1985 come to mind as I recall myself that night before I broke my wrist the next day: "Well, I finally made it / Take me to the edge ... / We'll shake out the dead." That's what I was doing at night with the ocean and on the next day.

[Standing]

So many of us are worn out – now and then or permanently – from being the living proof of death; and as such, we are the oxymoronic evidence of self-devaluation. "I'm only human," we say, which appears to state the fact that people make mistakes. Yet we are humane to forgive one another for our mistakes, rather than calling someone else's mistakes to their attention when we're not seeing eye to eye or when we're going over, in our minds, our mea culpas for the umpteenth time. *I'm only human* seems to place people in a position of culpability and to lower our humanity by emphasizing the exclusiveness of our species: we are only human and not divine. Divinity, manifest in the bodies of generous goddesses and gods, ourselves as rosy friends and lovers, forgives, and as it does so, divinity releases people from their self-made bondage in sin, guilt, and error of all varieties. Thus the erotics of forgiveness comes into focus. Divinity lives within the goddess and god, but people generally fail to experience their own divinity, because they are looking for the body of deity as made by artists across the eras and cultures of earth. They are looking for a symbolic body rather than in-the-flesh divinity.

How do you, living in a rose garden though you may not know it, perceive this phrase? *To err is human, to forgive divine.* Does it separate the human and the divine, into human as error and divine as forgiveness? Or does it suggest that although people make mistakes, the divinity within themselves can forgive those deviations from kindness, generosity, open-mindedness, and other qualities that comprise love?

People do let error bind them. The author Jerry Stahl, interviewed by Terry Gross on June 24, 2005, on her PBS (Public Broadcasting Service) show *Fresh Air*, stated: "We're all in love with our pain." One way to translate that is, We're all in love with our errors. Error causes pain to ourselves and others. So why hold onto error with such passion? One reason: it preserves the integrity of the familiar, and many of us have made error into a foundation of human existence. To move away from the familiar appears to entail leaping into a void. *Leap into the Void*: that's the title of a mid-twentieth-century artwork created by Yves Klein. The piece is startling the first time you see a reproduction of it in a book. Klein, dressed in a suit, appears to be flying. Then we notice that he's leapt out of the second-story window of a building on a quiet street. In actuality, he jumped into a tarpaulin, but in one version of the photo the tarp is excised, which emphasizes the daring of his act, the risk of injury or death. Yet, with his arms outspread, he looks like he's soaring. The image that Klein created in *Leap into the Void* is a metaphor for any leap – creative, imaginative, intellectual ... divine. We don't know where we're going. Ahh, a perfect chance to do the Non-Ado!

And we also know *exactly* where we're going; which is away from where we've been. That sounds simplistic, if not simple-minded, yet when we spread our divine – angelic rosy – wings we stop recreating and reworking error. We fall in love with something very different from pain, and we court different kinds of lovers. In Verse 23 of the *Tao Teh Ching*, Lao Tzu writes that "he who courts after Loss is at one with Loss." Likewise, those who court after error become one with error. And those who court after love become one with love. *[Sitting]*

Jill used to say that she needed her darkness to make her art. That reminds me of a belief that I'd probably held since I was a child and that came into my conscious mind in my early twenties: I couldn't be or wasn't an artist because I wasn't crazy. My father had painted from when I was very little into my teens and then created elegant collages into his old age, and both Mom and Dad knew a lot about art. Although he was a businessman, Dad was very much an art historian, and the bookshelves at home housed many volumes about art, mostly modern work. I copied Picassos when I was in second grade, and I read about art too, easily remembering an image and connecting it with an artist's name. Art was second nature to me. Probably in those art books, or maybe in the words of an elementary school teacher, or in comments made by Mom and Dad about their dear friend the renowned Chicago architect and often alcoholic Robert Tague – who my sister Ren and I called Uncle Bob – I "learned" that artists are crazy: melancholic and suicidal, sexually misfitting into culture at large, and addicted to drugs and other bad habits. I believed that artists are in love with error. And I didn't think that my position in the world of error, even though I was depressed from my teens into my late twenties, merited the name of artist.

Then, some year or decade later, I realized in one of those *satoris* – a truth that appears to come out of nowhere, like a lightning flash – that find us all now and then, that I was sane and I was an artist, and sanity helped my art. Out of nowhere? Ha! Out of sanity itself, which is related to love. For when we become healthier it is because we have become more loving, of both ourselves and others. Health is wholeness, soul-and-mind-inseparable-from-body living in ease, in contrast to dis-ease. Wholeness is being at one with ourselves. One: it is the number of completeness, in which everything is connected. It is the erotic number.

When do I know I am Goddess of Roses?

When I've gathered up the pieces of my heart from all the places that I've left them. In this life or in a past life: as an oracle trashed by the competitive jealousy of an old-guard medium; as a priestess seer who stopped seeing because horrors in the future were stacking up; as an actress who grew older in a century even more debilitated than ours by the belief in the overweening value of young women; as a child so tortured by the Holocaust that her spirit had crawled into a corner; as a mother who witnessed the slaughtering of the children in her tribe; as a woman who in some battlefield in medieval Europe held her husband, who was as open to love as she was, while he died. Drowning, alcoholism, isolation, sex without pleasure, numbings that resulted from depleted eros and from keeping eros at a distance. My gathering continues, and eros flowers from and on my very lips. Lately people say – from the "out of nowhere" that is a revelation to me – "I've never seen you grin like that!"

When did I know I am Goddess of Roses?

When it became clear to me that studying error does not solve it.

Lately I've been unearthing myself. I am an archaeologist, intent on piecing together fact from fiction but without a desire to study a history of pain and error. And too, I am an anthropologist of ecstasy, an Aphrodite with no need to repent. I am a shape exposed to sunlight, and both the finder and the sculptor of that shape.

[Standing]

How often we sculpt hard forms from the softness that is the relaxed heart.

Not only does the heart itself harden – arterial sclerosis; and we talk about hard-heartedness and hearts of stone – but also we let the arteries that convey ideas, such as entertainment and fashion media, everyday language in which cultural perceptions are embedded, and the foci and findings of scholars' research, become sclerotic. So we live in a mental sclerosis, and it's been passed on by generations of families. As well as scholars, some of whom are feminists. In their learning and smartness, academics name the damage. They imply or explain a form of heartbreak, in myriad permutations, without moving on or with, perhaps, lip service to change that is only minimally motivating. We need descriptions and accounts and embraces of pleasure in order to alter the dynamics of our psychic and bodily circuitry. Isn't this the problem, that we've become wired for pain? That people are inadvertently, unwittingly, and unconsciously heart-hardened and heartbroken most of the time? That very wiring causes people to replicate the pain. All those implications and explanations are rehearsals for more of the same, which are the dramatic productions that we call living.

[Sitting]

When did I know I am Goddess of Roses?

When Russell, in the first months of our love, called Joanna in her old age Silver Sex Lady. Thank you, Russell, for naming an erotic reality into which I Joanna, Goddess of Roses, am growing. In that name I see a graceful woman, well aligned in soul-and-mind-inseparable-from-body. Silver Sex Lady, Silver Siren, calling for lovemaking when and if I desire it, luring with a luster that comes without stopping from my innocent imagination.

When did I know I am Goddess of Roses?

When I was walking with a friend past a hedge and she exclaimed something like this: "That poor little branch, struggling to survive!" I distinctly remember her use of "struggling." Before she had spoken, I'd noticed red leaves extending upward through the mass of green. My thoughts had been: What a beautiful red! What a beautiful contrast with the green, and everything looks so healthy. So my friend's comment surprised me.

I didn't say anything to her about her comment, but the difference between our responses struck me, for it indicated a difference in consciousness. That little incident of literally not seeing the same thing began my cognizant awareness of the pained, ashamed, knee-jerk, and negative perceptions that numerous people project onto occurrences and behaviors that they witness, experience, or hear about. My consciousness was opening and softening – sweetening – in such a way that struggle felt awkward to me, uncomfortable, part of the supposed way things are that now appeared as perception, projection, and concept. Like the presumed dullness of all older people's natural hair color. That is a cultural concept and a projective habit.

I noticed people struggling with problems that they had imagined into reality: look and look and look for troubles and you'll see them everywhere. Someone assumed that I scrutinize my body, looking, looking, looking over every inch, seeing the disrepair that she sees on her own. She says she scrutinizes her body, so she imagines that I do as well, especially because so much of my work focuses on the body – my own and others', and in theoretical as well as experiential ways. I corrected her misperception with "I observe myself." Scrutiny – its object is the minutest detail, its goal the detection of error, so it damns the body by finding what it is looking for.

[Standing]

Scrutiny steals us away from the entirety of the body: how it feels to the eyes and the fingers; how it is a *whole* shape, a *whole* surface;

how we recognize people through their overall demeanor, through their posture, gait, and energy. The nineteenth-century English poet and painter Dante Gabriel Rossetti wrote, "The eyes the sungate of the soul unbar." That line appears in a love poem – of which he wrote many – and he was a master of the love poem; and, in the context of scrutiny, Rossetti's vision has leapt into my mind as an antidote: Goddess of Roses sees her eyes shining on her own body and others' eyes shining on their own bodies.

Scrutiny steals the heart. It steals our own hearts from ourselves, let alone stealing the heart out of any relation with another person when we scrutinize them. A beauty culture that teaches the public to scrutinize oneself is simultaneously teaching it to scrutinize everyone.

When did I know I am Goddess of Roses?

When I see Aphrodite crowned in white rose petals. They are a thicket of white. They are her hair itself, styled in the name of love.

When did I know I am Goddess of Roses?

When I see any sister goddess plaited in pearls.

When did I know I am Goddess of Roses?

When I see diamonds crowning Aphrodite's head. They are an array of sundance.

When did I know I am Goddess of Roses?

When I let the soul unbar the sungate.

You may think that Goddess of Roses is sentimental not to sit in a suffering gaze. Maybe the sunny vision seems easy, too easy. Maybe you'd tell Goddess of Roses that you need your darkness. Or maybe you'd tell her that your darkness is you and that it is normal to humanity. Goddess of Roses would not contest you. She would simply stay in the sun, not to mock you or to abandon you or to act superior, but rather because that's where she's at home. She might say that ease comes from the effort of erotic will, and that once you've found the sun, you feel the effort of suffering. Erotic will requires energy, but suffering is a labor that circles your undereyes in deep purple, that itches your inner eyelids, that shoots blood into the whites. Suffering as a daily modus operandi closes the sungate.

When did I know I am Goddess of Roses?

When I let eros guide my hearing.

How many times has Goddess of Roses heard or read the following statement? “I’m terrified of getting old.” Sometimes, “Like everyone” precedes it. When Goddess of Roses hears or reads that statement, she has recognized various feelings. She has felt a pall surround her. She has felt queasy. She has felt repulsed. Words are food, and she has felt sickened. Words can lodge in the abdomen. In through the ears and down the digestive tract of consciousness. A mass, glob, or obstruction may find a home for years in the belly. The words that have turned your stomach have turned you ill. When Goddess of Roses hears or reads the statement “Like everyone, I’m terrified of getting old,” she has felt a pang from her chest through her pelvic floor, and she’s sucked in her breath, just a little, because suffering is trying to take that breath away, to turn her into a cadaver right then and there. Suddenly, she recognizes the romance of suffering. People have such an affection for it, and they take it on like a lover, letting it sleep with them and invade their every dream. Ahh, suffering … an adventure in wayward inspiration.

Spiritus: meaning, in Latin, breath, life, the soul, and courage. Inspire: to take in breath, which is the breath of life, to become spirited. The breath that we take in may enliven or sicken us: what’s in the air? It is the air that carries words into our bodies. O, erotic air, carry my words into my own belly and beyond.

Goddess of Roses has let down her guard
She’s come down from the mountain
You were afraid that she’d be full of frowns
Oh, she’s a gentle fountain

[Sitting]

When did I know I am Goddess of Roses?

When I wanted an art of uplift. Spirit encouraged. Spirits rising.

[Standing]

For a general public, an essence of art is beauty and art serves to elevate the viewer. Those traditional values do not pertain to a great deal of today’s art. People educated in contemporary art practices know an aesthetics of ugliness, which began in Western art in the nineteenth century with Realism. Among other subjects, those artists depicted laborers and everyday situations, bodies and scenes that radically departed from the classical model of the nude – a body clothed in beauty, like a god or goddess – and from traditional ideas of ennoblement.

Twentieth- and twenty-first-century art includes countless examples of Realist progeny, from the mild, such as Man Ray's 1921 black-and-white photograph of washing hung out to dry, to the gross, such as Daniel Joseph Martinez's *Self-Portrait #7: George and Daniel. In an insane world it was the sanest choice* (2000), a color photo of a man shot in the head, blood splurting (digital manipulation gives realism to the shooting.) Such an aesthetics of the everyday and of the topically political and social is one identifying characteristic of contemporary art. In a statement for his exhibition "Without Anesthesia OR This isn't a Nice Neighborhood," Martinez speaks about suffering. The following statement appears on the website for SF Camerawork, where the show was installed from October 29 through November 30, 2002.

> Many of us suffer tremendous pain, and we have numbed ourselves to such a degree that we don't know how to feel anymore. We've lost touch with our own selves, our own bodies, our own souls. There are many different ways to uncover those things that have been numb for so long. Sometimes the nerve endings need to be laid bare. They need to be raw again. In order to heal a wound, sometimes you have to open it up to let the disease out. And sometimes you need to do that without anesthesia.

Goddess of Roses thinks that open and opened up wounds are everywhere.

She sees, hears, smells, and senses them leaking their poisons, their pain, in the classrooms where she teaches and the restaurants she frequents and the airports through which she travels. Leaking, from bodies, voices, gaits, and postures, the subtle angers, the twitching guts, the programmed responses to the unpredictabilities of life, whose delights are plentiful. People say that we're desensitized to horror, and Goddess of Roses says, We're desensitized to beauty, love, and gentleness.

How often Goddess of Roses has heard, read, or observed the following statement, which holds people in its toxic embrace:

"Every day I find some new and awful thing on my body – a line, a sag. You know what I mean." People who make such a statement assume that others do not stand in any relation to their bodies that is different from it. Self-loathing and severe self-critique are commonplace public speech – people confessing to journalists, on reality TV shows and in fashion magazines, the details and extent of bodily dissatisfaction unto detestation.

[Sitting]

Sometimes we are literally taught to focus on ugliness and wounds. My friend Erin told me that a writing teacher in college assigned the class to recount a horrible – the most horrible? – experience that they had had. "Why not assign writing about the best experience?" I wondered as Erin and I talked about the dearth of happiness in people's lives. Thinking once again of the *Tao Teh Ching*, those who focus on sadness become sadness, and I remember hearing in my early days as an art critic that it's easiest to write about art that you don't like because that results in a stronger piece. I always disagreed. Why would I want to take away my happiness, which was the process of exploring art that I enjoyed?

[Standing]

In the context of the psychological obviousness of Lao Tzu's wisdom, of the emotionally grueling aesthetics of some contemporary art, and of the fearful, dispirited statements about life and the body, without speech or images that transform the wounded spirit, eyes and ears are hellgates, and the spirit stays wounded.

[Sitting]

When do I know I am Goddess of Roses?

When I see changes, like contours softening at my throat, capillaries on my legs, looser skin on the backs of my hands. When I see that I am real. When, for the sake of beauty and humaneness, I am humane to myself, including ways that some feminists might say make me a slave to conventions of a beauty culture that stamps its approval only on those who look younger, sleeker, untouched by time or living – a world gone crazy over the surface appearance of bodies. I love the pleasure and effects of regular facials, sometimes with a glycolic peel or microdermabrasion. I've had laser work on my face, and it is clearer, creamier, and firmer than it would otherwise be. I have trained with weights for over twenty-five years and practiced yoga, on my own since my early twenties and in classes since my mid-fifties. I'm not immune to the culture I live in, and I conform to it in ways. I also spend time and money on myself the way that goddesses do, on feeling and looking happy.

When did I know I am Goddess of Roses?

When I dreamed the word *ahimsa* above my bed. *Ahimsa*, a Sanskrit word, is one of the five *yamas*, which themselves belong to what yoga practitioners know as the "eight limbs" of classical yoga. (*Asana*, the postures that have gained popularity in the United States, is only one of the eight limbs.) The *yamas* are spiritual practices, coming from within a person and exercised in the outer world, that manifest right behavior. In this context, "right" is not the opposite of "wrong," and it certainly does not mean righteous – proceeding from a sense of justice that probably proceeded from judgments cast in a moralistic frame of mind. In the plainest and purest way, the yogic "right" means true. Together, in this room, you and I are seeking the rightness of the rose. That search asks us for a lifetime of erotic effort. *Ahimsa* means nonviolence, do no harm. Phrasing this in the positive and with a historical example, Gandhi set in motion the transformation of India by rooting it in peaceful protest, the exercise of *ahimsa*. In the United States, Martin Luther King, Jr., impressed by Gandhi's methods and success, educated civil rights workers – and the entire country – in peaceful protest, what most of us know as "nonviolent protest." The right action of *ahimsa* involves peaceful practice towards oneself as well as others. Indeed, if we do not use peaceful words to describe ourselves to ourselves, and if our actions towards ourselves are not peaceful, we incapacitate our speaking and acting in peaceful ways towards others.

[Standing]

Do no harm: and we become harmless? In other words, weak, passive, so soft-spoken that no one can or cares to hear us? The connotations of harmless interfere with its truth. *Ahimsa* is one way to Do the Non-Ado. In other words, rather than being reactive to what we perceive as a slight from a colleague or to the pervasive self-criticism that beauty culture generates, we can observe ourselves – thoughts, feelings, bodily sensations – in order to be ourselves, not preconditioned automatons. Peaceful words and actions proceed from observation, which is different from analysis, speculation, or self-aggrandizing evaluations, because observation stills and calms us; it creates a state of peacefulness, no matter how momentary. To choose the observation of ourselves or of anything that our senses and sensitivities bring to us results in less and less violence, whether inwardly or outwardly directed.

[Sitting]

So *ahimsa* floated steadily above me in my bed. The word looked just as I type it – nothing fancy, and all lower case. The word was so real, and everything in my bedroom was as it actually was. Maybe I was doing some lucid dreaming, when, as you're dreaming, you know that's what you're doing. The physical and the metaphysical met up in my bedroom.

In the morning I felt amazed by the dream. It had enlightened me, and it has stayed with me.

[Standing]

Ahimsa enhances the powers of Goddess of Roses: the actualization of kindness and compassion, and they enhance the beauty for which she cares in metaphysical as well as physical ways.

[Sitting]

As I was writing about *ahimsa* announcing itself in a lucid dream, I happened to open a secondhand book given to me by Ariana. It's pop psychology from 1976, and the subject is love. On the title page, part of an old inscription reads: "Dreams are worth working on." Ariana adds her own sentiments below an arrow she has drawn that points to "dreams": "Yes they are!"

When did I know I am Goddess of Roses?

When the summer of the broken wrist became a summer of meditation, which some would call a metaphysical practice. Nothing formal. No one taught me – gave me a mantra, advised me to sit cross-legged or on a special cushion, said, "Concentrate on your breathing, don't worry about distractions, and let your breathing bring you back from them." Lying on my back on the wood floor of my living room was very comfortable during the weeks when my arm was in a cast. In the afternoons, the sunlit glow of the wood floor drew me down to a position and a level in which the comfort of gravity felt more profound than when I sat on the sofa or a chair. As I lay more or less in *savasana*, for my right arm in the cast had little mobility, I seemed to sink, all of my external body and my organs, equally into the gentle pull of gravity. *Savasana* is the *asana* of relaxation, of surrender, with arms, hands facing up, far enough away from the body to free the armpits, and legs a few feet apart, little toes turning to the floor.

[Frueh stands, holding the microphone at the sitting position]

Nectar-sweet, nuanced, and renewed, I stand here in my bold innocence, capable of asking forever, When did I know I am Goddess of Roses? The anecdotes, emotions, and philosophy are infinite, just as the history, lore, and legend of roses are, just as their scents and colors also appear to be. My words create a carpet for this room, like the roses, some say knee-deep, that covered the floors of Cleopatra's palace the first time that she and Mark Antony met. A layer of roses is said to have been strewn around her bed where they made love.

Savasana comes at the end of an *asana* practice. In *savasana*, all previous postures are absorbed in a processing that involves muscle memory, perceptual openness, and offering of the heart, the yoking – yoga means yoke – of body, mind, and spirit. The posture is one of surrender, in which you absorb what you've learned without thinking about it, without having to. *Savasana* is translated in English as Corpse Pose. The body is still … in its infinite aliveness … in order to absorb the beauty.

Frueh's assistants join her onstage. They remove her headband and her earrings. Then they unclasp her necklaces. She stretches her arms out to her sides, hands up, and her assistants remove Frueh's bracelets. They place the jewelry on the table. Center stage, Frueh turns her back to the audience and moves into a wide-legged forward fold – her hands are touching the floor – and then Shoelace Pose on her way to lying on her back, head towards the audience. The assistants lay roses from the vases around her, creating a carpeted halo. Frueh lies in savasana for a minute or so, and then the lights dim to darkness.

I performed *Goddess of Roses* at the University of Arizona, Tucson, Arizona, in 2007 and at Shelly Steffee, New York, and the Out of Bounds conference at Monash University, Melbourne, Australia, in 2008.

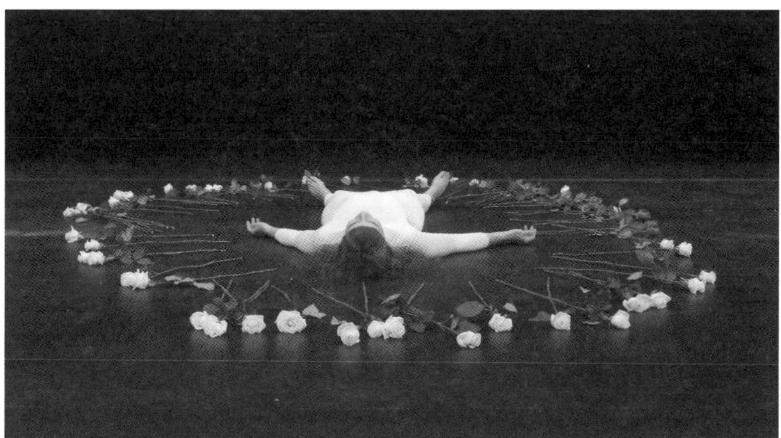

Figure 11 Joanna Frueh, *Goddess of Roses* (*savasana*), University of Arizona, Tucson, 2007 © Daniel Buckley, reproduced by kind permission

Sexual Advances, 2009

Stage right to center: a standing microphone, a black music stand, and a hip-high stool holding a glass of water. Stage left: a coffee table. The following items sit on it: a tube of MAC's Lady Danger lipstick, a bottle of Caron's Rose perfume, a mirror the size of a powder compact, several jewel-like bindis, tinchas, a set of ankle bells, and a small stack of white paper napkins.

Around ten feet away, along a wall, one thousand spoons of a light-colored wood, each holding a salty, sweet, bitter, or sour food, offer themselves to the audience. The centerpiece is a white ceramic platter filled with two dozen white rose blossoms.

Act I

Frueh enters stage left.

Clothing: a dress fit for a goddess and a night on the town. Ruched from the wide straps to the mid-calf hem and conforming to the shape of her body. Color: an unusually subtle and saturated pink – rosy-salmon. Pale pink satin damask ankle boots. No stockings. A deep sapphire-blue bindi.

Frueh brings the platter center stage and gently flings the roses into the audience.

Throughout the performance, any audience member who Frueh engages, asks for help, or approaches is a man. Frueh feeds herself from the table. She asks someone to choose a spoon and bring it to her. He may feed her or not. She may ask him to feed himself. Frueh reapplies her lipstick, by doing it herself or asking someone to do it. She may or may not use the mirror. Frueh makes mudra-like gestures.

Spontaneous interactions with the audience may happen at any time.

blason, French. A literary term originating in the Renaissance for a genre of poems in which the poet praises a woman by selecting parts of her body and enjoying them with suitably lovely metaphors.

sahasranama, Sanskrit. A Hindu scripture whose 1,000 lines describe the greatness, powers, and beauty of a particular deity. Each line can be recited as a mantra unto itself. The sequence of lines is non-hierarchical and attributes may be repeated in variant wording.

Frueh rings the tinchas. (In performance Frueh does not speak the numbers.)

1 I'm thinking of you when I take your T-shirt to bed at night
2 I'm thinking of you when I eat pasta
3 I'm thinking of you in the element of love: earth and fire, air and water, grounding ardor, flowing fortunes, and levitational alliances with spirits
4 I'm thinking of you in the present of erotic tender powerful time
5 I'm thinking of you in those amazing mystical moments of space and spaciousness and purity that auspiciously arise in our presence
6 I'm thinking of you talking with your friends at the Greek restaurant
7 I'm thinking of you as you think about yourself, your life
8 I'm thinking of your goldenness
9 I'm thinking of you singing
10 I'm thinking of your voice mixing with mine in song
11 I'm thinking of you when I wonder, still, why women get wet and men get hard
12 I'm thinking of you when I chime the tinchas in your name
13 I'm thinking of you in your sea-blue underwear
14 I'm thinking of you when you say about yourself, "I can be softer"
15 I'm thinking of your hearing me when I say, "I'm becoming softer"
16 I'm thinking of your saying to me, "You need a feminine man"
17 I'm thinking of your sculptural body
18 I'm thinking of your nudity in Classical Greek terms
19 I'm thinking of your writing about your "female hips"
20 I'm thinking of you playing tennis

21 I'm thinking of you when I see the deep rose sunset from my living room window
22 I'm thinking of you when the monsoon torrents throb against my skin
23 I'm thinking of you under the restless sky of the city in which you live
24 I'm thinking of you when I'm flying over an ocean to see you smile
25 I'm thinking of your love of the country in which you were born
26 I'm thinking of your feeling the lightness of this desert in which I live
27 I'm thinking of your saying when we are driving through this desert that I hold dear, "I feel at home here"
28 I'm thinking of you when I chant to Ganesh, the remover of obstacles, *Om gam ganeshaya namaha*
29 I'm thinking of you when I take the risks that this love so warmly invites
30 I'm thinking of you when I surrender
31 I'm thinking of you naked and next to me
32 I'm thinking of you sharing the silence of sleep with me
33 I'm thinking of you in the practice of being a *bodhisattva*
34 I'm thinking of you everywhere the box that people want to think outside of does not exist
35 I'm thinking of you showing me things about myself that I didn't know were there
36 I'm thinking of your softly sensuous penis deflating the hard evidence of the phallus fabled in the commerce of Cialis and Viagra, in the cultures where pillars of rectitude and spines of steel draw praise
37 I'm thinking of you and lyrics stream into my throat, like Wild thing, you make my heart sing, and It happens to be true / I only want to be with you, and I wanna stand with you on a mountain / I wanna bathe with you in the sea / I wanna lay like this forever / Until the sky falls down on me
38 I'm thinking of you my partner in the monsoon season when Violet Silverleaf blooms all over town
39 I'm thinking of you when you say, "Tears are healing"

40 I'm thinking of your tongue reaching the roof of my mouth

41 I'm thinking of your fingers in my vagina like no other's

42 I'm thinking of you whose hand on my knee conveys the power and the gentleness of ten thousand saints

43 I'm thinking of your hands on the piano's keys, your touch there like my mother's, bones and flesh light and swept by perfumed currents scented by an angel's wingspan

44 I'm thinking of you when I smell the sweat that your body has left for three days in the fibers of your T-shirt

45 I'm thinking of you with whom I sacrifice my hardness

46 I'm thinking of you who tells me, "You don't have to be coherent"

47 I'm thinking of your skin dazzling the sun, which misses you

48 I'm thinking of your saying, "There are no tests"

49 I'm thinking of you when I sit on the front porch during the gorgeous storm

50 I'm thinking of you when the enormous lightning bolts thrill the vision of this city

51 I'm thinking of your electrifying me

52 I'm thinking of you when the thunder vibrates deep within my heart and solar plexus *chakras* replenishing their strength

53 I'm thinking of you on first sight when we started shaking hands then knew our embrace to convey the spirit of this encounter

54 I'm thinking of you revealing the meaning of sacrifice

55 I'm thinking of you when I know that the thing sacrificed is the thing that holds a person back from love

56 I'm thinking of the shapely muscles of your legs

57 I'm thinking of the shapely muscles of your arms

58 I'm thinking of the upper auricle of your ear where the curve invites my touch

59 I'm thinking of your nipple hard and sweet to my tongue when our pleasure transmits straight to my vagina, clitoris, and their erotic sisters, the places that early twenty-first-century phrasing calls the G-spot, the U-spot, and the A-spot

60 I'm thinking of your puckered lips on my neck

61 I'm thinking of your neck right over the jugular vein and carotid artery

62 I'm thinking of you saying "Just you and me and the saguaros"

63 I'm thinking of you saying, "I can't believe I'm here," as we overlook a sea of saguaros and I say, "Believe it"

64 I'm thinking of you gazing at the hawk that soars overhead, first flying to our right and then back to our left

65 I'm thinking of your noticing a spider web on the leg of my jeans

66 I'm thinking of your black pants in the glint of a spider web

67 I'm thinking of your chest and stomach after you unbutton your black shirt and lie back basking in the sunlight with your eyes closed

68 I'm thinking of you not knowing that I want to jump on you

69 I'm thinking of you chopping garlic and slicing fennel

70 I'm thinking of you bearing fruit

71 I'm thinking of your cum like white lightning moving from my vagina into my pelvis and up to my heart and through my arms and out the fingertips and down into my legs and into my feet and out the toes

72 I'm thinking of you when I am full of faith

73 I'm thinking of you inspiring me

74 I'm thinking of you surprising me with the sound like a song and chant, long-lasting, of your coming

75 I'm thinking of your rich and graceful voice

76 I'm thinking of your voice whose sound gives me comfort

77 I'm thinking of you using the word *precious* from the center of its meaning, dear and beloved

78 I'm thinking of you illuminated by the many skylights and windows in your home

79 I'm thinking of your home feeling like a big ship

80 I'm thinking of your garden with the trees that bend and wail in the wind

81 I'm thinking of your garden in its many greens of winter

82 I'm thinking of your blue-enameled chairs and table in a courtyard of your garden

83 I'm thinking of your fluid influence as inside I am water streaming gently through the mossy channels down a mountain

84 I'm thinking of your assured and mild voice in my ears and cleaning up my cells

85 I'm thinking of you steadfast in love

86 I'm thinking of you kissing me, the first time, when I say, "I don't know what to do"

87 I'm thinking of you nurturing me with your cooking

88 I'm thinking of you in a city of gardens

89 I'm thinking of you caring for your parents with devotion

90 I'm thinking of your love for your three daughters

91 I'm thinking of you saying, "Now I feel perfect," after coming inside me the first time

92 I'm thinking of your smile when I say, "My parents would love you"

93 I'm thinking of you smiling when I apprise you that my father, dead for almost a decade, tells me that he hand-picked you for me

94 I'm thinking of your talking about the elasticity of time

95 I'm thinking of your age being the same as mine

96 I'm thinking of the lovely texture of your complexion

97 I'm thinking of the silver, white, and gray hairs curling on your chest

98 I'm thinking of resting my head on your chest

99 I'm thinking of your saying that it's time, together, to "reap the harvest" of our individual self-creations

100 I'm thinking of your saying, "I hope this is everything"

101 I'm thinking of you with whom intercourse actually *is* communication

102 I'm thinking of you with whom intercourse is an exchange of everything

103 I'm thinking of you with whom intercourse is connectivity

104 I'm thinking of you with whom intercourse is self-creation

105 I'm thinking of your penis in elegant arousal in my mouth

106 I'm thinking of your penis in all its small beauty held within my mouth

107 I'm thinking of your penis larger than my mouth can hold

108 I'm thinking of your passion and compassion

109 I'm thinking of your healing my distrust of men

110 I'm thinking of you telling me your dreams when we wake up in the morning side by side

111 I'm thinking of you biting my nipple through my clothing

112 I'm thinking of your cum tasting good

113 I'm thinking of your cum on your belly
114 I'm thinking of you reading about the Buddha
115 I'm thinking of your mild accent
116 I'm thinking of you creating yourself over half a century
117 I'm thinking of your saying, "Fantastic!" or another of your enthusiastic phrases when I suggest, "Let's go to Kyoto"
118 I'm thinking of your wanting to travel to India and Japan
119 I'm thinking of your wanting to go to a town and an *ashram* near a sacred mountain in Tamil Nadu and to Zen monasteries in Kyoto
120 I'm thinking of you creating the person you are with me
121 I'm thinking of you wanting to be the person you are with me
122 I'm thinking of you wanting me so that you experience what you expect love to be
123 I'm thinking of your knowing that finding what you expect love to be may take decades of a person's self-creation to occur
124 I'm thinking of you carrying an umbrella like Patrick MacNee as John Steed, one of the Avengers, does
125 I'm thinking of your part in our clear foundation
126 I'm thinking of your part in our purity, no lessons, tests, or subtexts
127 I'm thinking of you being the architect of the home you live in
128 I'm thinking of your home being your studio
129 I'm thinking of your piles, stacks, and collections
130 I'm thinking of your ladders, lamps, and beads
131 I'm thinking of you saying, "Pleasure"
132 I'm thinking of you sitting at the grand piano and electric keyboard
133 I'm thinking of you climbing up the narrow gray stairs to the loft
134 I'm thinking of you undressing for bed to the right of the top step
135 I'm thinking of your wind chimes streaming from the ceiling
136 I'm thinking of your garden pedestals topped with busts
137 I'm thinking of your comforter warming us

138 I'm thinking of your vast array of pictures, furnishings, and objects that I see when I'm gazing from the railing
139 I'm thinking of you climbing the ladder to heaven
140 I'm thinking of your long, dark wood dining table glowing
141 I'm thinking of your table seating many guests on the benches
142 I'm thinking of you walking past the vines that twine around a post just out of your back door
143 I'm thinking of your fruit bowl from which I choose a juicy pear for lunch
144 I'm thinking of you cooking when I say that the benches at the dining table feel like pews
145 I'm thinking of you working in the director's and the swivel chairs at your loaded desk
146 I'm thinking of your voice that holds and caresses me like your strong hands and arms
147 I'm thinking of the outdoor light that shines on you and potted cactuses through a wall of windows and French doors while you're working
148 I'm thinking of you at one with the saguaros
149 I'm thinking of your determination through your history to be real
150 I'm thinking of your many books
151 I'm thinking of your books that I would like to read
152 I'm thinking of your books about art
153 I'm thinking of your books about the country in which you were born
154 I'm thinking of you sleeping all night long by my side
155 I'm thinking of your bedroom when the soft light of late afternoon finds the two white dressers
156 I'm thinking of your bed that I straighten up for us
157 I'm thinking of your purple couch where we are watching Kurasawa's *Ran*
158 I'm thinking of you in the heavenly light at the top of the stairs
159 I'm thinking of your gravitas
160 I'm thinking of your meeting me at the Pink Fairy Palace, my nickname for a romance of a hotel in this desert of subtropical delights

161 I'm thinking of your drinking cappuccino at our first lunch
162 I'm thinking of your caffé lattes in the morning
163 I'm thinking of your sexy glamour wearing the black T-shirt that you gave me
164 I'm thinking of you in the black T-shirt, back to the fire in the Greek restaurant
165 I'm thinking of you speaking passionately about your identity in the black T-shirt at the Greek restaurant
166 I'm thinking of you being loved by your friends at dinner in the Greek restaurant
167 I'm thinking of you being honored by one of your friends who says in conversation that you're "a national treasure"
168 I'm thinking of your presence daring me to be my Self
169 I'm thinking of you daring to be yourself
170 I'm thinking of you being radically aware of living
171 I'm thinking of your wholehearted self
172 I'm thinking of your heart as a river, like the rain, bigger than this world that people call home
173 I'm thinking of you talking with me about our orgasms felt still in your bed long after we have come
174 I'm thinking of you feeling
175 I'm thinking of you feeling more and more
176 I'm thinking of you seeing me
177 I'm thinking of you seeing me in ecstasy
178 I'm thinking of you kissing me at the airport
179 I'm thinking of you seeing me across a crowded room and wanting our next kiss
180 I'm thinking of you wanting the day to end so that you can be in bed with me
181 I'm thinking of you telling me anything you want about your day
182 I'm thinking of you watching *Batman Begins* with me
183 I'm thinking of your making love with me at the end of a long day
184 I'm thinking of you loving me and hardly talking at the end of a long day
185 I'm thinking of you falling happily asleep with me by your side

186 I'm thinking of you speaking publicly
187 I'm thinking of your voice vibrating with ideas
188 I'm thinking of your body language and energy flowing with your love for me
189 I'm thinking of your clear love for me
190 I'm thinking of your opening the secret places
191 I'm thinking of your traveling the avenues of my inner sancta
192 I'm thinking of you receiving the gifts I bring to you
193 I'm thinking of you in rendezvous
194 I'm thinking of you making a lot of love with me
195 I'm thinking of your belonging in a life that's many bowls of cherries
196 I'm thinking of you experiencing everything
197 I'm thinking of you moistening my prophetic orifices
198 I'm thinking of you ringing the tinchas
199 I'm thinking of you sharing the sound of purity with me
200 I'm thinking of you offering your home to me
201 I'm thinking of you claiming the priority of Self
202 I'm thinking of you living from abundance
203 I'm thinking of you talking about the mundane and the miracles
204 I'm thinking of you knowing that the everyday and everything are one
205 I'm thinking of you drinking a glass of wine, Pinot Grigio, Sauvignon Blanc
206 I'm thinking of your daring
207 I'm thinking of the firmness of your penis that I feel through your pants
208 I'm thinking of your not needing the center of attention
209 I'm thinking of you centering me
210 I'm thinking of you moving towards something when it calls you
211 I'm thinking of your answering of prayers
212 I'm thinking of your walking into happiness
213 I'm thinking of you aligning in orgasm
214 I'm thinking of you when heart moves head
215 I'm thinking of you ocean-born like Aphrodite
216 I'm thinking of you being free

217 I'm thinking of you because the sky is overhead
218 I'm thinking of you because heaven is above and all around me
219 I'm thinking of you expanding the horizons of my heart
220 I'm thinking of you experiencing infinity
221 I'm thinking of your new origins within the body that is my Self
222 I'm thinking of your divesting me of armor
223 I'm thinking of you softening your defenses
224 I'm thinking of you in the glory of your skin
225 I'm thinking of you in utter loving ecstasy
226 I'm thinking of you leading with the heart
227 I'm thinking of you experiencing infinity with me
228 I'm thinking of your access to the heart
229 I'm thinking of your mystery
230 I'm thinking of your availability for enlightenment
231 I'm thinking of you catching my gaze
232 I'm thinking of you my firmament
233 I'm thinking of your freedom as terra firma
234 I'm thinking of you my child and mother
235 I'm thinking of you my friend and father
236 I'm thinking of you my newfound and eternal friend
237 I'm thinking of you beyond the bounds of perception
238 I'm thinking of you all at once
239 I'm thinking of your blessings in their silken splendor
240 I'm thinking of your smooth head in my hands
241 I'm thinking of you shaving your head
242 I'm thinking of your honoring the living and the dead
243 I'm thinking of your love unwinding the tangled innards of history
244 I'm thinking of you saying, "I'm real," when I ask you if you are
245 I'm thinking of you saying, "This is real," when you articulate the cosmic occasion that brings us together the first time
246 I'm thinking of you communing with the stars
247 I'm thinking of you on the terrace at the Pink Fairy Palace gazing at the lights in the Sonoran sky
248 I'm thinking of your loving light that brightens your friends' lives

249 I'm thinking of your energizing the universe
250 I'm thinking of you in the mysteries with me
251 I'm thinking of you with me walking down West Broadway
252 I'm thinking of you in Auckland
253 I'm thinking of you in my Dionysian bed
254 I'm thinking of your harmonies
255 I'm thinking of you in a restaurant called the Chocolate Buddha
256 I'm thinking of you when I eat a chocolate mousse tart with orange rind at the bottom
257 I'm thinking of your saying in front of our friends, "She's misty," when I tell all of you about my ruched and peony pink dress
258 I'm thinking of your silver-white hair growing in
259 I'm thinking of your saying, "Think of me"
260 I'm thinking of your faith in love
261 I'm thinking of your saying, "I do," when I say, "Trust me"
262 I'm thinking of your tart warm humor
263 I'm thinking of your brown eyes framed by your golden olive skin
264 I'm thinking of you saying, "Touch me, touch me"
265 I'm thinking of your thigh under my caress
266 I'm thinking of your pleasure in my hands
267 I'm thinking of you as still as the Buddha under the bodhi tree
268 I'm thinking of you wanting to be a saint for your parents as they die
269 I'm thinking of you with deep appreciation creating space for me in your life
270 I'm thinking of you sitting cross-legged on the floor playing with a child
271 I'm thinking of you lying in my arms receiving love and comfort
272 I'm thinking of your energy radiating like a halo all around your body
273 I'm thinking of you living a new life in our light
274 I'm thinking of your lips pressed to my lips colored in a red called Lady Danger

275 I'm thinking of you smiling at me with desire when you see me in the peony pink dress
276 I'm thinking of your strength resting in the softness of your heart
277 I'm thinking of your strong heart cradling all your softness
278 I'm thinking of your voice that soothes me like a lullaby
279 I'm thinking of your heart and mine held by heaven
280 I'm thinking of you looking in my eyes and saying, "Sweetheart" and "Dearest"
281 I'm thinking of you hearing "Darling" from my lips, my belly
282 I'm thinking of you sleeping soundly
283 I'm thinking of you darling
284 I'm thinking of you in a forest or a desert within the heady mix of our lovemaking voices loud as ecstasy insists
285 I'm thinking of your grand passion
286 I'm thinking of you singing in the rain
287 I'm thinking of you bared to the soul in Mediterranean sunlight
288 I'm thinking of your heart flowing and overflowing with mine
289 I'm thinking of your fingers in the salad bowl
290 I'm thinking of your hearty eating
291 I'm thinking of your completeness
292 I'm thinking of you my ever-present friend
293 I'm thinking of your body joining mine like two hands in prayer
294 I'm thinking of your oracular voice
295 I'm thinking of your persuasive prophecies: an open window; a switchboard where connections multiply; a reaping, us together, of the harvests that we've individually sown
296 I'm thinking of you singularly sweet like the first kiss you gave me when you took me by surprise
297 I'm thinking of you entering my home
298 I'm thinking of you coming inside my body
299 I'm thinking of you resting in my heart
300 I'm thinking of you in the present tense, it's Joy
301 I'm thinking of you standing with your sexy smile at my door
302 I'm thinking of you in a future of honey
303 I'm thinking of your immeasurable fineness

304 I'm thinking of your health and well-being vibrating throughout the heart of the world
305 I'm thinking of you undressed, standing for one eternal instant in every heaven surrounded by all the gods and goddesses whose reality is as mighty as your own
306 I'm thinking of your naked splendor shining in the desert sun
307 I'm thinking of you my lovemaking man
308 I'm thinking of your subtle ways of making love that wake me into more than orgasm
309 I'm thinking of your descent like mine from heaven
310 I'm thinking of your devotion to whatever unfolds and flows
311 I'm thinking of your sweet instrument of sound
312 I'm thinking of you bestowing goodness
313 I'm thinking of you bathed in rose-red light
314 I'm thinking of you being as bright as a thousand rising suns
315 I'm thinking of your bow-like mind releasing arrows of enlightenment
316 I'm thinking of your rose-red radiance
317 I'm thinking of your jewel of a heart
318 I'm thinking of your fingers making music that my friend tells me she could listen to while dying
319 I'm thinking of your easing words
320 I'm thinking of your easy way with words
321 I'm thinking of your love-soaked lips
322 I'm thinking of your melodic words creating eros every moment
323 I'm thinking of your flowing smile
324 I'm thinking of you emerging like a spring day from the winter
325 I'm thinking of you situating every cell in the waters of love
326 I'm thinking of your fragrant breath, like betel leaves, an ancient Hindu text might say
327 I'm thinking of your arms bedecked like a goddess's in golden bracelets
328 I'm thinking of your neck and chest adorned with quivering pearl necklaces
329 I'm thinking of your arrows bearing fruit

330 I'm thinking of you turning down the glare and turning up the true light
331 I'm thinking of your stylish clothing coming from secondhand stores
332 I'm thinking of your dark green, spring jacket that I want to borrow
333 I'm thinking of your solar energy radiating through your clothing
334 I'm thinking of you as the giver of fruit
335 I'm thinking of you in jeweled bells at your waist
336 I'm thinking of you dancing in jeweled anklets
337 I'm thinking of you walking like a languid swimming swan
338 I'm thinking of you in the effects and treasures of your breathing in and out
339 I'm thinking of your smile when I fly over an ocean to the desert that longs to kiss your skin
340 I'm thinking of you connecting in tranquility with all that is
341 I'm thinking of you taking off your dark green jacket
342 I'm thinking of your jacket on the back of a chair with an orange seat at my house
343 I'm thinking of your love bringing the benefit of healing to the planet
344 I'm thinking of you standing right before me in your overcoat and sunglasses, "Honey" wafting from your diaphragm to mine
345 I'm thinking of you kissing me in your wet anorak, our touch like an infusion of perfume into air
346 I'm thinking of your fingers floating through my hair
347 I'm thinking of your fingertips gently pressing my cervical spine
348 I'm thinking of you translating fire into water
349 I'm thinking of your voice holding me in its soft texture and strong currents
350 I'm thinking of you saying, "Sit on me, sit on me"
351 I'm thinking of your knack for freedom
352 I'm thinking of you loving my freedom
353 I'm thinking of you hearing that a hawk sat next to me
354 I'm thinking of your lips pouring garnets, rubies, roses

355 I'm thinking of you sleeping next to me all night
356 I'm thinking of your peaceful continuity with me
357 I'm thinking of you playing soccer
358 I'm thinking of you kicking the ball, connecting with perfection
359 I'm thinking of your uncontrivance
360 I'm thinking of your truthfulness
361 I'm thinking of your purity
362 I'm thinking of you untouched by academics' fixation on binaries of masculine and feminine
363 I'm thinking of you in the polarity of yin and yang
364 I'm thinking of you living in the heart of happiness
365 I'm thinking of you in the sounds I sing to you with all my heart
366 I'm thinking of your liberation
367 I'm thinking of your quiver of amorous arrows
368 I'm thinking of you steeping in our love
369 I'm thinking of you leaping like a jaguar
370 I'm thinking of your thousand-petaled roses
371 I'm thinking of your thousand-fold integrity
372 I'm thinking of your endless realness
373 I'm thinking of you singing mantras into me
374 I'm thinking of you seated calmly in all my *chakras*
375 I'm thinking of you pouring wine into my cup
376 I'm thinking of your boundless diamond-brightness
377 I'm thinking of your water cooling my fire and my fire heating your water
378 I'm thinking of your fire heating my water and my water cooling your fire
379 I'm thinking of your fire burning pain to ashes
380 I'm thinking of you being everywhere that real people are
381 I'm thinking of your pillow talk
382 I'm thinking of you ruled only by your Self
383 I'm thinking of your limitless facets of magnanimity
384 I'm thinking of you purging all obstructions
385 I'm thinking of your looks of love that radiate right through your Ray-Bans
386 I'm thinking of your unbewildering heart
387 I'm thinking of you at the canyon's edge by the Salt River

388 I'm thinking of you enwrapped in my legs
389 I'm thinking of you pulling into the lane way in your car
390 I'm thinking of you unlocking your front door
391 I'm thinking of your mobile smile
392 I'm thinking of your *chakras* inviting love's inventions
393 I'm thinking of your *chakras* spinning in the balance of your beauty
394 I'm thinking of you strong and winged, an ally of the genies sculpted for Assyrian kings
395 I'm thinking of you dancing in my kitchen
396 I'm thinking of your chest loving the light touch of my hair when I kiss your nipples
397 I'm thinking of your sweetness bold as the femininity of valentines
398 I'm thinking of you showering the world with happiness
399 I'm thinking of you girdled in gold jingling bells
400 I'm thinking of your navel with the bells below it complementing the color of your skin
401 I'm thinking of you sitting near the Sacred Way at Delphi by my side
402 I'm thinking of your usefulness to human beings and gods
403 I'm thinking of your heliotropic ecstasies
404 I'm thinking of your vitality
405 I'm thinking of you nourishing your life
406 I'm thinking of you nourishing my life and life force
407 I'm thinking of you gazing at the stars in the desert sky in May
408 I'm thinking of you gazing at the desert stars in February, March, and April
409 I'm thinking of you gazing in every season at the stars above an old adobe home
410 I'm thinking of your mouth filled full of starlight
411 I'm thinking of you filling me with starlight
412 I'm thinking of your facial lines whose fleshly and experiential beauty I love to touch
413 I'm thinking of you singing in South Africa
414 I'm thinking of you singing in my bed and flesh
415 I'm thinking of your starry-eyed sanity
416 I'm thinking of your blazing breath

417 I'm thinking of your mysteries opening in our presence
418 I'm thinking of your mysteries opening in our bed
419 I'm thinking of your mysteries welcoming all of my own
420 I'm thinking of you exceeding the cultural boundaries of age
421 I'm thinking of you exceeding the bondage called aging
422 I'm thinking of you, citizen of planet earth
423 I'm thinking of you, angel of the cosmos
424 I'm thinking of you looking at the yellow lilies on your dining room table
425 I'm thinking of you looking at a vase of oriental lilies whose pink reminds you of my scent and skin
426 I'm thinking of you standing sure and sexy like Govinda
427 I'm thinking of you dancing in a community of friends
428 I'm thinking of your energy shifting as you dance
429 I'm thinking of you luxuriating in our love
430 I'm thinking of you singing a different tune and beating your own drum to turn swords into plowshares
431 I'm thinking of you exulting
432 I'm thinking of you exalted
433 I'm thinking of your exaltation of art
434 I'm thinking of your heart as bright as a grown-up Snow White's red lips
435 I'm thinking of your feet bare in the sand next to saguaros
436 I'm thinking of your light step
437 I'm thinking of you walking smooth as flowing nectar
438 I'm thinking of your thighs free and full of *prana* like lungs fed by oxygen
439 I'm thinking of you walking towards me in the airport of this desert city whose sparkle you feel upon your first arrival
440 I'm thinking of you hearing every reason to be free
441 I'm thinking of you accepting every call to freedom
442 I'm thinking of you renovating your familial relations
443 I'm thinking of you knowing your surroundings the way that Bruce Wayne's master in *Batman Begins* says is necessary for a warrior
444 I'm thinking of you lifting the weight that's been in my legs for more years than I've lived this lifetime on the planet
445 I'm thinking of your eyes reflecting my gaze

446 I'm thinking of your subtle smile that reminds me of the serenity gathered in the lips and cheeks and around the eyes of the four-foot high Buddha head in my backyard
447 I'm thinking of your spirit jumping rope
448 I'm thinking of you moving in the right direction
449 I'm thinking of you welcoming travelers to the middle way
450 I'm thinking of your wisdom whooshing into all my *chakras*
451 I'm thinking of you planting seeds
452 I'm thinking of your hands in the soil
453 I'm thinking of you eyeing roses and tomatoes
454 I'm thinking of your humility like blue mist calming my meridians
455 I'm thinking of you laughing the atmosphere into good humor
456 I'm thinking of you using tools for healing souls, scars, and mild abrasions
457 I'm thinking of you listening to your daughter who suggests that you simplify your life
458 I'm thinking of your ordering caffé latte and macchiato
459 I'm thinking of you finding what you're looking for in Rome
460 I'm thinking of you talking with a friend in Venice
461 I'm thinking of you defeating evil demons known to humankind and deities
462 I'm thinking of you lifting the weight from everybody's shoulders
463 I'm thinking of you grasping burdens out of people's bellies and casting them to the stars for healing
464 I'm thinking of you trying on lipsticks, some pale some saturated, at our bedside
465 I'm thinking of you setting my mind awhirl with new thinking
466 I'm thinking of you unlocking your heart
467 I'm thinking of you increasing your *chi* using the Taoist method of moving it from your testes to your crown through the channels of your body
468 I'm thinking of you energized
469 I'm thinking of you fueled with *ching*, sexual *chi* that Taoists know to be the highest of all healing essences

470 I'm thinking of you circulating your *ching* with mine
471 I'm thinking of you decked in necklaces of many lengths, in arm bracelets around your wrists and biceps, in belts from your waist to lower hips of ancient Chinese beads of coral red, in anklets of white satin sewn with diamonds
472 I'm thinking of you reading to save your soul
473 I'm thinking of your soul saved by self-study
474 I'm thinking of your self-examination liberating you from chains of karma and undue obligations
475 I'm thinking of you forgiving yourself
476 I'm thinking of you filled with the simplicity of loving self-acceptance
477 I'm thinking of you spreading the word
478 I'm thinking of you singing the seeds
479 I'm thinking of you gathering the bounty of our love
480 I'm thinking of you knowing what you want
481 I'm thinking of you materializing your desires
482 I'm thinking of you knowing what matters
483 I'm thinking of you following what you know
484 I'm thinking of you free of karma like the wind
485 I'm thinking of you in our second day of ecstasy still feeling orgasms from the night before
486 I'm thinking of you dressed in sex and elegance
487 I'm thinking of you so at home in the eloquence of skin
488 I'm thinking of you wearing sandals of strong waxy flower petals
489 I'm thinking of you wearing sandals that I make of paper covered in my lipstick kisses
490 I'm thinking of you in a downpour of roses
491 I'm thinking of you walking with me through roses all around our ankles
492 I'm thinking of you catching blossoms in your hands
493 I'm thinking of you boarding an airplane for the homeland that is me
494 I'm thinking of you landing in my home country
495 I'm thinking of you rising in a *mandorla* of light
496 I'm thinking of you retaining your ejaculate and circulating its essence within your body as Taoist adepts do

497 I'm thinking of you exchanging your sex essence with mine as they circulate through us creating higher consciousness and greater health
498 I'm thinking of you reading books about *chi* and *prana*
499 I'm thinking of you clearing away cobwebs while loving the spiders
500 I'm thinking of you Everyman

Intermission. People eat food. Frueh is elsewhere.

Act II

Frueh asks someone to help her remove her boots and secure the bells around her ankles. She may execute footwork resembling that in Bharata Natyam.

Spontaneously, she asks people if they'd like a bindi on their forehead, and applies one to people who say yes,

Frueh rings the tinchas.

501 I'm thinking of you renewing our rapture when you hear my voicemails
502 I'm thinking of you texting me with acute news and kisses
503 I'm thinking of you seeing the sunlight through the French doors in my living room and study
504 I'm thinking of you seeing the light when listening to my voice from thousands of miles away
505 I'm thinking of your strength and flexibility climbing walls of granite
506 I'm thinking of you watching me eat chocolate
507 I'm thinking of you offering me wine
508 I'm thinking of you cooking soups and making coffee
509 I'm thinking of you eating meats and sardines
510 I'm thinking of your green eyes searching out the holds on granite
511 I'm thinking of your curly brown hair soft in the eyes and fingers
512 I'm thinking of you in white shirts and dark jeans

513 I'm thinking of your many pairs of cowboy boots
514 I'm thinking of your smile, so absolute that the cliché *dazzling* suits it perfectly
515 I'm thinking of you, every deity that breathes within the human body
516 I'm thinking of your sweeping joy
517 I'm thinking of your soaring joy
518 I'm thinking of your joy flowing from my crown within and down my body like a wave of honey
519 I'm thinking of you setting fire to the dead trees that clog the minds of depressed people
520 I'm thinking of you as the Way, the means of everything
521 I'm thinking of your quicksilver silliness
522 I'm thinking of your forever boyish beauty
523 I'm thinking of your immutable beauty
524 I'm thinking of your voice inside me like a mantra
525 I'm thinking of your voice clearing my glands and organs, bones and marrow
526 I'm thinking of the high vibrations of your voice
527 I'm thinking of you renewing your soul
528 I'm thinking of you being the change the planet wants to see
529 I'm thinking of you renewing the planet
530 I'm thinking of you helping the gay and the forgotten
531 I'm thinking of you flinging gems into the hands of strangers
532 I'm thinking of you painting in your studio
533 I'm thinking of your luminous handmade metal objects
534 I'm thinking of your voice loving me from far away
535 I'm thinking of your soft, smooth, and sexy voice
536 I'm thinking of you neither pushing upward nor sinking downward, in the balance of your humility
537 I'm thinking of you in tune
538 I'm thinking of you in the nuanced wakefulness, agility, and breakthroughs of our *chi* exchange
539 I'm thinking of you eating chocolate chip cookie batter with me
540 I'm thinking of you cooking risotto in our kitchen
541 I'm thinking of you being soul-and-mind-inseparable-from-body because I feel it when we make love

542 I'm thinking of you knowing that the oppressed must make their freedom
543 I'm thinking of you teaching students that Love, Core, Self, Heart, Essence, Being, Soul, and Consciousness are different names for the same thing
544 I'm thinking of you resonating Self
545 I'm thinking of you reading sacred texts
546 I'm thinking of your self-study
547 I'm thinking of you exploring yourself
548 I'm thinking of you opening the minds of fellow human beings
549 I'm thinking of you asking for my hand on your heart
550 I'm thinking of your calm confidence like the sage commander's in *The Art of War*
551 I'm thinking of your Aikido instructor readying you to read *The Demon's Sermon on the Martial Arts*
552 I'm thinking of your curiosity matching Arjuna's in the *Bhagavad Gita*
553 I'm thinking of your ability to see the largest picture, like Arjuna's friend Krishna, a musician, holy hero, and archetypal lover
554 I'm thinking of your cool head
555 I'm thinking of your Buddha mind
556 I'm thinking of you here now
557 I'm thinking of you because the sun is shining
558 I'm thinking of you because the sun shines
559 I'm thinking of you because people love you
560 I'm thinking of you standing in the wind blowing inland from an ocean
561 I'm thinking of you free as ocean breezes that I hear toning with your voice as we are speaking on our mobile phones
562 I'm thinking of you in this small world we call the planet earth
563 I'm thinking of you the big shebang-bang
564 I'm thinking of you looking at a photograph of me and my girlfriend in dresses with our arms around each other
565 I'm thinking of you experiencing your mother's giving birth to you
566 I'm thinking of you knowing what to do

567 I'm thinking of you knowing what to do with our love
568 I'm thinking of your preternaturally soft kisses
569 I'm thinking of you forever seated with me in the garden
570 I'm thinking of you at the breakfast table lit with two white candles, one in a holder embossed with an image of Lakshmi, goddess of abundance
571 I'm thinking of you walking with me in the Catalina mountains
572 I'm thinking of you grinding beans and serving us strong coffee
573 I'm thinking of you springing like a jaguar
574 I'm thinking of you running for the fun of it
575 I'm thinking of you springing like an action hero fairy into my heart
576 I'm thinking of you patiently treating my impatience
577 I'm thinking of your medicine steeped in the heart
578 I'm thinking of your talent for tenderness
579 I'm thinking of you ministering to me with the intimacy of rain on flowers
580 I'm thinking of you gardening
581 I'm thinking of your saying, "You're so flexible"
582 I'm thinking of your wonder at the flexibility of my hips and legs and pelvis
583 I'm thinking of your temple that is your body
584 I'm thinking of your intimacy with architecture
585 I'm thinking of you intimate with loving self-acceptance
586 I'm thinking of you as Shiva with hair flowing like the Ganges
587 I'm thinking of you dancing with dragons and tigers
588 I'm thinking of you relaxing into the position of Love
589 I'm thinking of you dancing way beyond the dreams planned by the ordinary and unloving ego
590 I'm thinking of you wearing the watch your father gives you in his old age
591 I'm thinking of you practicing Aikido
592 I'm thinking of you refining your intuition
593 I'm thinking of your trust in my intuition
594 I'm thinking of you talking with me for nine hours straight when time disappeared

595 I'm thinking of you listening to my singing voicemail, *Govinda hare / Gopala hare / he prabhu dina dyala hare*
596 I'm thinking of your simple verbal response on hearing me say, "Your cum tastes good"
597 I'm thinking of your melodious voice
598 I'm thinking of you loving the hell out of humankind
599 I'm thinking of you loving any hell out of every individual
600 I'm thinking of you residing, ready always to be seen, within the mists that seem to fog some people's minds
601 I'm thinking of your actions redefining pleasure, from amusement; entertainment; intoxicants ingested and observed that cause oblivion; and sexual expediencies in the name of love, into the sanctum of subtle bodily sensations
602 I'm thinking of your divine body
603 I'm thinking of you being a friend to Aphrodite
604 I'm thinking of you bringing water to the thirsty
605 I'm thinking of you cooking food for the hungry
606 I'm thinking of you preparing foods with olive oil and garlic
607 I'm thinking of you loving solitude and silence
608 I'm thinking of you chanting *swaha* and *namaha*
609 I'm thinking of you bearing mantras in your solar plexus
610 I'm thinking of you moving from the difference between force and balance, as yogis do
611 I'm thinking of you whose limbs surround me like the sunlight when, naked, I step from the French door of my study onto the patio
612 I'm thinking of your fulfillment of my desires
613 I'm thinking of your resemblance to Nataraja, Lord of the Dance, whose daring and precise grace refresh the world
614 I'm thinking of you watching me the *Lasya* dancer, wildflowers in my hair and worn as earrings
615 I'm thinking of your knees and penis, your chest and moist lips peeking through pale red trumpet flowers
616 I'm thinking of you when I lay me down to sleep
617 I'm thinking of you when I pray in the morning
618 I'm thinking of you awakening people from their ignorance of beauty

619 I'm thinking of you when the air is so good to breathe that I am as light as flying birds and feathers

620 I'm thinking of you when I'm putting on my lipstick

621 I'm thinking of you when I'm painting my lips the color of tiered coral bells that dance around your hips and pelvis

622 I'm thinking of you basking near my backyard Buddha like the lizards

623 I'm thinking of you with me watching a lizard on the Buddha's earlobe

624 I'm thinking of you in this delicate dance of words

625 I'm thinking of you in these simple turns of phrase

626 I'm thinking of you as my mind turns over some traits of goodness

627 I'm thinking of your happiness

628 I'm thinking of you sharing peaks and valleys of orgasm with me

629 I'm thinking of you making love with me for hours

630 I'm thinking of you walking to the B-Line and to the Epic Café with me for cobbler with vanilla ice cream, some cups of coffee, a piece of German chocolate cake, a carne asada burrito, and the prosaic pleasures of conversation and observing our fellow human beings

631 I'm thinking of you coming to me in the midnight air

632 I'm thinking of you my wine, meat, and chocolate

633 I'm thinking of you without embellishment

634 I'm thinking of your lips vibrating with many names of love

635 I'm thinking of your name written by angels

636 I'm thinking of your name pronounced by the petals of roses

637 I'm thinking of you producing the seasons in your heart

638 I'm thinking of you harmonizing the seasons in your heart

639 I'm thinking of you responding to every change with ease

640 I'm thinking of you paying attention to your pleasure

641 I'm thinking of your spontaneous enjoyment of the world

642 I'm thinking of you naming what you see when you see it rather than *ex post facto* trying to reinvent the past with unconscious current anxieties and attempting to preempt the future with prognostics based on nothing but statistics and other fetishizations of facts that vaguely and absurdly

measure the human liability that believes in the accountability of numbers
643 I'm thinking of you listening to singing birds in my backyard
644 I'm thinking of you surrounded by blue dragonflies, levitating above a high desert creek
645 I'm thinking of you in bed with me and listening to the desert rain
646 I'm thinking of you smelling the desert rain
647 I'm thinking of your well-groomed fingernails
648 I'm thinking of you driving along the coast
649 I'm thinking of you witnessing the high and steady billowing clouds
650 I'm thinking of you whose fullness in your apparent absence gives proof to my faith
651 I'm thinking of you unconditionally
652 I'm thinking of your firm belly pressed to mine
653 I'm thinking of your conventionally hard cock unconventionally alive
654 I'm thinking of your digestion working smoothly underneath the skin my tongue is kissing
655 I'm thinking of you seeing palm trees and mountains from the windows of my home
656 I'm thinking of your footsteps in the mountains
657 I'm thinking of you brightening my eyes
658 I'm thinking of you saying, "Finally," as we begin to make love for the first time, when the distance created by schedules and continents dissolves, when my trust in you and me is clearer than my desire can almost bear
659 I'm thinking of you singing, I know that I've been saved / Cause the angels in heaven done written my name
660 I'm thinking of your measureless capacity for freedom
661 I'm thinking of you sweating with me in the garden
662 I'm thinking of you with your computer, writing on my patio
663 I'm thinking of you in the hundred-degree heat
664 I'm thinking of you being hot, or so a girlfriend of mine tells me who is close to half the age that you and I share
665 I'm thinking of you whispering in my ear the names of saints and family members

666 I'm thinking of you whispering in my ear the names of friends and artists you adore

667 I'm thinking of you grounding yourself anywhere you choose

668 I'm thinking of you earthing in my arms

669 I'm thinking of you firing up my spirit

670 I'm thinking of you liquefying my fears

671 I'm thinking of you airing out my consciousness

672 I'm thinking of you taking off my necklace of black tourmaline and silver

673 I'm thinking of you brushing my hair away from the nape of my neck

674 I'm thinking of you as mysterious as Woman is said to be

675 I'm thinking of you letting the universe have its way with us

676 I'm thinking of you my teacher

678 I'm thinking of you my student

679 I'm thinking of you learning by observing phenomena, such as the actions of your heart and the energy of trees

680 I'm thinking of you being still and being here

681 I'm thinking of your solar plexus pressing against my thoracic spine

682 I'm thinking of your pelvis at my sacrum

683 I'm thinking of your defined deltoid and trapezius muscles

684 I'm thinking of your blood's pressure and velocity

685 I'm thinking of you in a flock of phoenixes

686 I'm thinking of you within a band of unicorns

687 I'm thinking of you climbing down the branches and arriving at the root

688 I'm thinking of you soaring like ethereal music

689 I'm thinking of your eyes just like a fawn's

690 I'm thinking of your scent as sweet to me as ylang ylang

691 I'm thinking of your brilliance bright and quick as lightning

692 I'm thinking of your sentient intelligence

693 I'm thinking of you calling me on the phone to tell me you can't wait to see me

694 I'm thinking of your saturated calm like sapphire and emerald lakes I've seen in Canada

695 I'm thinking of you blooming again and again

696 I'm thinking of your passionate remembrance of visiting the Lightning Field
697 I'm thinking of you creating with me
698 I'm thinking of your yielding strength
699 I'm thinking of you settling the dust
700 I'm thinking of your spinal column curving and rotating as we make love
701 I'm thinking of your skull growing like a newborn's
702 I'm thinking of you minutely and enormously
703 I'm thinking of you describing climbing holds
704 I'm thinking of you retelling many times certain stories from your youth
705 I'm thinking of you rereading over decades the words of your favorite Hindu sage
706 I'm thinking of your classy walk
707 I'm thinking of you certainly
708 I'm thinking of you bathing in clear water
709 I'm thinking of you smelling my skin as the sun turns your arms and torso darker
710 I'm thinking of you bathing in my sweat
711 I'm thinking of your organs producing light, your glands producing smells, your groin close to my lips
712 I'm thinking of your evident excitement
713 I'm thinking of you covered in my many scents from cum to Caron's perfume named, simply, Rose
714 I'm thinking of you knowing when to relax and when to be swift
715 I'm thinking of you listening to the wind through my hair
716 I'm thinking of you traveling with me where there are no roads
717 I'm thinking of you roaming with me without weariness
718 I'm thinking of you centered in my heart and my vagina
719 I'm thinking of your eyes and ears clear of entanglements
720 I'm thinking of your heart in harmony with tides and trees
721 I'm thinking of your ability to unknot the knotted
722 I'm thinking of your capacity to unmix the mixed up
723 I'm thinking of you uncongesting the congested
724 I'm thinking of you untangling overgrowths

725 I'm thinking of you saying that you cherish me, as my best friend in high school wrote me in her love note
726 I'm thinking of you adapting as you act
727 I'm thinking of you establishing sweetness, the foundation from which all other flavors derive
728 I'm thinking of you soft as water, which can penetrate through stone and metal
729 I'm thinking of you energetically
730 I'm thinking of you echoing with Om
731 I'm thinking of your three middle fingers caressing the back of my cervical spine
732 I'm thinking of your celestial teachings
733 I'm thinking of your arts of longevity
734 I'm thinking of you sharing the arts of health with me
735 I'm thinking of you deeply penetrating me
736 I'm thinking of your consummate style
737 I'm thinking of you moving the world with a single word
738 I'm thinking of you where rivers flow and mountains rise
739 I'm thinking of you in flowing waters and in mountains that befriend the sun
740 I'm thinking of your solar energy
741 I'm thinking of you whenever I want to
742 I'm thinking of you attuned to the arrival of phoenixes that fly in front of people and all around them
743 I'm thinking of you traveling oceans, continents, and galaxies without leaving your house
744 I'm thinking of you traveling far within yourself
745 I'm thinking of you relaxing the hearts of children
746 I'm thinking of your responsiveness
747 I'm thinking of your initiative
748 I'm thinking of you like a mirror, which conceals nothing and causes no harm
749 I'm thinking of you ringing bells and ripening fruit
750 I'm thinking of your self-direction
751 I'm thinking of you where paved roads and passports do not exist
752 I'm thinking of you waging love with me, we, in the world, love's champions

753 I'm thinking of you leaning on sturdy pillars
754 I'm thinking of your smooth passage
755 I'm thinking of your primal luster
756 I'm thinking of your love superior to the logic of linking rings
757 I'm thinking of you stretching the tendons of your heart
758 I'm thinking of you strolling through my neighborhood of trash and palaces
759 I'm thinking of you looking up into the mesquite and yellow-flowering paloverde trees
760 I'm thinking of you clothed in my slow kisses
761 I'm thinking of your wardrobe, caresses from my alabaster thighs and fingers
762 I'm thinking of you sitting in a pew beside me in the mission called the White Dove of the Desert
763 I'm thinking of you exuding sex
764 I'm thinking of you smiling at me jumping rope in my summery cotton skirt
765 I'm thinking of you clarifying bowls of water so that we can see ourselves in them
766 I'm thinking of you on the patio, stretched out, opening your eyes to the lizards on the rocks and trees and the two doves in the bird bath beneath the eucalyptus tree
767 I'm thinking of you seeing the small while emulating seas and rivers
768 I'm thinking of you emptying your moods
769 I'm thinking of you renewing yourself like plants, which live because the seasons change
770 I'm thinking of your hot pursuit of me
771 I'm thinking of you within our galactic equanimity
772 I'm thinking of your elan
773 I'm thinking of your spirit leading your body
774 I'm thinking of you staring at steam from my teacup
775 I'm thinking of you taking our clothes out of the dryer
776 I'm thinking of you decanting yourself into me
777 I'm thinking of you knowing which way the wind blows
778 I'm thinking of your endlessness so like the desert blue sky on this one more day in paradise
779 I'm thinking of your foolproof beauty

780 I'm thinking of you full of history and free of it
781 I'm thinking of you shifting the direction of the wind
782 I'm thinking of you making the kindest, gentlest, most passionate love with me
783 I'm thinking of your countless sparkles
784 I'm thinking of your inimitable luster
785 I'm thinking of your radiance that causes peacocks to fan their tails and the blossoms on orange trees to release their heady scent
786 I'm thinking of you heart to heart in bed, in love inevitably
787 I'm thinking of you investing in lotuses and roses
788 I'm thinking of your utter trusting decency
789 I'm thinking of you harnessing love and applying it like salve and perfume
790 I'm thinking of you listening your way into me, my bones and marrow
791 I'm thinking of your passion building up like lava
792 I'm thinking of you living in the neighborhood called heaven
793 I'm thinking of you at home, at ease, and young at heart
794 I'm thinking of you sweetheart
795 I'm thinking of you looking at me silently across the dining room table
796 I'm thinking of you telling me about your finances and dreams
797 I'm thinking of you trusting me completely, like the tissues of saguaros trust the water that they hold
798 I'm thinking of you fostering my growth by quenching my thirst
799 I'm thinking of you manifesting the design of heaven
800 I'm thinking of you my twin

Intermission. Same as previous intermission.

Act III

When the spirit moves her, Frueh goes into the audience with the perfume and sweeps it across the forehead of people, asking beforehand if it's okay with them.

Frueh rings the tinchas.

801 I'm thinking of you praying with me in a pew at San Xavier del Bac
802 I'm thinking of you crying with me as we pray
803 I'm thinking you as I light a candle for your family in the chapel
804 I'm thinking of you when I'm climbing to a grotto and dust clings to the suede toes of my shoes
805 I'm thinking of you wanting our clothes off
806 I'm thinking of you saying, "Let's take off our clothes or we'll go crazy"
807 I'm thinking of your disinterest in my lingerie
808 I'm thinking of you turning me on my belly
809 I'm thinking of you making love with me in front of the glass block window at the head of my bed
810 I'm thinking of your consciousness changing my patterns and habits
811 I'm thinking of your refuge in the one hundred beautiful things that enter your eyes in my backyard
812 I'm thinking of you entered by the at least ten thousand beautiful things that are always in your view
813 I'm thinking of you serving the sights that enter your third eye
814 I'm thinking of you, who has never practiced yoga, amused by your own statement about what you imagine as an eventuality, "I see a door at the end of a hall and on it is written YOGA"
815 I'm thinking of you seated on a mat beside me in a yoga class here in this desert city
816 I'm thinking of you, my balm, my hideaway
817 I'm thinking of you, my haven and retreat
818 I'm thinking of you sheltering me
819 I'm thinking of you full-on
820 I'm thinking of your pacifist passion
821 I'm thinking of your pacifist sexuality
822 I'm thinking of your pacifist sex
823 I'm thinking of you meditating with me in many positions
824 I'm thinking of your white-gold light spiraling with mine up from our physical bodies when are making love, to the ceiling, out the roof, and far and wide

825 I'm thinking of you rising to the occasion

826 I'm thinking of you immersed in my good wishes

827 I'm thinking of you untroubling the waters

828 I'm thinking of you preparing potions that reek of roses

829 I'm thinking of you inspired by me so long ago, in some past life, a *devadasi* dancing in a temple in Thanjavur

830 I'm thinking of you blessing the hearts on people's sleeves

831 I'm thinking of you blessing pigs and diamonds

832 I'm thinking of your individuation

833 I'm thinking of your fairness emanating from you, without words

834 I'm thinking of you walking the walk

835 I'm thinking of you putting your money where your mouth is

836 I'm thinking of your sufficiency

837 I'm thinking of you digging in the garden, holes where demons lie down and die

838 I'm thinking of you digging holes so deep and wide that every soul can root anew and resurrect itself

839 I'm thinking of you delivering sunken treasure from what seemed to be its final resting place

840 I'm thinking of your sophistication among intellectuals and airline passengers

841 I'm thinking of you relying on everything that gives you life

842 I'm thinking of you eating foods that are in season

843 I'm thinking of your tongue tasting

844 I'm thinking of your teeth chewing

845 I'm thinking of you preferring cotton clothing, wearing armor when necessary

846 I'm thinking of you expecting wetness from water and fragrance from flowers

847 I'm thinking of your fingers on the iPhone

848 I'm thinking of you in the middle of my night

849 I'm thinking of you in the dawning of my day

850 I'm thinking of you navigating my *chakras*, a sailor deeper than sailing who has chosen to be *in* the seven seas

851 I'm thinking of you loving us

852 I'm thinking of you refreshed by us

853 I'm thinking of you balancing exertion and surrender

854 I'm thinking of you blissful in my embrace
855 I'm thinking of you embracing me into bliss
856 I'm thinking of you balancing focus and abandon
857 I'm thinking of you standing your ground and holding your own by flying in place
858 I'm thinking of your steadiness in terms of profuse simplicity
859 I'm thinking of you getting your beautiful butt on a plane over here
860 I'm thinking of you wafting to me from afar, an incense that is burning all around me
861 I'm thinking of your saliva
862 I'm thinking of your saliva on my skin
863 I'm thinking of you diving into me
864 I'm thinking of you glancing toward me when I'm applying lipstick
865 I'm thinking of your expanding repertoire of love songs
866 I'm thinking of your devotional eroticism
867 I'm thinking of your pulse
868 I'm thinking of your dovetailing with me
869 I'm thinking of you saying Grace at dinner
870 I'm thinking of you inviting me to share with you a bottle of wine begun by you and your parents
871 I'm thinking of your headdress that looks indeed like gold dust, the saffron powder from the flower of the kadamba
872 I'm thinking of you kneeling face to face with me within the liquid grip of angels
873 I'm thinking of your emergence from the airplane ready for this blessed desert sun
874 I'm thinking of you waking up my thighs
875 I'm thinking of your enjoyment of me when you say, "You're so wet"
876 I'm thinking of you calling my attention to my vagina when you say, "You're so alive there"
877 I'm thinking of you going nowhere in particular with me as we find each other over and over
878 I'm thinking of you placing one foot in front of the other
879 I'm thinking of your centers and edges
880 I'm thinking of your unknowable heart

881 I'm thinking of your unhidden ecstasies
882 I'm thinking of your daily allegiance to our love
883 I'm thinking of you near and far
884 I'm thinking of you ocean-wide and filled with subtle currents
885 I'm thinking of your headdress of spun and spinning gold
886 I'm thinking of your belt of bells that shimmers with the sound of a flock of chirping, whirling dervish birds
887 I'm thinking of you surveying my little garden of rocks
888 I'm thinking of you reflected in the ethereal blue-green garden gazing ball next to the granite Buddha head
889 I'm thinking of you in the sprawling midst of two spiral galaxies that began their intercourse around 300 million years ago
890 I'm thinking of your flat-out distance from the word "colliding," with which experts name the mutual engagement of those galaxies
891 I'm thinking of you in the breathing room of this is all there is
892 I'm thinking of you in the breathing spaces and birthing rooms
893 I'm thinking of your gorgeous drifts of mind
894 I'm thinking of you delighting in my poetry, my dancing hips and shoulders, the action of my words
895 I'm thinking of you sallying forth, drifting back
896 I'm thinking of your frankness of feeling, your wakes of emotion
897 I'm thinking of you, my beautiful, sexy man
898 I'm thinking of you comfortably resting your heart in mine
899 I'm thinking of you in Martha Graham's words, an "athlete of God"
900 I'm thinking of you meeting my friends
901 I'm thinking of you greeting my sister and her partner
902 I'm thinking of you laughing at something that I say
903 I'm thinking of you feeling cool in the summer and warm in the winter when I'm around
904 I'm thinking of your very nakedness
905 I'm thinking of your reassuringly hard thighs
906 I'm thinking of your speechlessness

907 I'm thinking of your love of words and silence
908 I'm thinking of you holding the power of my speech
909 I'm thinking of you held in my silence
910 I'm thinking of you looking at my nakedness
911 I'm thinking of you loving my nakedness
912 I'm thinking of you looking at my nudity with your head slightly cocked, a little smile on your lips
913 I'm thinking of your tongue in my navel
914 I'm thinking of your fingers trailing over the roundness of my belly
915 I'm thinking of your glow that's radiating through your navel
916 I'm thinking of your sweet ass
917 I'm thinking of you coming to me
918 I'm thinking of you dreaming your world into being
919 I'm thinking of you dreaming the doors open
920 I'm thinking of you everywhere and wherever you are
921 I'm thinking of you moonlit and open-armed
922 I'm thinking of your arms around me in the moonlight
923 I'm thinking of your salty forearm
924 I'm thinking of the pliant changing pressures of your lips
925 I'm thinking of you following my fancy footwork with a kinesthetic gaze
926 I'm thinking of you placing garlands of roses where my feet have stomped and jumped
927 I'm thinking of your soul music
928 I'm thinking of you garlanding my naked waist in roses, a white band of petals that touch my hipbones where your kisses do
929 I'm thinking of you looking over the geography of heaven
930 I'm thinking of your tools, including paintbrush and piano
931 I'm thinking of your fine arts
932 I'm thinking of you saying, "You look good"
933 I'm thinking of you texting, "thank you beautiful joanna"
934 I'm thinking of you in the spirit of the moment
935 I'm thinking of your breath in my lungs
936 I'm thinking of you the way any young lover does
937 I'm thinking of you with the heart of the most loving longtime wife

938 I'm thinking of you dreaming with me in words
939 I'm thinking of you with me in the deep of night when sleep, a transparent sparkling cloud, surrounds us
940 I'm thinking of you simply thinking of you
941 I'm thinking of you protecting me from freezing temperatures
942 I'm thinking of you in the spaciousness of dreams
943 I'm thinking of your dreams forever coming true
944 I'm thinking of you distilling me the fully opened flower
945 I'm thinking of you telling me once we're in bed for the night, "You smell like beautiful herbs"
946 I'm thinking of you in the spaces of my simultaneously evanescent and penetrating fragrances
947 I'm thinking of you cradling roses in your arms
948 I'm thinking of your seismic grandeur
949 I'm thinking of you fitting into my plan and me fitting into yours
950 I'm thinking of your skills and innate power of observation
951 I'm thinking of your observant sensitivity
952 I'm thinking of you river rafting in the rapids of Love
953 I'm thinking of your astonishing me, deep in my eyes to say, "There are many kinds of oceans"
954 I'm thinking of you in the space between smite and smitten
955 I'm thinking of you charming snakes and children
956 I'm thinking of you bowing to the jewels in cobras' eyes
957 I'm thinking of you dancing with serpents
958 I'm thinking of you savoring me, no sets, props, or scenery
959 I'm thinking of you deep into the texture of sand, in the desert and on my skin
960 I'm thinking of your devotion to eros
961 I'm thinking of you creating a new body in our eroticism
962 I'm thinking of you enchanted as I decorate the air with hand gestures called *hastas* in Indian classical dance
963 I'm thinking of your mood guided by my body's arabesques
964 I'm thinking of you in the tempos and sequences of our bodies scrolling in and out, our transferences of weight, new dances, unrepeatable
965 I'm thinking of your energy unabridged
966 I'm thinking of your love bridging the continents
967 I'm thinking of your deluxe interior

968 I'm thinking of you struck with wonder at all that you have built

969 I'm thinking of you standing on sacred ground wherever you walk

970 I'm thinking of you surpassing description, even the inherent logic of poetic abandon

971 I'm thinking of you building a temple of your body so that you can live in heaven every moment

972 I'm thinking of you showing me that the proof is in the pudding

973 I'm thinking of you imbibing the universe in the song of a bird whose singing comes to us through the wide open French doors as we sit over our morning tea and coffee

974 I'm thinking of you feeding my heart with the lightest of texted kisses

975 I'm thinking of you arousing me with just a word or plain-spoken silence or a perfectly placed touch

976 I'm thinking of your serene face while you're dancing

977 I'm thinking of you raising physicality to bliss

978 I'm thinking of you coiling a huge snake around your throat, a necklace of undulating color

979 I'm thinking of your entrainment to my strength and stamina, *Ananda Tandava*, where I am jumping to my toes then striking the floor with my feet, crossing one leg high over another in a balancing that whirls into a toe squat with my hands in a *hasta* meaning I offer you my love

980 I'm thinking of your surprise when I say, "You have a sensual mouth," you tell me that no one has said that before, and I respond, "They didn't know what they were looking at"

981 I'm thinking of the candor in your voice

982 I'm thinking of your composure

983 I'm thinking of you kissing the soles of my feet

984 I'm thinking of you lingering long within my gaze, my eyes lined in soft black and flaming from the heart

985 I'm thinking of you at my doorway, sensing already the subtleties of fresh flowers, sheets, and skin, stepping inside, soothed and stimulated in the beauty of a home and woman prepared for your pleasure

986 I'm thinking of you seized by the brilliant colors of my clothing
987 I'm thinking of your thankfulness for my joy
988 I'm thinking of you my ecstatic
989 I'm thinking of you my husband
990 I'm thinking of you loving my power
991 I'm thinking of you living, which some call throwing caution to the wind, misunderstanding that to take risks with the heart, through the throat, and in the spirit is an essential meaning of the verb *to live*
992 I'm thinking of you as the excellent scent of honeysuckles accompanies my walk to the library for a book about the deification of eroticism in Hindu temples, as a lizard scampers in front of my feet
993 I'm thinking of you when the cactuses are about to bloom
994 I'm thinking of you when it snows in this valley and melts by noon
995 I'm thinking of you turning towards me and me turning towards you, roses empowered by the sun
996 I'm thinking of you tasting my nipple harden
997 I'm thinking of you delivering the goods: cadence and percussion, the melodies in caverns, the proportions of sanctuary
998 I'm thinking of you – bullseye, quintessentially simpatico
999 I'm thinking of you without thinking at all.
1000 I'm thinking of you, lover and beloved, as I offer these, my highest salutations

Frueh rings the tinchas.

She thanks the audience and joins them in conversation and whatever food is left.

I performed *Sexual Advances* at Cabinet, Brooklyn, New York, and Tucson Yoga, Tucson, Arizona, in 2009. For the Cabinet performance Paul Ramirez Jonas prepared a feast. I presented an excerpt of the performance at the Performances Galore session of the TFAP (The Feminist Art Project) sessions at the College Art Association Conference, Los Angeles, California, in 2009.

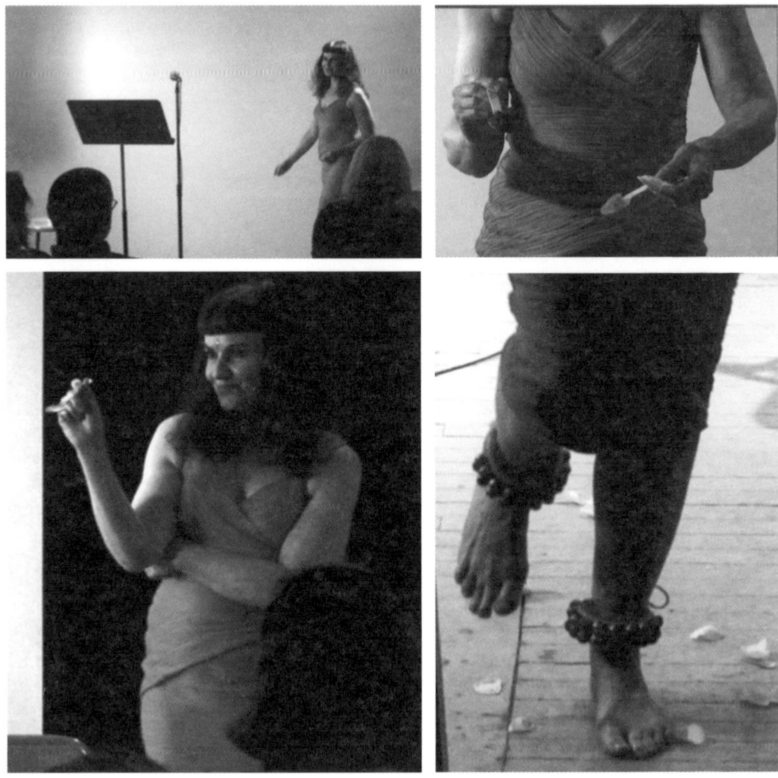

Figure 12a–d Joanna Frueh, *Sexual Advances*, The Cabinet, Brooklyn, 2009, video stills © Paul Helzer, reproduced by kind permission

The Dark Lord and his Wily Mistress, 2009

I costumed myself for this reading but used no props. An off-white skirt, all chiffon ruffles, came to just below my knees. Over a white and modestly sheer cotton tank top I wore a navy blue tuxedo jacket, very feminine with its extravagantly sized satin collar and petite peplum and its fit, low-cut and close at the waist. Lace-up boots to the bottom of my calf and of ivory-colored leather struck a Victorian note. I wore my hair in its usual loose style and echoed the bright red of the Wily Mistress's lips on my mouth.

Singing with all my heart

The Dark Lord was a mess. Even though he looked alluringly dapper in his dandyish clothing. Often black and always eloquently simple, it spoke of sex and elegance. It spoke the language of Armani, perfect tailoring fitted to the confidence of a slender muscularity. In actuality, the Dark Lord covered his golden nudity in selections from secondhand stores. Why spend money on clothing when style, one's personal style, was of the essence? Everyone attracted to his self-reliant aura who walked by him day or night caught their breath in fearful longing that either he or they would grab the other in an embrace that could last no shorter than eternity.

I would want him if I were you. If I were you, I would sing to him with all my heart.

Many kinds of oceans

In laughter long ago the Dark Lord and his Wily Mistress gave each other those nicknames. Women wanted him to seduce them, but he was no vampire, and men wanted to kiss her full lips, painted an unnameably brilliant red, while at once fearing and adoring the arrestingly direct and intimate words they spoke, but she was no femme fatale.

The names gave them pleasure deeper than the luster of mythic figures that literature and cinema invited people to desire through the enjoyments of identification and terror. Deeper than the cliché of deep blue seas and the detestation of deep thinking by people who called intellectuals eggheads. Deeper than the conversations of the Lord and Mistress that a smart, romantic psychotherapist would call lovemaking. Deep, like the breathing through which meditation materializes the physical world. Deep, like their orgasms that lasted hours after the end of intercourse. Deep, like innocence rather than transgression. Deep, like your native tongue when you talk to me of stars.

Turpitude

Moral conflict plagued the Dark Lord. He had bought a gun and during the past month lay in bed all night next to his Wily Mistress, scheming. He invented scenarios in which to kill people, and the line from Johnny Cash's "Folsom Prison Blues" kept repeating in his head: "I shot a man in Reno just to watch him die." Killing had become a compulsion.

She had almost fallen asleep one night when he startled her with a menacing rendition of the "Folsom Prison" line. "Jeez!" she exclaimed in compassionate frustration. Another woman would have called him a fucking idiot.

Lullaby

The Wily Mistress sang her Dark Lord a lullaby.

Clear the space and clear the air
Clear the heart of every care
Clear the oceans bring the rain
Clear the earth of every pain

Dragon tiger power flow
Tiger dragon prowling low
Flying high and everywhere
Bring me all my heart does dare

Dragon dragon burning bright
In the starry splendid night
From the heavens through the ground
All is love and all is sound

He thanked her: "It's an incantation."

Their dreaming skin

If someone looked into his eyes, which was rare, they saw redness lining the lids. He'd been taking uppers for nearly a month because he didn't want to sleep. A recurring dream, every night if he let himself even doze, disturbed him so much that he would rather feel jagged, jangled by a drug, than debilitated by what had become a nightmare. In it he lived in a sewer. From that stinking abyss he could smell roses every now and then if a breeze blew in from a sky so far away that he felt as though he were glimpsing heaven in a galaxy yet to be named or even seen by astronomers.

Through a meager tear, unnoticed by the Dark Lord, the red rim of one lower lid looked like a jewel. His Wily Mistress was stretching out in undulations beside him in their bed, and her white skin – you might call it rose-petal white – dreamed. She felt his tear with the tip of a finger, and I would do the same if I were she. He had talked about the dream many times before stopping its nightly appearance with medication. Using the tact that blesses the territory of love, she offered, "Oh, my Dark Lord, that dream has a sense of redemption about it."

The dream's images and impact pursued him. They chilled his voice. "My Wily Mistress, that dream could be the equivalent of a merciless lover, who likes to fuck you rather sweetly, then hurt you in every way possible all at once."

Her skin kept dreaming and his skin dreamed alongside and along with hers.

City of changes

The city in which the Dark Lord and his Wily Mistress lived usually comforted him. Its speed was fast enough. Its inhabitants greeted strangers on the street. The servers in its dives and dining halls genuinely thanked customers for their business. But now the city cudgeled him. It cranked him into a high gear of madness.

He perceived fraud and famine and overweening luxury. He was walking in the midst of liars and other delusional souls who fed their egos with uncertainty and a sick poetry of flagrant criminality sung automatically, under the breath. He saw himself as one of the violently disaffected: "I shot a man in Reno just to watch him die." Meddlers in his life called him friend so that they could become nosier and more voyeuristic.

The Dark Lord was existing in a surly, putrid city of garbage that never got picked up, of people covered with poultices and patches.

The city had been built next to a huge lake, which a child might call an ocean, and the climate was moderate all year round. Most days the sky changed and changed. Could he?

Shit. Destiny had mismanaged his life.

Calling it alive

"Dark Lord!" Her whisper caressed his lips and he parted them. She lingered in her next inhalation and consciously exhaled from her mouth, which she puckered, directing her breath between his teeth. The almost inaudible groan released from organs, fluids, and space lower than his throat excited her more, so naked body to naked body, she licked his right nipple and pleasure shot straight from where her tongue touched his chest to the posterior of her vagina, the place called the A-spot in twentieth-century terminology. He called it alive.

Crazier than ever

"You're crazy, my Dark Lord," she said in all honesty. "Crazier than ever," he agreed.

Why him? Why me? Why such defiled emotions? Redundant speculation and repeated recriminations would drown the heart of less wily mistresses and of a lord less willing to spin, like a dervish, in the nexus of currents that he or some planetary spleen had set in motion.

He tapped his teeth with his fingers.

He described his condition, "My life is imploding," and they looked into each other's eyes and laughed, the way they did at the words *sundown* and *sunset*, for who could parse into perfection the details that made each word itself? Who could exactly define the strains of meaning that had called each word into being?

Washing the Buddha's face

A stone Buddha head four feet tall smiled in the rooftop garden outside the penthouse home of the Dark Lord and his Wily Mistress. The previous owner of the property had left the statue at their request. The top of the Buddha's head was a planter. Lantana, fuchsia, honeysuckle could have trailed down from it like wild locks of hair, but the two gardeners left the planter empty, as if any human choosing of its contents interfered with nature, not to mention the Buddha's very smile.

Every day she took the hose, set the nozzle on *mist*, and washed the Buddha's face.

Lucky seven

The mystic attractiveness of the number seven escorted the Dark Lord wherever he went: from the seemingly prosaic number of the days in a week to the power of the *chakras* in the human body to the chutzpah of Christ rising on the seventh day. The Dark Lord and his Wily Mistress had found a home on the seventh floor, and their given names were seven letters: Rosario and Rosalba.

As deep as seven was for him, *rose* being the first syllable of each of their names swirled her into the oceans of their love.

She performed for him the Dance of the Seven Veils. It was not the Salomeian striptease that Oscar Wilde and film had made it. When she danced ecstatically, shaking her head back and forth, rotating her hips easily from her free and easy pelvis, he experienced her as a beacon and a balm, and he felt lifting sometimes from one *chakra*, sometimes from more or all of them, a veil akin to a cataract covering an eye.

Water

"Looks like some kind of rain," thought the Wily Mistress and threw a cloak of plush velvet over her shoulders. If you were watching, her naturally dramatic gestures might take you by surprise, because you might mistake them for a symptom of narcissistic self-consciousness if you were to see them in public. You might mistake her, as people often did, for the femme fatale that she was not. You might be like men who misread the playful climate that she manifested all around her, such as the celestial breeze that seemed always to be flowing through her hair, for seductive cunning. The Dark Lord's heart responded to her atmospheres and alignments by opening more and more.

Dusk was falling and the sky looked strangely pink, not the usual tonalities of that color before it disappeared into the night. The length of the cloak, to the ankles, and its weight would have kept most women from wearing it in impending rain. The fabric would get ruined and it would weigh them down. The Wily Mistress did not give such things a thought. Ultrafeminine and foppish, her costume took her to the park by the lake, where she imagined that in the midst of vines and brilliant-colored flowers she was strolling through a Victorian garden in the mid-nineteenth century.

Her stroll conveyed purpose, so it was an unusual gait. Which may be why a man to whom she said hello asked, as you yourself most likely would: "Are you queen bee or stallion? Bitch or stud? Left or right? Distinct or dissected?" Lucky for him that "Angel or devil?" didn't come up. Not that she would have cussed him out or punched him; but that pairing of angel and devil so bored her sense of fun that hearing it might have stopped the breezes through her hair – if only for a millisecond. "I am an approximation of each and each one precisely." Quickly she added, "Better yet, I am beast and *bodhisattva*," and with those words light from her poured into the Dark Lord. She knew it without seeing it. "What the hell?" crossed her mind. She heard the Dark Lord translating the phrase correctly, as "Why not?," and she heard it as clearly as any conversation that loved ones, alive or dead, have with one another in the expanse of oceans.

Namaha

Having left the gun at home the Dark Lord returned there to get it, so that he could kill someone in an act that he imagined would be random, dispassionate, and a complete waste of his time. Eyes closed like always, the Buddha smiled at him.

The populace knew that saints lived in their city. Some in stylish skyscrapers, some in hovels. Some shit in the street, and no one seemed to notice. Maybe the Dark Lord hallucinated that, and maybe he had hallucinated leaping to the top of a two-story building when he was a child and falling to the ground only feet from his goal. Maybe he could try again, but nothing had compelled him. Maybe broken bones scared him. Maybe a heart broken by the inability to fly scared him more.

The Dark Lord did not fondle the gun in his pocket. That was stupid, a sexual cliché that caused him to roll his eyes even as he scanned the sidewalks near and far for a target. Someone to shoot on the spot – and the cops would appear from greasy spoons and bars and in cars whose sirens wailed into his *chakras*. Someone to charm into a drink at an upmarket bar, to get to know in a superficially sophisticated urban way before walking to a close and quiet street where the Dark Lord's dispatch would shock anyone but a saint.

There was one now. Saints, thought the Dark Lord, stayed cool through anything. Otherwise, they were not saints. In coolness they could know their surroundings – ahead, behind, above, below them. In coolness they could act lightly even when situations appeared to be sluggish, stalled, and wracked with extreme emotion. In coolness saints kept their hearts in balance with the cosmos, what Taoists knew as the watercourse way – all in motion, like the Wily Mistress's hair, like the sky above the city, like the oceans, like the voice, especially when it sang.

"*Om gam ganeshaya namaha*," sang the saint. "*Om gam ganeshaya namaha, ganapataye ganapataye.*" If I had been there, I would have counted her steps because their slowness intrigued me. If you had been there with me, maybe we would have followed her in her walking meditation, her processing through the city at an infinitesimal pace. Surely we would have chanted with her, learning the words as we heard them, and we would have sung them so many times that counting either steps or the repetition of the mantra would have melted away, along with any obstructions that we faced. *Om gam ganeshaya namaha. Om gam ganeshaya namaha, ganapataye ganapataye.* I greet you and bow to you, Ganesh, remover of obstacles.

Like the Dark Lord we would have known the Wily Mistress's light within us as we chanted, and I would have been thinking, for a minute, that dogmas initiate people into the formal constraints of a practice or belief and interfere with love, whether we give it the name of oceans, flowers, saints, or lucky seven, and that mantra frees the rhythms of those oceans, the blooming of those flowers, the coolness of those saints, the veils mystifying life just enough that when we look in a mirror we see opacity.

The saint with whom the Dark Lord chanted had written a book in which a student of hers asked many questions and the saint responded. "What gets in the way of my knowing myself, the light, and love?" asked the student. "Your mind that wanders and that fixates, your perverted ways," answered the teacher.

The Dark Lord gave the gun to the saint, in whose hands it immediately dissolved.

Grace

The Dark Lord knew where to find his Wily Mistress. By the lake in the place that they called the Victorian Garden. On his way he noticed the clouds that gathered over the water and glided over the city. Suddenly, roses rained down in every neighborhood and onto every freeway. Multitudes of thornless roses that were whites, including the color of her skin, and reds, including the color of blood from martyrs' bodies, dried to crosses, earth, concrete, and other consecrators of death sentences, that came to life when saints sang these words: I told every little star just how sweet I think you are / Why haven't I told you? The roses caused no accidents and the next morning bouquets appeared on breakfast tables in homes and every class of restaurant.

At the outskirts of the Victorian Garden, the Dark Lord watched his Wily Mistress weaving together whites and reds. "Garland of roses": his parents had told him the meaning of his name, Rosario, when he was a little boy. She turned towards him. "Better late than never," he said.

They walked home holding hands, through piles of flowers and the Good evenings of passersby. The wreath that she had woven crowned his head. She had placed it there. Near home they took off their shoes and dropped them gently on the pavement in the alley behind the building. He stood between her and the wall, only a couple inches from both, and she pressed against him so softly that if you were close as a cat underfoot between the two of them, you would have sworn that his jacket and her cloak had not touched at all. He had closed his eyes before she closed hers, and an agreement, in the space that exceeded the limits of atmosphere, in the love that has no name but itself – not romance, marriage, friendship; not wife and husband, partners, lovers, or companions – connected them. Caresses came from that agreement and they circulated, heart to heart and through fabric, over and into every inch of skin.

The Dark Lord spoke and the Wily Mistress looked into his opened eyes. "Time to fly." Side by side they held hands and leapt, up to the garden, to absolute grace.

The Buddha was happy that roses were overflowing from his head.

I read *The Dark Lord and his Wily Mistress* as part of my keynote presentation at the Art History Graduate Student Symposium at the University of Arizona, Tucson, Arizona, in 2010.

I AM Desire, 2010

Frueh walks onstage from sitting in the audience. A black music stand, a microphone and stand, and a high stool, her usual gear, await her, as does a pink plate, placed on the stool and stacked with a pyramid of Joanna's Chocolate Bars, her especially melt-in-your-mouth treats (with whole macadamia nuts). The stool also holds a clear glass filled with water. The rose of her dress, snug and ruched from the sweetheart neckline to the hem at the top of her calves, is a much brighter and deeper color than that of the plate – flamboyantly gorgeous but not flashy, which also describes the design of her dress that recalls a night-on-the-town frock of a 1950s Hollywood star.

Frueh's creamy shoulders, arms, and legs create a luminous contrast to the chiffon-like length of pink. Satin ankle boots in pinkish mauve, laced up with matching organza and high enough to be sexy but not too high for walking comfort, add to the play of minimalist elegance.

Lipstick: the fully saturated pleasure of MAC's Dubonnet, richly winey. Hair: worn long and off the face with a side part; silver-white, in the naturally espresso warmth, undulating just to her temples.

Desire is benign, but people think otherwise. They squirm in its grip, they are buffeted by its whims, they are unmoored from any happiness or peace because desire pushes them into immoderate and intolerable appetite.

I say, "That's another country, not desire. That's a country of boundaries not infinite frontier. That's a country of constriction by barbed wire and walls of fire, the kind that are the borders of a Christian hell. That's a country where the patrolling goon called conformity enforces a childhood and continuing education in sadistic unfulfillment. That is a country where people call desire the cause of their own clamor and commotion. That is a country where people believe that desire drives them, as if they are beasts of the burdens of pleasure."

Freedom, peace, and happiness constitute pleasure when a person is receptive to desire rather than pushing it away by denying, despising, or trying to control it, all of which are reactions to fear. Fear of desire, which people define as an object, whether material or mental, outside of themselves – such as success in work, ice cream before bed, or an alluring woman wanted for her body. Desire experienced as an external object that is a goal, whether obviously out of reach or soon attainable.

When a person grabs for objects or craves them, desire has a goal. If that goal is achieved, another desire or bunch of them take its place, so people experience desires as compelling. That desire, over there, outside of me, compels me to act – or to stave off action (for moral, financial, emotional, ideological, or intellectual reasons).

When a person is receptive to desire, receptive over and over and over and over and over and over again, she finds that desire does not create a stream of separate desires, but rather that she herself IS desire. She embodies it, she wafts it, she expresses it, she communicates it.

When I AM desire, sin, barbed wire, and the goon go away. When I AM desire, it is always present and therefore not a goal. When I AM desire, I am always fulfilled.

Frueh eats a chocolate bar. She enjoys it, so eating takes the time that is the equivalent of the pleasure that she feels. She eats as many chocolate bars as she feels like eating and shares them with audience members too, and she talks playfully and pointedly with them as she eats. Perhaps she says as she offers the plate to someone, "If you take one, you've got to say, 'I AM desire,' with conviction." Perhaps she says, before she delivers the second part of the text, "When I AM desire, the world brings gifts."

Here is the plenty of a peaceful rod
Here is the abundance of a father's kisses
Here is the abundance of curls with which humid weather endows my hair
Here is the abundance of the next breath
Here is the luxuriousness of taking you at your word
Here is the plenty of our matched hearts that do not require an address – hey, hi, hello, or even dear – do not demand a closing – love, much love – in our emails to one another
Here is the luxuriousness of releasing pins and needles

Here is the abundance of flowers in a vase on the table from the garden that I grow
Here is the plenty of deciding for myself
Here is the luxuriousness of a daughter's white blouse over light skin on which her mother's pearls are resting
Here is the abundance of sea to shining sea, which is the human body, made mostly of water, head to toe
Here is the plenty that lets life happen while we are mastering ourselves, because that mastery has loosened reactions to every little thing as if it were out to get us
Here is the abundance of saliva, which Taoists define as a healthful elixir that we can swallow consciously
Here is the plenty in the difference of your every kiss with me
Here is the plenty of Rita Hayworth's incandescent Gilda
Here is the plenty of seeing me as I am
Here is the abundance of seeing as far as the eye can see and farther
Here is the abundance of beauty that grows from mud, like the lotus
Here is the plenty of singing the unsung
Here is the plenty of walking forward in shoes that fit, worn with socks that don't slide around, on feet whose muscles and tendons are as easy as the Buddha's mind
Here is the plenty in unfueled memories, because when aflame, they burn down the house of love with their overzealous ardor
Here is the abundance when crossing a threshold that you can call your own
Here is the abundance of things changing in their own time
Here is the plenty of you, all of you, in sunlight
Here is the luxuriousness of our limbs as we help them rise and root

Frueh sings:
Dona nobis pacem, pacem Dona nobis pacem

I performed *I AM Desire* at an evening of performances at Club Congress, Tucson, Arizona, in 2010.

Index

Page numbers in **bold** refer to figures